T0244519

SNOWBLINDNESS

SNOWBLINDNESS

Let's talk about storytelling, colonialism, Netflix, and my great-grandfather

PREFACE

With many thoughts and reflections on why, if, how, and when, *Snowblindness – Let's talk about storytelling, colonialism, Netflix, and my great-grandfather,* has finally found its way to becoming printed and published matter. The making and publishing of *Snowblindness* and its formative artistic research was concretised and developed before and throughout the global pandemic that began in 2019, and the project has formed the design discipline I practise.

2021 marked 300 years of Danish presence in Kalaallit Nunaat (Greenland). Since the independence movement of the 1950s, debate and criticism of Danish colonial presence in Greenland has increased. This book brings together various myths, stories, and questions, and offers multiple views and reflections on the relationship between design practice and storytelling. It primarily focuses on Nordic colonialism through an autoethnographic lens.

As the *Snowblindness* research and collaborations developed, new and surprising encounters occurred. During the process I learned that global production and streaming giant Netflix wanted to make a feature film about a Danish polar explorer – my great-grandfather – who throughout this book is referred to as EM. EM are the initials of the Danish polar explorer (1880–1971) – one of many other titles – who, in 1919, adopted my grandfather. Throughout this book I purposely only call my great-grandfather EM as a cover name. This cover name is firstly a choice from my side, based on a wish to care for and protect my family, should this book ever be printed in many editions or debated heavily. Secondly, throughout this work I am trying to debate the idea of mixing documentary with fiction/semi-fiction, and exploring what these genres add to the design discipline (also treated in the chapters:

THOUGHTS ON METHODOLOGY

REFLECTION ON 'TRUTH' & THE 'COLLECTIVE MEMORY')

A cover name allows for other interventions, as it is not presented as fact, but instead creates space for imagination. This is especially important since EM was a public figure. Netflix's surprising interest appeared meanwhile decolonisation movements gained heightened attention worldwide, encouraging a questioning of the value of various policies and regimes. One could feel the need to know why Netflix were interested in producing a film like that in times such as these.

I started this work not because EM was an important figure in Greenland and the Arctic region, nor because of the loaded historical meaning to the documentation of his narrative. The urgency to develop this body of research into a book grew into a personal necessity; I had to investigate and question my own link to, and influence in, the North Atlantic, outside of the familial domain, in a self-reflective and open manner – a connection and concern that has been both a source of conflict and a sort of gold deposit when developing work through my design practice. I lived for four years in Iceland, visited Greenland, and have a sincere interest in and concern for the Arctic, its people, its resources, and the possible futures for the region, as it has become a high-tension zone whose trajectory sparks global interest.

GEOPOLITICAL ISSUE

At quite an early stage of the sculpting of this book, collaborations revealed themselves to be a key element. Firstly, in search of stories and documents, various archives, museums, institutions, and individuals guided me further than I could've gone alone.

ARCHIVES & EVIDENCE

Secondly, graphic designer and friend Anna Bierler became a crucial collaborator, as we started to experiment with collected material and to engage with the work through different types of media.

EDITING & SHARING

Thirdly, integral to the making of this book is the way the collaboration with my father, Olaf Havsteen-Mikkelsen, took shape. I was urged by several different actors to invite Father (as he is named throughout the book) to take part in the editorial process from almost the very beginning of the research. Father helped in moments of commenting on and discussing content, and allowed for the presence of trust and vulnerable stories. For that I am very thankful, as well as for the conversations we had when reading this book together and discussing sensitive matters of myths, history, and heritage. The conversations were treated with careful consideration in the editorial work and in the design process, which is something I will return to throughout the book.

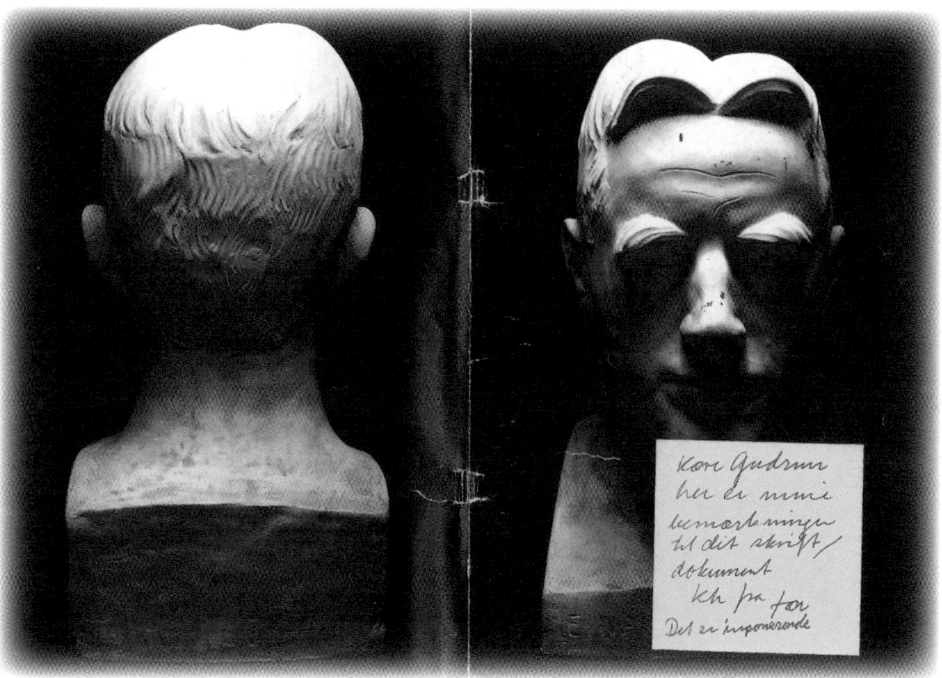

In April 2020, Father wrote: Dear Gudrun, here is my notes to your text/document. Love from Father. It is impressive.

001.JPG

In April 2020, Father wrote: Was it not Iver that wanted to eat EM, because he was walking behind him with the gun. I think they were both afraid of that.

EM was a captain. He was captured three years on Greenland's East Coast with his engineer and friend, Iver Iversen. EM was so hungry he wanted to eat Iver. EM was my great-grandfather.
(source from Father)

Narratives on EM

Narratives on EM is the working title on issues that deals with colonialism, myths, history and contextualized narratives in the Arctic. It is an auto-fiction on my great grandfather, Captain Ejnar Mikkelsen.

Gudrun Havsteen-Mikkelsen

Should you not put an (EM) behind Ejnar Mikkelsen ? A bust we have at home my birthplace

In April 2020 Father wrote: Should you not put an (EM) behind EM? A bust we have at [your] birthplace.

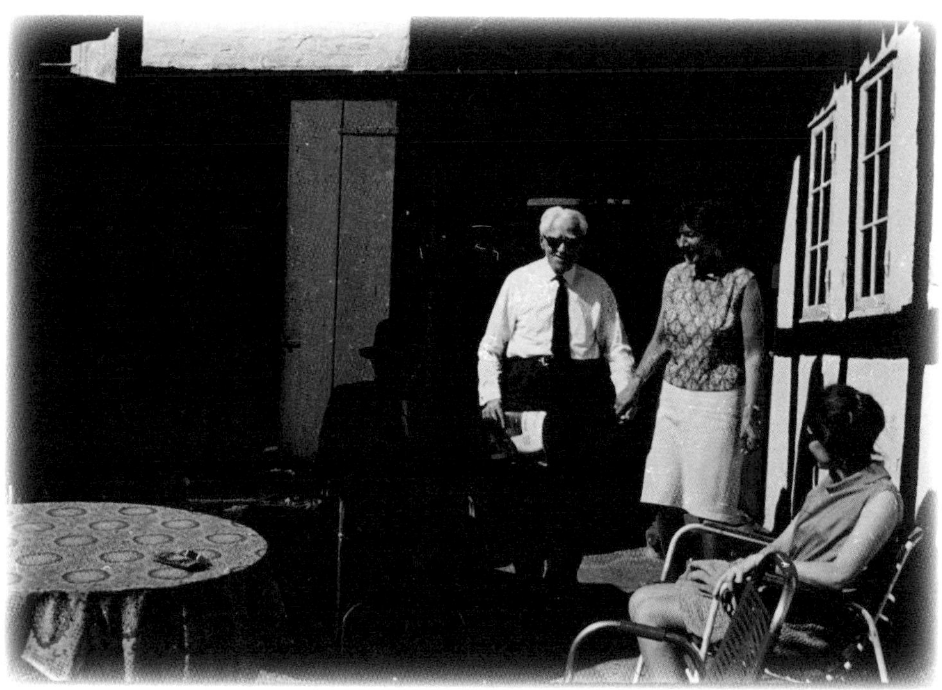

In April 2020, Father wrote: You have already said that EM was your great grandfather, is it necessary to mention it on each page? Suggest you do not write EM was my great grandfather on each page.

In February 2020, Father said: "It is called: between under- and over arm."

EM was a sailor. He could crack a walnut in his elbow. He was called the ironman and did things beyond human capacity. EM was my great-grandfather. (source from Father)

005.JPG

EM was a Danish polar explorer. He went to the North East of Greenland to find the assumed dead bodies of the two polar explorers, Mylius-Eriksen and Jørgen Brønlund. EM did not find Mylius-Eriksen, but he found his diary in Denmark-Fjord. EM was my great-grandfather. (source from Frederiksen's book)

006.JPG

007.JPG

CONTENTS

EDITORIAL

This book invites you to wander through a design research and into interwoven connections of images and texts, narratives and imaginaries. The book contains various semi-fictional texts, essayistic reflections, and conversations, in a more or less autobiographical format. The different texts are connected to various kinds of sources; conversations with contributors, private or archival documents, and published literature, manifesting in multiple dialogues.

The semi-fictional texts are indicated by their materiality; they are printed on 10% black-coloured Munken Polar paper. Each semi-fictional story is connected to the making of an object, and in return these objects are connected to the research; tools to come closer to the case study. The objects and artistic research guide the reader along my understanding of what it means to create work in different media, and in this case to unfold and communicate investigations into colonial heritage and myth-making echoed in 'collective memory'. The semi-fictional texts relate to the autoethnographical approach – a lived experience – either in the form of memory or conversations, which are occasionally stated as fictional or taken directly from specified sources in another context.

The essayistic and reflective texts do something else. They aim to guide the reader through the research and reflections as situated in a design practice. These texts – reflections, notes, and conversations – are often interrupted by smaller intermezzos of conversations with relatives, locals in Greenland, archivists, artists, and more, which relate to the content of specific chapters. These intermezzos move out of the static horizontal grid and take space in the margins of the page. The conversations, often presented as email correspondence, are trans-formulated, translated, edited, and are certainly not verbatim transcriptions. The edits are made due to issues of privacy; they are untraceable for a reader, as I wish to cause no harm to the contributors in the making of this book. This is also the reason why some names are obscured; indicated by fictive initials and narrowed down to only last names, or only indicated by names of a company or institution. The selected conversations are a series of fictionalisations of actual correspondences, which have been just as important for the research as for the final execution of the book.

Near the end of the book you will find the sources. These sources highlight the work's connection to other writings, in which I have found both great inspiration and inexhaustible knowledge. The sources also indicate the archives I have been collaborating with, people Anna and I have interviewed for our podcast, and the moving images that have been a part of the *Snowblindness* research and translation.

Some of the texts have been translated from Danish to English. This is mostly true for passages of EM's writings, as well as the various email correspondences I had with relatives, archivists, and publishers. Where the contributor wished to remain anonymous, I have carefully transformed the text into my own formulation, and in some cases have merged conversations together, leaving only the essence of the context intact. Where the contributor wished to be quoted, the proofreader and I were very careful when translating these parts, and tried to make as few changes as possible to retain the original voice and content. Where the contributors wished that conversations should not be included in the book, Anna and I covered the conversations with the same metallic layer, as it is echoed throughout the book on images and texts, which made these passages unreadable and hidden. These precautions and protocols when dealing with conversation-as-material are observed to respect issues of privacy and ethics, to avoid plagiarism, and for the protection of agency contracts.

The images in the book appear as a stream of narratives, feeding a conversation to the chapters and the text images, as the images and texts are connected to one another (both the semi-fictional texts and essayistic reflections). In their specific order that touches the horizontal line in the middle of the pages, they become one entity in dialogue with each other, as though they are having a conversation about the idea of 'collective memory' The 'collective memory' or the 'Basic Narrative' is the dominant historical story that is frequently retold, rewritten, and perceived as a universal history, mostly dictated from and in the Western/European world. There is often not one 'collective memory' but many formulations and examples of collective memories, depending on who the author is and who the receiver is, and where this 'collective memory' is communicated. When writing the 'collective memory' I am referring to the dominant historical context retold in Denmark, on the relationship between the Nordic countries and 'Rigsfællesskabet' (the Danish Kingdom). When writing 'collective memory' without the 'the', I talk about the general existence of a dominant historical narrative, in mostly the Western/European world. and territories of opacity. This element brings a more coherent recognition to the reader, as they dive into the narratives and design choices throughout the book. Each image is paired with a footnote number, all of which are mapped out in the

IMAGE INDEX

at the very end of the book, in the appendix, which gives information (or the most precise estimation) about the origin, date, and source of every image.

Finally, throughout *Snowblindness*, the footnotes offer a crucial contribution to the understanding of the research and content. The footnotes function both as links to other writings, actors, and events, and as an editorial voice accompanying the dialogues that I, Gudrun, had with my collaborators, (my) Father, I write Father with a capital 'F' throughout the book, which functions as a cover name for my Father. However, in this publication I am not writing any falsehoods, or committing 'libel'. I am very aware of the responsibility for the wellbeing of my family, and I consequently use cover names in the *Snowblindness* texts, though Father has agreed to contribute as a source of knowledge, an external text editor, and a collaborator. and Anna. Though the footnotes appear in a smaller font size, they also take space as small interruptions, comments, and edits inside the text, with the insistence that they should neither be overlooked nor forgotten.

Finally, it is not necessary for the chapters to be read in chronological order. The reader should feel free to jump between chapters as they please, as the images and texts all communicate with – and are in reference to – one another.

INTRODUCTION

What are the notions of 'truth' underlying this work? Is it the multiplicity of voices – a way to offer alternative perspectives on history (read 'collective memory'), or is it a way we come to terms with a colonial past? Nele Wynants, ed., *When Fact is Fiction: Documentary Art in the Post-Truth Era* (Amsterdam: Valiz, 2020), 14. While 'truth' is such an enormously loaded and contested term, my agenda is not to reveal a certain 'truth', I believe there exist different versions of a 'truth', which depend on the interpretations of the author and the receiver. A universal 'truth' regarding matters of the past that is equal and true for everyone simply does not exist. We have to take care in these moments, as universal terms could support colonial discourses, which I seek with this book to confront and to challenge. but instead to expose various 'truths' that are connected to the narratives both in- and outside of the 'collective memory'. Here I use 'collective memory' to refer to the dominant historical context consistently retold and rewritten, and usually perceived as a 'universal story', mostly dictated from and in the Western/European line of sight.

Snowblindness came to exist not only out of an individual urgency and specific perception of my 'truth', but also from the understanding that this urgency and thought seemed to be shared, and critically reflected upon, by many design colleagues, writers, filmmakers, artists, and actors in today's creative disciplines. In the design field, there is a need to critically redefine and re-situate the discipline. There is a need to acknowledge that the design discipline in itself is deeply linked to the rise of capitalism, the culture of mass-production, and the exploitation of both natural resources and human labour, and that design still contributes to the logic and discourses of Western societies, Claudia Mareis and Nina Paim, eds., *Design Struggles: Intersecting Histories, Pedagogies, and Perspectives* (Amsterdam: Valiz, 2021), 15. as design theorists Claudia Mareis and Nina Paim write in *Design Struggles*. How can *Snowblindness*, in practice, implement a decolonial approach to its design? How can it give emphasis to more voices that seek to critically challenge the dominant modernist idea of the design 'tradition', and how can it seek to address the colonial and imperialist entanglements that haunt the discipline? *Snowblindness* may not present any solutions, but it hopes to apply a curious and open reflection through its texts and visuals. The artistic research behind *Snowblindness* does consider the 'collective memory' and colonial legacy while leaving crucial space for comments, edits, and opacity, for both the reader and the people involved in its making.

In search of vision and collaboration, I investigated the 'collective memory' of Nordic colonialism in my own design practice. *Snowblindness* uses an autoethnographical approach when including personal narratives and experiences to illustrate the relations between a colonial past and its treatment in design, translation, and research, which can offer a wider cultural and social commentary. This book contains reflections on methodologies in the design field; how to access, how to re-contextualise, Meaning something that generates new meanings that change over time and how to edit content. It thinks through how to share, include, and make material public, and how to debate the 'collective memory', challenge colonial discourses, and understand ethical responsibilities in the process of design research. It exposes the struggles and triumphs of artistic making, working between fiction and reality, which seeks to be relevant and recognisable for others while seeking to function as thorough cultural critique.

The story of how *Snowblindness* came to exist can be traced back to the first Danish and Norwegian encounters in the Arctic region, and then throughout the several epochs of missionary, colonial, and security control that followed. In the name of God, science, and rescue, the Danish Kingdom gained territory: Kalaallit Nunaat (Greenland). Under the Danish flag my great-grandfather, EM, sailed in Arctic waters and imprinted his narrative on maps, books, and people. His engagement in Greenland and the Arctic garnered much admiration and honour, especially among Danish circles.

Sadly, colonial dynamics are still present in Greenland today, and these colonial dynamics also still mark other countries that in one way or another are involved in colonial processes and exploitation. The relationship between the countries are marked by the different partners' perception of the colonial history, whether that is the perspective of people from the post-colony, or the post-colonial power. As several scholars and researchers have observed, the relationship between Greenland and Denmark can be classified as 'typical' in the post-colonial landscape, where even after the official termination of colonialism the relationship is still marked by its highly asymmetrical power relations. Kirsten Thisted, "De-framing the indigenous body," *Nordlit* 29 (2012): 280. This is something I was very aware of during the research process and editing for this book. I use the connection to Greenland, with my familial relation to EM, to find a reflective and questioning voice on the matter of post-colonial history, and thereby encounter a unique position as a designer and editor in the discussion of the vision – and its narration – of decolonising

Greenland. It is important for me to state that I do not wish to act as an historian, and especially not as an ethnic Danish citizen dictating history. Instead I wish to question history, and to make space for a multiplicity of narrations and voices. I have tried to understand and consider the Greenlandic-Danish relations and the stories involving EM in the context of their time and geopolitical situation. This has been necessary in order for me to better understand my own background, where it is common, and even encouraged, to believe what EM did in Greenland, or what the Danish Kingdom did in Greenland, The Danish Kingdom (meaning the Danish Government at the time EM lived). July 2020, Father added: "EM did not always agree with the Danish Government, upon what needed to be done in Greenland and at what pace." as something 'good'. But what the Danish Kingdom did in Greenland was also highly problematic. I have tried to be reflective and responsible, for the content and discourses in the research and in this book, by questioning and analysing structures, methods, narratives, and practices, while yet still taking responsibility for the wellbeing of the contributors and myself. This is elaborated in more detail in MY STRUGGLE WITH SEEING CLEARLY.

Though this research might seem to advocate only for a transparent agenda and practice to remove the blindfold and to see clearly, the book responds just as much to a need for opacity. Only with trust and care for the actors, collaborators, and contributors involved in the project can a transparent dialogue occur. Opacity enabled us (the people involved in the book) to handle the vulnerable matter with mutual respect and care, as it opened up for new dialogues and narratives. This inclusion of dialogue and comments when unfolding a colonial past helped me to overcome a blindness in my own practice. By approaching my own background with trust and the acknowledgement of the right to opacity, it is possible also to challenge a collective 'snow blindness' and to debate coloniality. This is all something Anna, Father, and I discussed in relation to design translations and editorial decisions throughout this book.

I believe, within my practice as a designer, that I have the freedom to relocate, discuss, and translate material, also if that material is formed from historical documents and visuals, and eventually release improvements in the act of re-situating and recontextualising material in a new form within another discipline. In that way, I will hopefully contribute to the idea that other communities and voices feel that they can benefit, take space, and challenge 'collective memory's' lack of vision and inclusivity.

In making this book I do not wish to pass judgement on anyone, or to make any assumptions of other people's understanding of history and 'collective memory'. I am, however, interested in what it means to access, edit, discuss, share, and preserve certain narratives – narratives that are either directly or indirectly connected to my own heritage and practice. This is how, in collaboration with Anna, we came up with the title and subtitle *Snowblindness – Let's talk about storytelling, colonialism, Netflix, and my great-grandfather.* Snow blindness is defined as a painful eye disease caused by light when the sun is reflected into the snow, which then in an overexposed form of light burns the eyes. If snow-blinded, one cannot see clearly. In this research, 'snow-blinded' refers to a blindness within the reproduction of the collective's colonial narratives (and yes Netflix's narratives too), which seems to be out of sight without including other stories or counter-narratives to the production of a dominant history and 'collective memory', also treated in the chapter REFLECTION ON 'TRUTH' & THE 'COLLECTIVE MEMORY'. The title *Snowblindness* acknowledges this blindness and tries to confront it when dealing with storytelling (the practice of design), the mechanisms of colonialism, and the influences of contemporary media culture such as Netflix, all in relation to the case study of EM.

As a contemporary designer from a post-colonial power it is important for me to make this book, as it debates my own position and urgencies in the design discipline itself, making me reflect upon under which context and conditions, and with which media, I can create work. This book confronts a present coloniality, Some actors would even claim that Greenland was never a Danish colony, but instead claim that Greenland was considered part of the old Danish-Norwegian kingdom that came into Denmark's 'custody' after 1814, and that the word 'colony' was used in the Greenlandic context for the newly established cities on Greenland's west coast, and not comparable with the other territory that the Kingdom of Denmark possessed in the 17th century, as Thorkild Kjærgaard notes in his writings. Thorkild Kjærgaard, "Grønland og Hermond Lannungs private udenrigspolitik," Weekendavisen, accessed September 6, 2021, https://www.weekendavisen.dk/2017-8/boeger/groenland-og-hermod-lannungs-private-udenrigspolitik). It is an opinion I highly disagree with, as in my view it arrogantly neglects the cause of the very harmful events that happened during Danish rule affecting many Inuit and Greenlanders. and debates storytelling, encouraging a questioning of History (with capital H), ethics, and aesthetics. It is in an autoethnographic lens throught which I too try to confront my own blindness.

Snowblindness also arises from a collaborative need for Anna and I to leave space for various and multiple narratives, which is elaborated much further in EDITING & SHARING. It is our aim that this book will appeal to collectives and a broad range of individuals, whether they are artistic practitioners, or people interested in journalism, history, and postcolonial studies. This book responds to the need to review the design discipline, and reflects on 'reality' by trying to create meaning in the exchange between author and interpreter, and by making connections between the past, present, and future. *Snowblindness* tries, through reflections on memory and experience, to draw connections between materials and narratives and to guide a meaningful design and research practice. *Snowblindness* tries to remove the blindfold to access vision. In this very search for vision, it is important for me to state that this book is made with love.

He mostly talked about the stories, the success stories, he had.

In January 2020 in the moving image *Dialogue w. EM through my father* EM/Father said: "He mostly talked about the stories, the success stories, he had."

008.JPG

009.JPG

In April 2020, Father wrote: South of Scoresbysund

EM (born 1880) was a Danish coloniser. He founded the colony Scoresbysund/Ittoqqortoormiit in 1924-25. The colony consisted of inhabitants from Ammassalik/Tasiilaq, which is located about 1000 kilometre south from Scoresbysund. There is a bust of him there, which was recently covered with black paint. EM was my great-grandfather (source from Frederiksen's book).

010.JPG

011.JPG

012.JPG

Pia Arke in *Stories from Scoresbysund:* What does 'incorpo ed in the ranks of Danish Greenland' me Is the answer to be found in Angmagssa [old Greenlandic for Ammassalik], Scoresbysund and Da borg's common history, the exercise of D ish sovereignty over the virtually uninh ited territory of East Greenland? But w deceives us and makes that history subli and limitless is its second edition, wh states that it was to relieve famine and ease in Angmagssalik that Scoresbys was colonised.

In April 2020, Father wrote: In The Hauge, Ebbe Munch was ambassador in London and Lord Chamberlain for the Queen.

In February 2020, Father wrote: It is not Ella Mikkelsen, if it had been, she would not put her arm under H.P. Nielsen.

EM (born 1880, died 1971) was a Danish inspector. He prevented Norway to take territory over East Greenland. He was an important actor in the Danish sovereignty claim over Greenland and took part in the East Greenland process at the International Court of Justice in Den Haag in 1921-1933. EM was my great-grandfather (source from Father and Frederiksen's book).

EM was a polar explorer. He was captured on Greenland's East Coast for 2 1/2 years. He lived in a wooden house. This house was once his own ship, named Alabama. EM was my great-grandfather, and I have his eyebrows (source from Father).

017.JPG

Danmark

In January 2020 in the moving image *Dialogue w EM through my father* EM/Father said: “He was not thinking of himself; he was thinking of the people on the East Coast of Greenland.”

He was not thinking of himself,
was thinking of the people on the East Coast of Greenland.

019.JPG

1. Tale holdt ved indvielsen af Mikis Hus af Emil Madsen.
Fangstmand og næstformand i Scoresbysunds Kommunalbestyrels

Nu har vi fået vort ønske opfyldt.
Velkommen alle i Mikis Hus!. Nu er gaven til Jer blevet
Mikis Hus skal bruges på denne måde, at alle beboere i Scor
sund distriktet kan komme og bruge huset som værksted (la
håndværk, skæresrbejde), her kan fremvises film og der k
holdes dansemik og laves kaffemik.
Som I alle ved, har man lige fra oprettelsen af Scoresbysu
kaldt os for "Mikis folk". Lige fra 1924 har han arbejdet
os, til gavn og glæde for os. I år havde han for sidste ga
hårdt for at hjælpe os, idet han skaffede os et ungdomshus
Han rejste rundt i Danmark i tre måneder og havde så travl
at han næsten ikke sov. Det lykkedes ham til slut at skaff
penge nok til opførelsen af huset.
Nu står huset færdigt, og vi skal indvie det. Og ikke mind
må vi takke vore venner i Danmark, som har givet os penge
til formålet. Til slut vil vi takke fangerne i Kap Hope og
den svenske tømrer og takke arkitekt Allan, som med dygtig
og velvilje har opført huset. Vi vil som tak udbringe et
foldigt Hurra for Miki og for dem, der gav pengene.
For første gang vil indbyggerne i Scoresbysund indsamle
penge. Huset er først og fremmest en gave til fangerne og
vet til gavn for hele befolkningen i Scoresbysund.
Dette har jeg sagt på Kap-Hoper-nes vegne.

020.JPG

EM was a captain. He later became the chairman for the East Greenland's Home Rule Agency. EM was my great-grandfather (source from Frederiksen's book).

INVOLVEMENT OF NETFLIX

Over the last years, large publishing companies have encountered a new competitor: Netflix. The global streaming platform and the other publishers are all competing for consumers' time and money. Keeping their enemy close, the biggest publishing company in Denmark, Gyldendal, have negotiated a contract with Netflix to make a feature film focusing on the adventures of a Danish polar explorer. With the consent of the descendants of this explorer, two publishing companies in Denmark, Gyldendal and Lindhardt & Ringhof, have gained the rights to republish his books and to digitalise them as e-books, audio-books, and print-on-demand material in various languages.

These books of 'adventure' are written by EM who, one could argue, is a key narrator of the stories that make up 'collective memory' of Greenlandic-Danish history. EM's stories and experiences have now been encountered by the big machinery of Netflix. The production of a dominant Westernised popular culture, and therefore 'collective memory', has likely been a point of interest for Netflix ever since it was established, as a cornerstone on which to build their business. Netflix's methods as a production company have seen them develop as one of the most popular and well-known distributors of film, television, and moving image content of the last fifteen years, which has boosted their capacity to effect media regulation and carry out data-mining, challenging traditional forms of entertainment, Allison N. Novak, "Framing the Future of Media Regulation through Netflix", in *The Netflix Effect: Technology and Entertainment in the 21st Century*, eds. Kevin McDonald and Daniel Smith-Rowsey (London: Bloomsbury Academic, 2016), 50. and influencing a whole generation.

As I see it, the publishing and streaming companies are both the consumers and the producers of 'collective memory' and the narration of the colonial moments in Greenland. This 'collective memory' does not seem to include a plurality of narratives and narrations by the Inuit people – the native population of Greenland – in the (re)making of 'the' story. The 1922 film *Nanook of the North* The director claimed that the film is documentary realism, when it was actually a staged film with handpicked 'actors'. by Robert J. Flaherty is a prominent and disturbing example of how native people and their stories have been used to feed a Western discourse in the Western film industry through use of Western methods, aesthetics, and ethics. I fear that the coming Netflix film *Against the Ice*, based on EM's book *Farlig Tomandsfaerd* (English translation: *Two Against the Ice*), will fit the mechanisms of colonialism and capitalism all too well.

The sensational nature of this collaboration between Gyldendal and Netflix reached new heights when it became known that Nikolaj Coster Waldau, the internationally popular Danish actor who gained fame from appearing in the TV series *Game of Thrones,* would not only be co-writing the film script together with the Danish instructor Peter Flinth, but would also be cast as the polar explorer himself. Much of the film is to be filmed in Iceland, a location very popular for new film productions, but with very little connection to the landscape of the actual events and their colonial imprint on the people of Greenland, and EM's quests. The current and continuous problem, as I understand it, is that it is mostly third parties that handle and distribute certain historical material, Manu Luksch, "From the Cellar to the Cloud", in *Lost and Living (in) Archives: Collectively Shaping New Memories*, ed. Annet Dekker (Amsterdam: Valiz, 2017), 108. and that these third parties, regardless of whether they are publishers or streaming services, feed 'collective memory', national spirit, As the 1924 film *The Great White Silence* by Herbert Ponting came to advocate for the British Empire. and the 'cultural archive', and romanticise these narratives.

From: Me Sent: 6. August 2020, 09:00 To: Gyldendal Rights & Permissions

Subject: 'Farlig Tomandsfærd' and Gyldendal's collaboration with Netflix

Dear Gyldendal Rights & Permissions,
I am writing to you regarding EM's *Farlig Tomandsfaerd* and the agreement you at Gyldendal are about to negotiate with Netflix. I am familiar with this collaboration you have with Netflix, since I am the child of Father, and he the grandson of EM. The reason why I am interested in your collaboration with Netflix is due to a research I am currently developing for my master degree in Design, where I am making a project around colonial heritage, and history/myth-writing in relation to design methodologies. EM and his work are a part of my case study in this project. In the last 10 months has the project taken shape with several translations such as objects, graphics, text and video. I have become aware that Netflix will soon make a draft-contract with you at Gyldendal, here I refer to an email you sent around the 2nd of March to XM, who forwarded your email on the contract process to Father, which Father then forwarded to me. I am in that regard very interested in what draft of contract Netflix has submitted to you? What narrative and 'take' will they have on *Farlig Tomandsfaerd*? Do they have plans to film other books by EM too, or make a film about his life? When will this film start its production? Why do you, as Denmark's finest and biggest publisher, collaborate with a film-streaming service such as Netflix? What will you get out of this collaboration? And what do the relatives of EM get out of that collaboration too? If you want more information about my project or background for this interest, please let me know. Looking forward to hearing from you.
Kind regards,
Gudrun

From: Gyldendal Rights & Permissions Sent: 2. September 2020, 10:23 To: Me

Subject: SV:'Farlig Tomandsfærd' and Gyldendal's collaboration with Netflix

Dear Gudrun,

Thank you for your email and questions about *Farlig Tomandsfaerd* and Netflix. I can unfortunately not help you with much information about the project at the moment, since the manuscript is not ready yet. In addition, we are subject to a strict confidentiality clause, so we can not disclose information about the agreement. However, what I can tell you at this moment is that no films are at this moment planned with Netflix. Gyldendal collaborates with many different producers in Denmark and the rest of the world in terms of sales of film and TV rights, Netflix is one of many in other words.

Kind regards,

Gyldendal Rights & Permissions

From: Me Sent 1. January, 2021, 15:02

To: Gyldendal Rights & Permissions

SV:'Farlig Tomandsfærd' and Gyldendal's collaboration with Netflix

Dear Gyldendal Rights & Permissions,

hank you for your reply in September. It truly interesting if the manuscript and a ible film adaptation of *Farlig Tomands-* will happen, in light of a growing focus reenland, the Arctic region and the 300 ar anniversary of Hans Egede's arrival to enland, followed by the colonialisation. very curious if the project has found its ling ground, and if you at Gyldendal has any closer to a deal with a film service/ ovider? My family and I are very curious the process. Hope to hear from you, best wishes for a happy new year!

Kind regards,

Gudrun

From: Gyldendal Rights & Permissions Sent: 19. January 2021, 22:33 To: Me

Subject: SV:'Farlig Tomandsfærd' and Gyldendal's collaboration with Netflix

Dear Gudrun,

Today, Netflix has released the news about the film *Against the Ice* (Farlig Tomandsfærd), you can read more here: https://about.netflix.com/en/news/nikolaj-coster-waldau-and-joe-cole-star-in-netflix-feature-film-against-the-ice

We look forward to the film being released on Netflix sometime this year, I have asked them for a more accurate date, but have not heard from them yet. Peter Flinth wrote today

that he is editing the film right now.
Kind regards,
Gyldendal Rights & Permissions,

From: Me Sent 10. July, 2021, 18:59
To: Gyldendal Rights & Permissions
Subject: SV:'Farlig Tomandsfærd' and Gyldendal's collaboration with Netflix

Dear Gyldendal Rights & Permissions,
Thanks for the link to the news of Netflix film *Against the Ice* earlier this year. It will be exciting to see Peter Flinth's interpretation of the book *Farlig Tomandsfaerd.* I have just learned that the premiere has been postponed to the spring of 2022. Have you at Gyldendal heard anything about the film's character, interpretation and content, as the premiere is approaching? And do you know if there has been any local East Greenlanders looking through/working on the manuscript too? Or whether there have been external connoisseurs of EM's literary works in the script, or at the film adaptation in Iceland? I ask out of interest for specific interpretation of the narrative and what it adds in the 'collective memory'. Hope this mail finds you well and that you have a good summer too.
Kind regards,
Gudrun

It has been difficult to gain any insight or information on the making of the Netflix film, even for the descendants of the polar explorer. By emphasising the relation I have to the copyright holders, as well as explaining my position as a designer and a researcher, I tried to access information about the process of the film and the contract between the publishing house and Netflix, but still I had no significant luck.

Netflix seems only to be expanding. They even have their own button on TV remote controls! Netflix's development will undoubtedly shape media, technology, and future policy debates. As it is predicted by external observers, Netflix will likely provide key insights into how societies will be moving forward culturally, Kevin McDonald and Daniel Smith-Rowsey, eds., *The Netflix Effect: Technology and Entertainment in the 21st Century* (London: Bloomsbury Academic, 2016), 15. maybe in the same way as the photographic medium authorised and authored time and place as we know it, which is also treated briefly in the chapter ANOTHER STORY ON EM

Perhaps it is Netflix's position, as Susan Sontag predicted before the company came to exist, that film is made purely for the purposes of entertainment (that is, commercial) without a self-critical reflection of their productions. Sontag anticipated that these commercial films, the kind streamed by Netflix, are 'astonishingly witless; the vast majority fail resoundingly to appeal to their cynically targeted audiences.' Susan Sontag, "The Decay of Cinema," The New York Times, accessed June 13, 2021, https://www.nytimes.com/1996/03/17/magazine/l-the-decay-of-cinema-007358.html.

Unfortunately, it is not possible to share the details of the conversations between the descendants and heirs of EM in this publication due to reasons of privacy and due to agency contracts. What I can reveal is that the film *Against the Ice* will have its world premiere during the Berlin Film Festival 2022, and that a private Netflix screening-event will happen in Denmark for those involved in making the film and for the descendants of EM. The trailer for the film *Against the Ice* was realised and made public in January 2022. January 2022, Father noted: I don't understand why a woman appeared in the end of trailer, unless it was a dream he [EM] had.

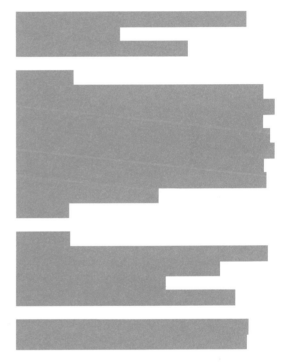

It seems to be true that fiction never really exceeds the absurdity of reality.

Extract from audio recording from the premiere for the descendants in Copenhagen, February 2022.

Production team: More than half a billion people share and see the films at Netflix. The Netflix distribution channel is huge ... It is an amazing story of two men in the sublime North, that we want to tell the world, and we are so proud of it.

Peter Flinth: Without Netflix this movie would not succeed. And it would have been very heavy if... For the first it would be impossible to make it on that scale without Netflix.

HISTORICAL CONTEXT

2021 marks 300 years of Denmark's engagement in Greenland after the first missionary and colonial project led by Hans Egede. Hans Egede (1686–1758) was a Danish-Norwegian priest, missionary, and coloniser. Ever since, Greenland and Denmark have been a part of each other's history, for better and for worse. But as discussed by the Danish anthropologist Kirsten Hastrup in her article 'Colonial Moments in Greenland', 'far greater consciousness of the Greenlandic point of view on this ["shared"] history has been necessary I would like to note that it is still very necessary to include the Greenlanders' and Inuits' voices. to really establish the kind of new, equal "partnership" that is the goal of the current negotiations about an expansion of the Home Rule Act.' Kirsten Hastrup, "Colonial Moments in Greenland: Mutable Tensions in Contact Zone," *Itinerario*, vol. 43, no. 2 (2019): 255.

Rigsfaellesskabet (The Danish Kingdom) consists of the nations Denmark, Greenland, and the Faroe Islands. Greenland is physiographically a part of the continent of North America, but is politically and culturally associated with Denmark, as Denmark is the late colonial power. The majority of Greenland's population are Inuit, and the national language only quite recently changed from Danish to Greenlandic. Even though many of the administrative and everyday texts, signs, and oral communications are still in Danish, and Danish is still widely spoken in mostly resourceful Greenlandic families. Greenland has been colonised over several periods in history, all of which have greatly impacted the area and its people by bringing environmental degradation, the spread of disease, economic instability, ethnic rivalries, and human rights violations, to mention the worst examples. The Danish supremacy has taken many different forms over the centuries, and while I will not unfold these in great detail in this book, it is important for me to state that I acknowledge that the colonised space in which people are geographically and historically separated has caused conditions of coercion, radical inequality, and intractable conflict, Hastrup, "Colonial Moments in Greenland," 244. Quote by Mary Louise Pratt. and that Greenland is no exception to this matter, though the Danish 'collective memory' has tried to 'polish its self-image as a good, friendly and mild colonial power.' Michelle Arrouas, "Danske stat lille naturfolk," Information, accessed September 4, 2021, https://www.information.dk/kultur/2016/10/danske-stat-lille-naturfolk. I support a Greenlandic independence should the Greenlandic people wish to detach themselves from the Danish state, whenever the Greenlandic public and Government of Greenland propose and vote for independence. I acknowledge that Danish supremacy in Greenland has taken many double-sided forms. The majority of actions by the Danes may have sprung from good intentions, but ultimately they left many scars and much damage throughout history; damage that good intentions cannot fix or heal.

This book does not seek to justify any of these positions or intentions, nor does it take anything as an absolute. Instead I would like it to address the space where these trajectories intersect – where narratives and subjects become co-present – to try to understand better how we deal with these spaces and narratives both today and in the future. This book and its research attempt to investigate the above by using as a case study my great-grandfather: EM.

EM was a captain, polar explorer, and coloniser. He was an important and prominent actor in Arctic territorial discoveries as well an important actor in the establishment of a new colony in East Greenland for the indigenous people. These events resulted in Danish sovereignty over all of Greenland through a trial called the Eastern Greenland case or *Grønlands Processen* in The Hague, The Greenland Process in The Hague, which was a trial in The International Court of Justice, The Hague, between Denmark and Norway on Greenland, 1921–1933. at which EM was a member of the Danish delegation. This was a delegation that fought in The International Court of Justice for Greenland to remain as one territory under Danish control, and not to split or share the territory with Norway.

Father (from an interview in February 2020):
"When the decision was made in The Hag about the conflict between Norway and Denmark, where should Greenland, East Greenland, belong to. He [EM] was very much responsible for that Greenland shou not be halved."

EM supported the Danish trade monopoly in the interest of the Greenlanders, and he pursued (as did many others) a very specific colonial project based on a difficult negotiation between the urge to protect the traditional culture and the urge to modernise and change this same culture. Hastrup, "Colonial Moments in Greenland," 253.

Father (from an interview in February 2020) while looking through his family album:
"Scoresbysund was a place where grandfather, your great-grandfather, moved them [Inuits from around Ammassalik] to. To Scoresbysund from Ammassalik, 1000 kilometers North, because the livelihood was not so good in Ammassalik, since they could not live of th fish they caught there. He moved them to Scoresbysund, where they could live and h better fishing opportunities ..."

It is important to understand here, throughout this book, and in conversations, that 'colonialism is composed of significant moments and particular national visions [a context], rather than uniform ideologies.' Hastrup, "Colonial Moments in Greenland," 253. This idea is demonstrated by EM, writing when the colony Scoresbysund/Ittoqqortoormiit was established in 1924:

'The flag ... it is raised, is caught by the summer breeze, unfolds, flutters merrily from the pole – looks splendid against the gloomy background of the mountains, against the pure blue of the sky: Comrades Scoresbysund has been incorporated in the ranks of Danish Greenland; we have add a foot breadth to Denmark's soil – may good fortune find a dwelling in the new colony!' Pia Arke, *Stories from Scoresbysund* (Copenhagen: Pia Arke Selvskabet & Kuratorisk Aktion, 2010), 12.

Although EM fought for Danish control of Greenland, his motivation was not ideological, but aimed to support what he believed could benefit Greenland and Denmark, the nation and kingdom.

EM wrote about his experiences, adventures, and discoveries in the Arctic/Greenland in several publications and articles, which became very central to Danish self-understanding and outward image. These writings were published internationally over six decades and given to almost every young Danish man as a confirmation gift. One could say that these generations of young men were schooled in stories about the great adventures made by Danes in the sublime North. Here, especially the events that took place during *Danmark-Ekspeditionen* Danmark Ekspeditionen (or translated 'Denmark-Expedition') was a Danish expedition to Greenland's Northeast coast from 1906 1908 led by the Danish polar explorer Ludvig Mylius-Erichsen who was accompanied by 28 other men, including the cartographer Niels Peter Høeg Hagen and the Greenlandic polar explorer Jørgen Brønlund. The main task of the expedition was to map, at that time, the completely unknown northeastern coast of Greenland, which included carrying out geological, botanical, zoological, meteorological, oceanographic, and archaeological studies. Ole, Ventegodt, "Danmark Ekspeditionen," Den Store Danske Encyklopædi, accessed September 4, 2021, https://denstoredanske.lex.dk/Danmark-ekspeditionen. and EM's *Alabama-Ekspeditionen* (1909–1912), which was an attempt to find the bodies or other traces of Mylius-Erichsen and his colleagues during *Danmark-Ekspeditionen,* were of great importance to Danish self-understanding. These stories, told by the polar explorers, recreated the narrative of Denmark being 'a little nation of great achievements', after Denmark lost one third of its kingdom in 1864. These publications formed a genre in its own right, with writings full of adventures, explorations, politics, dangers, and heroes. EM was one of those heroes.

In January 2020 on the moving image *Dialogue w EM through my father* Gudrun said:

"And what were the difficulties?"

... I'm no
you show
so we do
being sur
And the
somethin

Brother,
Maybe I
literally,
anthropo
In relatio
Although

Email fro
Dear Gu
through

Brother,
no I have
I told Mo
But she w
I didn't sa
Did dad w
But I ca
fictitious

ut I think I would be much better off proofreading if
ore, and talked more openly with him about it. Just
between each other and that there is no risk of him

where you are from, so people do not think it is

2020, 20.29:
er. Thank you for your honesty. I wish you could understand what I am
a and what I am doing. There is nothing escaping [Sandberg]. And there is
at is not already known by the individuals who have become familiar in

t I sent you.
ds Love from

rt, I can just read text. And if you don't want to read
ke care to call your methods something akin to
different kind.
em, I think you should try sending it to mom.
u who you want to listen to.

0, 11.44:
would see your assignment before handing it in? I would be happy to go

2020, 13.36:
to dad about my job, and urged him to read it before my assessments.

t EM and I asked her if she had read it, she hadn't.

a passage that might help you to emphasize the
out the particular form, "performative biography,"

In July 2020, Father corrected the manuscript for the book *Snowblindness:* ~~Kind regards~~ Love from

026.JPG

027.JPG

028.JPG

unknown Greenlandic woman from Ittoqqoetoormiit said: "He was cute, but he could also be fucking annoying" (source from Nikolajsen's film *Scoresbysund – kolonien er mit eget barn*).

029.JPG

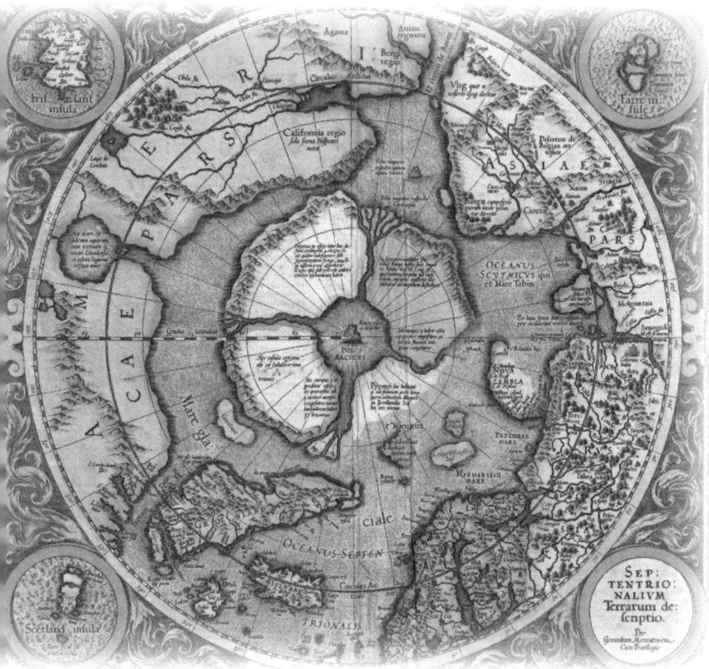

030.JPG

031.JPG

CHRISTIAN IX's PALÆ
AMALIENBORG
1257 KØBENHAVN K.
TLF. (01) 14 41 23

15. oktober 1971.

Fru Ella Mikkelsen,
Vilhelmshåbsvej 6,
2920 Charlottenlund.

Kære Ella,

Til din orientering vedlægger jeg en kopi af et brev, som jeg i dag har sendt sagfører S.E. Jørgensen. Jeg håber, at vi kan få sagen trukket igennem, men på grund af ministerskiftet må vi nok have en smule tålmodighed.

Den 22. holder vi møde i Scoresbysundkomiteen, denne gang i Aalborg. Vi vil bl.a. tage stilling til opstillingen af Fischers buste af Miki på Langelinie, som du ved, vi tidligere har fået principiel tilladelse til af Københavns borgerrepræsentation.

Hvis det passer dig, vil jeg gerne aflægge et besøg hos dig, når jeg kommer hjem fra Aalborg.

Hilsener
Din hengivne

Ebbe
(Ebbe Munck)

Bilag

032.JPG 033.JPG 034.JPG

In February 2020 in the moving image *Aftermath: Narratives on EM* Father said: "There were places where nobody had been, so he wanted to discover the land. In those days there were places on Earth that were 'white'... and that was land that had not been colonised or not been visited, you see."

In those days there were places on Earth that was *white*

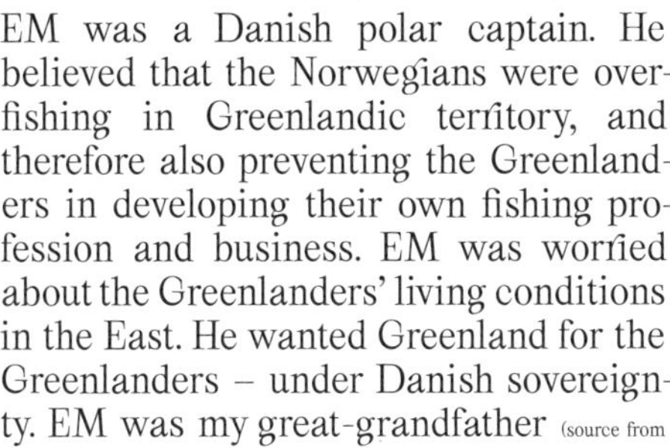

EM was a Danish polar captain. He believed that the Norwegians were overfishing in Greenlandic territory, and therefore also preventing the Greenlanders in developing their own fishing profession and business. EM was worried about the Greenlanders' living conditions in the East. He wanted Greenland for the Greenlanders – under Danish sovereignty. EM was my great-grandfather (source from Father and Frederiksen's book).

In April 2020, Father wrote: EM was responsible for moving people to Scoresbysund in order for the Greenlanders to have a better livelihood.

035.JPG

036.JPG

MY STRUGGLE WITH SEEING CLEARLY

Coloniality reaches beyond domination, conflict, ethnicity, labour, and gender. It is the relationship between subject and object, and its ongoing conditions. I have become aware of these conditions, which have set the scene of a space, which I can no longer ignore or sneak around, as something I will have to confront. As my design practice and research are situated in relation to these conditions – conditions of Nordic colonialism in relation to my own background – it is revealing a problem for me to negotiate. My struggle, and the design discipline's struggle as a whole, is to participate critically and to practise in other ways, in attempts to reach a more 'pluriversal' understanding and vision. Or, as it is mentioned in the introduction to the book *Design Struggles;* '[D]esign today struggles to confront this modernist and post-war heritage, which rests on colonialist and imperialist foundations.' Mareis and Paim, *Design Struggles*, 15.

In reading postcolonial theory and history, I became aware of my own naivety and the lack of vision I had on this matter, and sought to understand what I needed to unravel and understand in order for me to create work around the Arctic region as both a Danish woman and the great-granddaughter of EM. When reading works by Sara

Ahmed I came to understand that 'whiteness could be described as an ongoing and unfinished history, which orientates bodies in specific directions, affecting how they "take up" space.' Sara Ahmed, "A Phenomenology of Whiteness," *Feminist Theory* vol. 8(2) (2007): 150.

> '[A]fter all, bodies are shaped by histories of colonialism, which makes the world "white", a world that is inherited, or which is already given before the point of an individual's arrival. This is the familiar world, the world of whiteness, as a world we know implicitly.'
>
> Ahmed, "A Phenomenology of Whiteness," *Feminist Theory*, 153.

In these readings of the studies by post- and decolonial researchers and scholars, I became aware of my own blindness; the often hidden or invisible expressions of exclusion and the cultivation of 'the universal'. In Denmark, there is unfortunately little awareness of its most recent colonies Greenland and the Faroe Islands; their histories under Danish rule are not common knowledge. Greenland and Faroe Islands 'received' Home Rule respectively in 1953 and 1948, but still have four mandates in the Danish Parliament, as they are a part of the Danish Kingdom. Iceland finally became independent from the Danish Kingdom in 1944. And not to forget the United States Virgin Islands (the Danish West Indies), which the United States of America bought from the Danish Kingdom in 1917 for 25 million dollars in gold. This lack of historical understanding and reflection nationally, as well as internationally, is something I would like to address. It seems to be that the dominant historical context is, as usual, taking up space and 'whitewashing' other perspectives, narratives, and visions.

I, along with many others, am a product of post-colonialism, Post-colonialism is a term that indicates that colonial rule and times are over, and is a term I question, since the power imbalances that were once installed though colonisation still remain today. and thereby also a product of an unfinished colonial heritage. Some would claim the ghost of colonial moments still haunts Greenland on many different levels, and that the epoch of decolonisation to some extent has not yet arrived, since the imperialistic worldview has lived on for generations and is unfortunately still practised. The Danish State is still in control of Greenland's Foreign and Security policy, which also affects their infrastructure, trade, resource explorations, collaboration partners, etc. Racist exclusions are still present in public relations between Greenland and Denmark, just as they are globally. However, the discourse articulated on the level of governance (in Denmark especially) claims that 'we are equal partners'.

To move closer to the subject of this book, I have become increasingly interested in Arctic (geo) politics and thereby also in self-reflective questions regarding my engagement. What landscape does the 'collective memory' and my own background bring to the debate and to my own design research and practice? What does the 'collective memory' disclose about the continuities of a dominant Danish agency through past, present, and future? I see a need for clearer vision, and the need to know (the narratives of) the past, as well as to observe a relocation of agency. I see a need for an epistemic and ontological pluriversality, where other narratives must be present, and where at the same time there is space for opacity. 'Opacity' as used by the French poet and philosopher Édouard Glissant. Glissant defines the term as something that exposes the limits of schemas of visibility, representation, and identity that prevent sufficient understanding of multiple perspectives (Zach Blas, "Opacities: An Introduction + Biometrics and Opacity: A Conversation," accessed July 20, 2021, https://zachblas.info/writings/opacities-introduction-biometrics-opacity-conversation/), but also something that overcomes the risk of reducing, normalising, or assimilating the singularities of cultural differences by understanding. In optics, opacity is understood as a measure of visible light and in Adobe's Photoshop software opacity is the extent to which something blocks light.

I wish for a better understanding between narratives, and I wish for spaces that allow critical remarks and reflections on the past. I wish for an attention to these matters in the design discipline, where a new set of questions is asked. I wish for a shift. As Dutch theorist Gloria Wekker writes in *White Innocence*, 'no one colonises innocently, [and] no one colonises with impunity either.' Gloria Wekker, *White Innocence* (Durham: Duke University Press, 2016), 3.

When visiting Greenland in 2017 to deal with another project My BA graduation project, *The Mining Project – an ex-colonist mining for gold in Greenland*, 2017, from Iceland Academy of the Arts. I came across, for the first time, a story that threw an unknown shadow over EM. I am aware of my privileges as a white Danish, and therefore European, woman, and I am aware of the horrors people from the Global South in the past and also in the present have suffered due to slavery, colonialism, racism, and genocide. I am aware of the contemporary colonial politics spanning the last century, the acknowledgement of which was awkwardly absent from my educational upbringing in Danish educational institutions. But alongside this awareness there are also moments that people from my own background have not articulated or criticised when discussing the colonial moments in Greenland, which EM was involved in, when he established the colony Scoresbysund/Ittoqqortoormiit. It therefore came as a shock for me on my visit to hear a Greenlandic woman tell me about EM and her mother's friend's experiences of him. It filled me with shame.

Me, November 7, 2019, 18.00

Dear Bendo,

I hope you and Gujo had a nice trip to Denmark last week. It is good to be updated with your lives, now that I do not pass by Greenland and Nuuk that often.

I am writing to you regarding something, which has occupied my mind since we talked about postcolonial dilemmas and agendas in Danish/Greenlandic politics and relations. Do you remember telling me about EM and his journeys in Greenland/South Greenland? EM was not my biological great-grandfather, but I still feel there are some unspoken aspects about the events that happened between the Greenlandic people and the polar scientists/adventurers who acted in the Arctic. You said something about the Greenlandic women running away from him because they felt intimidated by him/his tions... Or is it completely wrongly remembered? This fall I started a Master in Design the Sandberg Institute. I am still working the themes of the Arctic, the connection Greenland's natural resources and the endence movement. As a Dane, I feel that have a co-responsibility towards Greenland promotes the wishes of the Greenlanders does not use the same old post-colonial ments that unfortunately many politicians Christiansborg [the Danish Parliament] use, but especially the co-responsibility the Greenlanders who suffered from these explorers and the Danish Government's convenient deeds in Greenland. I therefore wanted to ask you if you can describe the you told me when I visited you in March 2017 about EM and the Greenlanders' views him. Or can you recommend that I contact ome who knows the story better? My plan to make a small booklet about this issue *ratives on EM.* Through text and graphic dia. I wish to reflect on my own position in ection with the language and histories we each other about the relationship between mark and Greenland, and reflect critically Denmark's intervention and movement in enland. I hope you are doing well with all hildren and grandchildren. And finally, do feel obliged to answer you probably have a lot to look after.

Best regards from Gudrun

Bendo, November 7, 2019, 18.11

Hey Gudrun!

Lovely to hear from you. I am a bit confused if it was Lauge Koch [another polar explorer operating at the same time as EM in Greenland] July 2020, Father said: "EM could not stand Koch. They had a very different view on Greenland and the inhabitants". my foster mother's friend thought of or if it was EM. Think, though, it was the last one. Unfortunately, I do not know anything other than what is to be found on Google.

Very good luck with your Master. Though the Greenlandic woman does not recall the story she shared with me in detail in 2017, or whether it was EM or Koch who stood behind these misbehaviours, the stories or myths of the actual events still linger on and are connected to the polar explorers' adventures.

Being reflective and self-critical of one's own privileges, positions, and actions is of course necessary when addressing colonialism in the Western world – a Western world that still benefits tremendously from inhumane resource extraction, and exploitation of land, water, animals, and humans – and when discussing and presenting these matters of concern. Can I judge EM for something that he might have done or might not have done in the past, even though he cannot defend himself now? Even though the women who were victims of his misbehaviour have not raised any case against him (but to whom could they communicate this misbehaviour)? July 2020. Father said: "We can not know what happened." Even though it was another time with other social norms? Or is it 'enough' to create awareness and to facilitate access to other narrations and voices? Is it 'enough' to reflect on the context of the paradigm in which the events happened? Under what conditions am I bound to my social and political background and environment when working with this subject? And am I still ignorant in understanding and seeing the coloniality in my own behaviour, communication, and practice in everyday life working as a designer and being a European citizen when dealing and operating in a geolocation other than the one I was born into?

One cannot say that it is a 'complicated issue' without giving in to the discourse of the coloniser. One cannot decolonise design when the design field as a whole still believes that one can do the right thing by colonising subjects whilst continuing to maintain control over the directions and outcomes of decolonisation. Decolonising Design/Ahmed Ansari and Matthew Kiem. "What is needed for change? Two Perspective on Decolonization and the Academy" in Mareis and Paim, *Design Struggles*, 159.

Even though, according to some parts of my family across generations, and also in terms of a Danish self-image and understanding, it seems to be highly sensitive material to work with, I still believe that as a designer my role can be to treat this subject critically and reflectively, and that I am entitled to do so. With this story and with the process of making *Snowblindness* I am not interested in judging or 'blaming'. I am, however, interested in questioning these subjects of concern, and negotiating their relation to global histories and geopolitical dynamics. But most importantly I want to navigate how the process of making *Snowblindness*, with all its configurations, has re-situated my own design practice and methodology; my use of editing, connecting, documenting, and archiving material, as well as writing, and creating visuals and physical aesthetics.

I have dealt with matters of the Arctic region in earlier works, but after encountering the methodologies practiced at the Sandberg Instituut, Postgraduate programme of the Gerrit Rietveld Academie, based in Amsterdam, the Netherlands. my research took a much more personal turn. This resulted in a family conflict as well as a categorical problem for myself. In the beginning, dealing with my own background in a design project occurred to me as very alien and irrelevant. I did not want to have this all-too-familiar, very personal, and sensitive 'navel-gazing' approach in my work. In my previous understanding, this would only be interesting to a few people. *The Snowblindness Podcast Series 'Let's talk about what it means to collaborate with your mum – working with relatives in artistic processes'* also talks about the issues of relevance and professionalism when working together with one's family. In a collaboration with Anna Bierler and PUB (PUB is an interdisciplinary initiative by students of the Sandberg Instituut, which functions as a hub and platform to identify interdisciplinary connections and accelerate collaborations amongst the students or third parties) we created the *Snowblindness Podcast Series*, and in conversation with visual artist Carmen Dusmet Carrasco (1991) we talked about working with relatives in artistic processes. Anna Bierler and Gudrun Havsteen-Mikkelsen, "Snowblindness Podcast Series w. Carmen Dusmet Carrasco," https://extraintra.nl/initiative/student-council/event/snow-blindness-podcast-series-1. However, shortly after diving into the research it became clear to me that these issues spoke to a much larger audience about a wider concern. These notions of colonial heritage, dominance, and colonial guilt are not unique; many people and many societies will be able to recognise their own story in this book, comparing how oneself, one's own relatives, and one's surrounding institutions deal with 'collective memory', which, in many cases, comes from the only written and archived narrative distributed, which has also shaped our identities.

In this research, and in 'my struggle with seeing clearly', it became urgent for me to understand and to reflect on when and how to share information, and how to eventually make certain information public. In this process the following questions arose: How I can influence the debate with relevance, and communicate a missing critique? Under what conditions can I as a designer, or a reader, 'benefit' from making information public? Under what conditions can I as a designer, and as a relative, attempt to be honest and transparent, while still being aware of the responsibility for the wellbeing of those implicated? And who has the (copy)right to what information, to what narrative, and to what memory?

As discussed, and treated in several cultural studies on archives and preservation in connection to postcolonial territories, I still see a need to make new ways to preserve history and to gain access to underexposed narratives, information, and material. Even though it seems easy for researchers and scientists to access such documents, as Dr. Temi Odumosu Dr. Temi Odumosu is a senior lecturer in Cultural Studies at Malmö University, Sweden. observes in her lectures, Lecture 'What Lies Unspoken: A remedy for colonial silence(s) in Denmark' by Dr. Temi Odumosu, held online November 4, 2020. there is still information that public and private archives have not succeeded to preserve, and information that they deny 'outsiders' access to.

I find it quite ironic, as it seems that certain information is only accessible as long as it corresponds to the 'collective memory' and the 'cultural archive', or to be more specific; information that deals with colonial actions written by European men of the colonial power. I will not try to propose another system of archiving or preserving material and information for museums, universities, or archival institutions in this publication. I simply wish to raise questions of accessibility, and to observe the need for changing outdated archival practices, And luckily this is also something that is happening. We see that indigenous people are collaborating on alternative ways of imagining information creation, circulation, and the practices of access in creating, using, and reusing digital technologies. (Kimberly Christen, "Does Information Really Want to be Free? Indigenous Knowledge Systems and the Question of Openness," *International Journal of Communication 6* (2012): 2881. since these methods seem to be practising and perpetuating colonial structures, in archives and institutions as well to design methods of decolonisation inside the archives and broader operational systems.

For many years it has seemed as though the imperialist and colonising nations of Europe and the West were comfortably forgetting their colonial pasts and instead celebrating the 'freedom' and 'openness' that gave humanity inexhaustible quantities of materials and resources for the 'common good.' Christen, "Does Information Really Want to be Free?", 2876. And for the same reason many of us are forgetting the dynamics of what it means to perceive a narrative that is aligned with 'collective memory'. It is essential for me to understand these dynamics and to make other perspectives and voices heard; those that have been absent from the Danish 'collective memory' in Greenland and those that have been drowned in self-congratulatory Danish narratives, in the attempt and act of 'decolonisation' by 'forgetting' the actions from the past, and instead emphasise the recent investment deals on heavy infrastructure in Greenland, Danmarks Radio, ritzau, "Nye lufthavne i Grønland bliver en realitet midt i politisk drama," https://www.dr.dk/nyheder/indland/nye-lufthavne-i-gronland-bliver-realitet-midt-i-politisk-drama. and the acknowledgements of being 'equals' in the political climate. In 1984, Stewart Brand, a debater for free use of the Internet and free use and distribution of information, said: '[I]nformation wants to be free because the cost of getting it out is getting lower and lower all the time ... By "free" I am not referring to price, but rather to the freedom to copy the information and to adapt it to one's own uses.' Christen, "Does Information Really Want to be Free?", 2874. I do not wish to follow Brand's example to the end, but I do believe that it is important to distribute 'other' narratives and information that challenges 'collective memory's' production of history. This should be accessible within and outside of institutions. As long as these other stories do not have the tendency to reproduce any mechanisms of coloniality or violence. A plurality of voices is crucial in the discussion of colonial pasts and postcolonial presents. This, the notion of copyright, and thoughts on archival practices within a design practice are all ideas I will return to in the chapter ARCHIVES & EVIDENCE.

The *Snowblindness* research truly challenged me. It pushed me to work outside of my usual realm or 'comfort zone' because I had involved my family in the project by asking them to edit, comment, and reflect on certain issues, which previously blocked or limited me from making actual work, making design decisions, edits, and visual translations of the researched matter. The act of including my family members, Father especially, in my research brought me closer to understanding the mechanisms and meaning behind editing and sharing narratives, and eventually deciding which of these narratives should stay hidden and which should be made public and preserved, as well as deepening my understanding of how these mechanisms are situated in a research and design practice.

With this book it is my intention to reflect upon the ways a designer can use different methodologies to (re-)construct narratives and materials, in this case challenging the 'collective memory' of Nordic colonialism. I do not wish to discuss how design is defined from the 'outside', or how design defines itself from within the field. Instead, I am more interested in addressing how design, storytelling, and its methods can facilitate a much more experimental and reflective approach The 'outside' society is first and foremost my own background and thereby also myself. Secondly the 'outside' society is both actors in and outside of the design/art arena, whose discourses and narratives also take part in 'collective memory' production. than the usual understanding of what design is, which is mainly referring to problem-solving. 'Design for debate' is currently being discussed among designers and researchers, often in relation to a speculative approach towards social futures. The concept 'design for debate' allows designers and thinkers to debate the implications of different futures before they happen [outside of the work]. Anthony Dunne and Fiona Raby, "Design for Debate," accessed May 15, 2021, http://dunneandraby.co.uk/content/bydandr/36/0. In the making of *Snowblindness*, the design debate has taken place 'inside the work', since I am, as a designer, embedded within the narrative and the research I unravel. Always being in between the boundaries, or a co(i)mplication, of the interpenetration of subject/object is expressed by Michael Renov using the term 'domestic ethnography', or autoethnography. Renov states that 'domestic ethnography' is a kind of supplementary autobiographical practice that functions as a vehicle of self-examination through recourse to the familiar other, but where the practice of care is defining the relation between the domestic ethnographer and subject. Michael Renov, "Domestic Ethnography and the Construction of the 'Other' Self," in *Collecting Viable Evidence*, eds. Michael Renov and Jane Gaines (Minnesota: University of Minnesota Press, 1999), ch. 7, 2-3. The designer or artist practising 'domestic ethnography' is never fully outside the work.

When dealing with research into the connection between my own background and Danish (or Nordic) colonialism, it is crucial to question whether my research could harm other people – in this case it would most likely be the people that are closest to me, or people involved as contributors to my process. Can the images and texts appear violently? Have I 'used' my family source to gain material to develop this research? Is any design project worth a family conflict? And what about the notions of public-ness and archives; what can I share and what should be kept invisible? There have been moments of true struggle, where I questioned my right to practise the almost selfish activity of writing, unfolding, and debating my story through design work, whilst trying to challenge my own practice through collaboration and involving other narratives and voices.

In these moments of questioning, the *Snowblindness Podcast Series* Podcast series of two sessions in collaboration with Sandberg Instituut's independent radio platform PUB. was developed. It was conceived in parallel to and correspondence with the *Snowblindness* research, in collaboration with Anna, as an act of decentralising media, as a broadcast (aired twice in April 2021). Here we were in conversation with visual artist and filmmaker Carmen Dusmet Carrasco to discuss her experience of collaborating with relatives in artistic processes, in the episode 'Let's talk about how it is to collaborate with your mum'. This interest and urgency discussed in a podcast format is presented and added in this book as extracts, in the attempt to incorporate this plurality of different voices and perspectives in design research and processes. In the conversation we talked about what it means to make autobiographical work and still obtain a certain quality and honesty, especially when working so closely with relatives (in Carmen's case she made the film *The Swimming Pool* Carmen Dusmet Carrasco, "The Swimming Pool," accessed April 2, 2021, http://www.carmendusmet.net/video. with and about her mother).

In the podcast, Carmen reads an extract from her writings on the subject:

> It seems that through vision – and some self-reflection – we become entangled with the world. "*Either because one seems to have been transported hundreds of feet beyond the edges of the body out into the external world, or instead because the images of objects from the external world have themselves been carried into the interior of the body as perceptual content, and seem to reside there, displacing the dense matter of the body itself.*" In a way perception is a process through which we position ourselves within objects and other subjects. Sometimes, the things that reside in front of our eyes are difficult to look at; they are painful and confront us with situations we are not ready to accept. Images from the external world may be too violent for us to allow them to be carried into our bodies and need to be looked at with some distance. I have encountered that distance through my camera's viewfinder. The compact display is designed to showcase the field of view of the camera's lens. It acts as an extension of the body providing a material separation between the observer's eye and the seen object or subject. The stories I'm about to share with you are related to the physical and metaphorical distance I experienced through the viewfinder. They are stories of woman that have also found a necessary distance through devices that extend their bodies, as a means of defining their approximation to the world around them. Carmen Dusmet Carrasco, "A Matter Of Optics", [illegible] Design Department, Sandberg Instituut, 2020, 33.

The first translation of the *Snowblindness* research did not appear, as in the case of Carmen, through the camera's viewfinder, but in the form of printed matter. The booklet *Narratives on EM* image and text, colour, 156 pages investigated the different narratives and myths surrounding EM. The image material and narratives inside came from various sources – both private and public archives – which is also treated in the moving image translation *Aftermath: Narratives on EM* Gudrun Havsteen-Mikkelsen, "Aftermath: Narratives on EM", mix of found footage and own footage, 06:35–10:35, accessed March 18, 2021, https://www.youtube.com/watch?v=jQOcB4Zffts. and the semi-fictional text

ANOTHER SILVA RERUM?

The image material on the left page in *Narratives on EM* was often presented without any connection to the specific moment described in the text on the following right page, see eventually This allowed me to make new connections and the possibility for other realities to emerge; realities sometimes different

138.JPG

from the 'collective memory', but stories which nonetheless were shared among local Greenlanders or stories shared between my family members – both communicated as a truth. The image material was mostly provided by Father and shared with me together with stories, which were either confidential or public. Other stories came from contemporary local Greenlanders (treated in Pia Arke's Pia Arke (1958-2007) was born in Scoresbysund/Ittoqqortoormiit. She had a Greenlandic mother and a Danish Father. Several of Arke's works are quite critical towards the colony Scoresbysund that EM established. and Nikolajsen's work) and from different biographies about or memories of EM.

Father's role in this design work and research has been a source of far-reaching knowledge, and he was a key player when trying to understand the complexity of the meanings of a colonial heritage. Father has been very helpful in granting me access to his archive, to family albums, memories, and knowledge of EM, Greenlandic matters, and colonialism. There has been an openness, trust, and shared interest that I did not expect, and also a willingness to discuss matters of an unpleasant character, such as some of the narratives' stories of EM shooting or harassing people in East Greenland. Discussing this matter of concern with Father was indeed difficult, since I did not wish to change or convince Father about other narratives and rumours being more 'true' than his perception (and how could I ever be the judge of that?), especially when Father, in earlier talks, refers to EM as one of his greatest role models. Some of Father's memories of EM framed him as a loving grandfather who achieved great acknowledgement and honour for his deeds. Once, Father even cut his eyebrows so that they could grow as big as EM's.

From: Me Sent: December 12, 2019, 15:23 To: Father

Subject: with love and a little request

her, have you inherited some objects from
Hope you are well and that it is peaceful
around you after the family visit.
With love
Gudrun

From: Father Sent: December 12, 2019, 23:44 To: Me

Subject: with love and a little request

Dear Gudrun,
Yes, some books and furniture are from
their home in Vilhelmhåbsvej 6. His scraper
to shave his beard with and other things, a
document folder, which I use when attending
choir practice. Alan got most of his Greenland
stuff.
With love from your father xox

From: Me Sent: December 13, 2019, 13:04 To: Father

Subject: with love and a little request

Alright, thank you for your mail! I am

speculating on making a little installation in relation to his arrangements in Greenland with my own work. Is it OK if I borrow some objects for this after Christmas? We can also talk more about it when we meet.
With love
Gudrun

From: Father Sent: December 13, 2019, 15:10 To: Me

Subject: hi and a little request

Dear Gudrun,
I have a Greenlandic oil lamp standing on
desk, which was my grandfather's. It meas
48x24x7.5 cm. The musk's skull I have
hanging in the hallway is from 1958. I brou
it home when I was there with my grandfa
and your great-grandfather.
With love Father xox

From: Me Sent: December 13, 2019, 21:37 To: Father

Subject: with love and a little request

Father, can I ask you about these issues [achievements and myths of EM], and record the sound – in English?
With love
Gudrun

From: Father Sent: December 13, 2019, 23:40:06 To: Me

Subject: with love and a little request

Please feel free to ask me in English when
you get home. I think I have some more thi
from Greenland lying in the drawers that I
find until you get home.
Love from father xox

'My struggle with seeing clearly' was also situated in questioning how, when, and where it is acceptable to share reflections on one's own colonial background. This was especially entangled with the knowledge that parts of my family, in order to protect the family reputation, would not acknowledge that another narrative connected to our shared ancestry was something that could be 'true' for others. I had troubles approaching and communicating critiques and myths of EM (critiques that had been debated by other actors and critics in other forums, and to some extent in contradiction to what I have been raised to believe), which Father and the rest of my closest family would likely not be aware of and likely not tolerate, so I thought.

Out of fear of harming the people I love, I tried to hide my research and critique, and unfolded 'myths' contra 'truths' about EM and my own colonial heritage by discussing another concern; Greenland's coming independence (which presented just as many implications as solutions and became another categorical problem). I wanted to reject the research into my colonial heritage and basically finish the project off, since it seemed as though it was not possible for me to treat the subject any further, due to the possible conflict it would generate. This was in January 2020. However, the questions of access, opacity, and moments of editing in a design practice lingered on. I started to write my reflections and struggles down. I committed myself fully to writing, and I tried to maintain a critical self-reflection on the material and research I was investigating, and to the texts I was writing. It was in the relationship between the two – the written and the writing – and through collaboration that the project *Snowblindness* came to exist. In the writing and in the making, it was as if I was disclosing a secret, and letting myself and other readers understand the weight and the very layered patchwork of narratives, findings, shame, uncertainty, and imagination embedded in the design process too.

To act upon all these writings (narratives about and by EM, my reflections related to the subject, my semi-fictional stories, etc.), I had to invent a strategy against any predetermined interpretation or judgements from my family suggesting that my critique and my feelings of shame would not be acceptable or possible to treat as subject matter in a project. The strategy I needed had to include collaborations and moments of sharing and discussing content with my collaborators, and, here especially, Father, as the main collaborator. This strategy had to include Father's edits and writings in the design work. But most importantly, this same strategy had to ensure that it would not expose any person in a harmful manner. With these considerations in mind I shared the struggles embedded in the design process, and confronted the colonial guilt, Def.: "White guilt, or European guilt [or white/European shame], is the individual or collective guilt felt by Europeans for the harm resulting from the context of the Atlantic slave trade, colonialism and the legacy of these events. In certain regions of the Western world, it can be called white settler guilt or white colonial guilt, which refer to the guilt more pointedly in relation to European settlement and colonization." Wikipedia, accessed May 13, 2020, https://en.wikipedia.org/wiki/White_guilt. with Father in conversation. Confrontations of guilt or shame in relation to the colonial moments in Greenland, the colonial moments in relation to EM in East Greenland, and the 'collective memory', first and foremost had to be situated and discussed through self-reflection. After months of further investigations

CONVERSATION WITH ANONYMOUS FAMILY MEMBERS

and discussions (with some family members who were worried about me making an 'artistic father-murder'), also treated in add chapter title hereI finally decided to share all the various narratives present in the booklet, *Narratives on EM*, with Father. This act became the strategy for continuing the project, practising 'domestic ethnography'. I shared the content in the booklet with Father, together with my struggle behind the research, while documenting and recording this encounter through the camera lens' viewfinder. All this, of course, in agreement with and acceptance from Father.

In February 2020 I interviewed Father for three days, introducing him to my work and the various narratives in the booklet. Father did not validate the issues around the 'unknown' or the stories that were critical of EM, but rather categorised them as rumours or misunderstandings. Father seemed neither sad nor disappointed about my investigation into the myths of EM and his enterprises, but more impressed with how I worked with the material and narratives related to our family in different media.

Since Father and I are both 'products' of EM, and since both of us 'are formed by the rules that allow us to speak and that we will exert on others', as Alfredo Cramerotti writes it in *Aesthetic Journalism*, Alfredo Cramerotti, *Aesthetic Journalism: How to Inform Without Informing* (Bristol: Intellect, 2009), 73. my struggle with colonial heritage had to be discussed and re-situated in relation to the researched material. I had to understand the very location of my struggle in order for me to unfold and take on the challenge of being 'snow-blinded', or of not being able to 'see clearly' in my design process, and by doing so share my struggle with Father. Father did not neglect my struggles to make work on Nordic colonialism with the family connection to EM. Nor did Father neglect the other narratives to be told; instead he understood the need for these other narratives to be heard, though he would disagree with some of them. In dialogue, Father acknowledged that the time when EM was alive was another, that people today are more enlightened, and that Father also understood the need I had to continue the research and include his comments in the work, as Father's comments both demonstrated a certain adaptation to the 'collective memory' as well as a correction of the 'collective memory', as we discussed matters of coloniality at present times in Greenland. In that way, it was not only Father's narratives and perception of history that were addressed and discussed, but also the counter-voices from other sources, with or without comments from Father. Father invested himself for hours in commenting on narratives and images, particularly if he was convinced that some of these were communicating a rumour, a misunderstanding, or simply missed important details. These conversations with Father and his comments on and around the narratives of EM allowed for new design decisions to be made.

In the *Snowblindness* research I had to delve into the old actions and power relations of coloniality, as old sentiments about the illegitimacy of the [Danish] state linger on in Greenland, and thereby keep coloniality alive. Hastrup, "Colonial Moments in Greenland," 256. Analysing these old actions and power relations, I understood that coloniality had also been kept alive in me due to the narratives formed and retold through the 'collective memory' in my educational upbringing. It has been important for me to understand, while developing this research, that colonialism is always contemporary, even though it is not ideologically uniform, and that colonialism remains within postcolonial configurations. Hastrup, "Colonial Moments in Greenland," 257. Coloniality keeps being an unfinished business, since structures of colonialism are inscribed in and remembered by bodies and territories across generations and borders. It is therefore crucial that designers of today, as individuals, are aware of these configurations, and are openly discussing the presence of colonialism (and coloniality). And, furthermore, it is crucial that designers are exploring how to challenge and change figurations of coloniality in 'collective memories' that exist across language and territories, archives and public spaces, as these narratives often claim that they are articulating the 'truth'. Or, as it is proposed in *Design Struggles:*

> In order to rethink the [design] discipline today, we must expand its definition while avoiding its past universalisms, always situating and particularising its historical claims. Moreover, the agency of design needs urgent reappraisal, a process of elevating, recovering, and creating perspectives and imaginaries beyond the dominant Western solutionist and anthropocentric model of thought. Mareis and Paim, *Design Struggles*, 12

In order to rethink, the challenge lies with ourselves. Most often, we want to tell our own story while not really being receptive to hearing a different version of it, due to the potential the other version has for calling our identity or position into question. Annet Dekker, Josien Pieterse, and Stef Scagliola, "The hidden value of oral history in an 'open' society" in *Lost and Living (in) Archives: Collectively Shaping New Memories*, ed. Annet Dekker (Amsterdam: Valiz, 2017), 128. How can we learn quickly to occupy enough distance from our own stories, norms, and values, in order to genuinely hear the other side of the coin? How can we ensure space for opacity and honesty?

Dr. Temi Odumosu investigates the other side of this coin in the field of postcolonial studies. I had a chance to ask a question in an online lecture on Danish Colonialism on November 4, 2020.

My question:

"Thank you Dr. Temi Odumosu for a really interesting, urgent, and important talk. I am curious how you move around dealing with different colonial moments and collective memories? Here I am especially thinking of the unspoken stories in Greenland."

Dr. Temi Odumosu's answer:

"So, the last place I really went to was Greenland actually, in October last year, I did major travel, I mean, we did, as a part of the art and colonialism project. It was one of those life changing moments, where you also come to understand colonialism differently though different kinds of experiences of land, place, and context. But if you, by the question, also mean how I navigate the Danish imaginary or the Danish relationship to these histories,

then it becomes infinitely more complica
'Cause one of the challenges during the w
in 2017 [research on *What Lies Unspoken*
Remedy for Colonial Silence(s) in Denma
What Lies Unspoken: Sounding the Colonial Archive was a sound interventi
Dr. Odumosu, during that year, as part of the *Living Archives Research Project*
in exhibitions at the National Gallery of Denmark and the Royal Library of Denm
lecture explores the intentions, processes, and challenges of developing a
project in the Danish cultural sector, when responding to national
of unfinished histories.] was understanding what was
layered and nuanced. In the sense that... S
the referendum that happened in 1916 incl
ed the Faroe Islands, right, and also inclu
Greenland in terms of, like, negotiating
property, negotiating territory, so... But it
was very difficult to sort of have that com
plex conversation of how... About coloni
intersections. So it just became about the
Caribbean, and to a lesser extent West an
Central Africa, although not really, when
fact 2017 2017 marked the centennial of Denmark's sale of the
West Indies to the United States of America, today called the US Virgin Islands.
have been an opportunity to talk about al
those colonial intersections as they kind
reverberate but are seen through the sail
the island, but in fact still have conseque
in the way that Denmark thinks about its
relationship, and the concepts of possessi
what colonial possession is, also its relati
ship to Norway which, you know, most of
colonial work was done under the flag of
Denmark-Norway, which we tend to forge
We think of it as just Denmark, but it was
really Denmark-Norway for most of histor
So, I think the challenge was kind of, at le
in terms of the work I have been doing...
been to sort of have a more complex or m
layered... Or having a denser dialogue ab
what colonialism is, and how it binds com
munities and bodies across space and tim
That was quite tough to do. Yeah."

When in dialogue with Father, it is hard not to imagine that what EM did for Greenland was done with the best vision and best intention for the country and its people who, I have been told from various sources, he loved so much. A quote taken from Nanna Nikolajsen's film, *Scoresbysundkolonien er mit eget barn* (2010). However, I still find it relevant to discuss the nostalgic conditions shared among explorers and colonisers, rose-tinting their 'innocent actions' as a way to capture people's imagination (the consumers and the 'collective'), and to conceal their complicity in domination Wekker, *White Innocence*, 109. through mapping, mythologising, aestheticising Kathryn Yusoff, "Configuring the field: Photography in early twentieth century Antarctic exploration' in *New Spaces of Exploration*, eds. Simon Naylor and James R. Ryan (London: I. B. Tauris, 2010), 67.,

and storytelling on matters of Nordic history and colonialism into the 'collective memory'. This is also something Wekker analyses in her work, aware of both the victims of Nordic colonialism and the victims of 'collective memory'. Wekker, *White Innocence*, 12.

Since EM's very first explorations he was convinced that the unique culture of the Inuit people, one of the only un-colonised people left on the planet at that time, was to be 'protected'. EM dedicated his life to East Greenland, but he also went there to discover, to move Inuit settlements, to gain influence, and to establish his name as a polar explorer, coloniser, and captain.

The scope of this research reaches far further than what I am capable of revealing with this book, however I still see *Snowblindness* as an important opportunity to incorporate a plurality of perspectives into the research, making, and design processes, and also into the collaborations, which I believe we will see much more of in future design practices. This is something the *Snowblindness Podcast Series* also tried to emphasise and reflect upon in the conversation with Inuuteq Storch. *The Snowblindness Podcast Series* in collaboration with Anna and PUB, in conversation with photographer Inuuteq Storch (1989) on 'Let's talk about what it means to find something and use it – working with archives and photography to highlight forgotten narratives': Anna Bierler and Gudrun Havsteen-Mikkelsen, "Snowblindness Podcast Series w. Innuteq Storch," https://extraintra.nl/initiative/student-council/event/snowblindness-podcast-series-2.

Still, readers and listeners create their own associations, no matter what. I am responsible for what I address in this book, but not for the reader's interpretation. For me, the urgency to translate this research (and the embedded autoethnographic approach and reflections) into a design work remains, so we must keep questioning whilst being in reflective dialogue with ourselves and others, to challenge the production of a dominant History.

To end this chapter of reflections on design practice, it is commonly understood that it is crucial for designers to collaborate with various industries, specialists, institutions, and communities to produce and publish work, as those actors are ultimately the transmitters of said work, urgencies, and even value in society. It is not my attempt to discuss the designer's role – today or in the future – in terms of value, collaboration, or industry, but it is important for me to state that this research has, to a large extent, been dependent on help and comments from colleagues, friends, family, and especially Father's written, visual, and oral archive and memories. I will, at a later moment in the chapter

EDITING & SHARING

treat the notion of publishing in relation to opacity, honesty, and collaboration, and thereby also the urgency and embedded strategy with and for this book.

EM was an inspector in Green-land. He was the spokesman for the hunters and fishermen in Greenland's East Coast. EM was my great-grandfather (source fro[m] Frederiksen's book).

EM was a Danish polar explorer. He saw it as his national duty to make sure that the outside world knew of Denmark's rights in the Arctic. EM was my great-grandfather, and I have his eyebrows (source from Frederiksen's book).

In April 2020, Father wrote: Is that not a myth that you have his eyebrows.

037.JPG

038.JPG

In February 2020, Father wrote: Bought by Olaf in Scoresbysund in 1958, here in Strandgade 17 Troense.

EM was a polar scientist. He was an expert on the musk in Greenland. He was the first to write the musk diaries, which resulted in a preservation of the musks and its population. EM was my great-grandfather (source from Frederiksen's book).

039.JPG

040.JPG

EM was a polar scientist. He wrote musk-diaries, which resulted in hunger in East Greenland. Only the Danish polar explorers were allowed to kill the musks, in order to feed the sledge dogs on their expeditions. EM was my great-grandfather, but not by blood (source from Pia Arke's book *Stories from Scoresbysund*).

In April 2020, Father wrote: Ella & EM were married on 1.7.1919 his former wife Naja Marie Holm (24.9.1887-18.8.1918) died of the Spanish flu.

In February 2020, Father wrote: 1.7.1919 in Korsør Sct. Pauls. Ella and EM at my parents' wedding 11.7.1936 in London.

EM was a conqueror. He married in 1919 my great grandmother Ella. Ella was the cousin of his former wife, who passed away shortly after their marriage. Ella survived him. EM was my great-grandfather, but not by blood (source from Father).

042.JPG

043.JPG

044.JPG

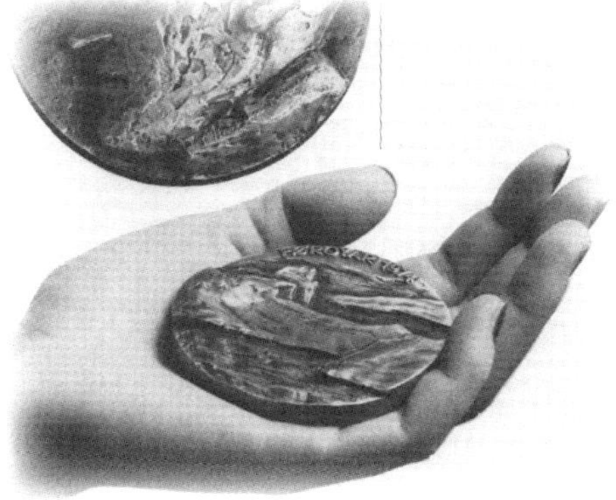

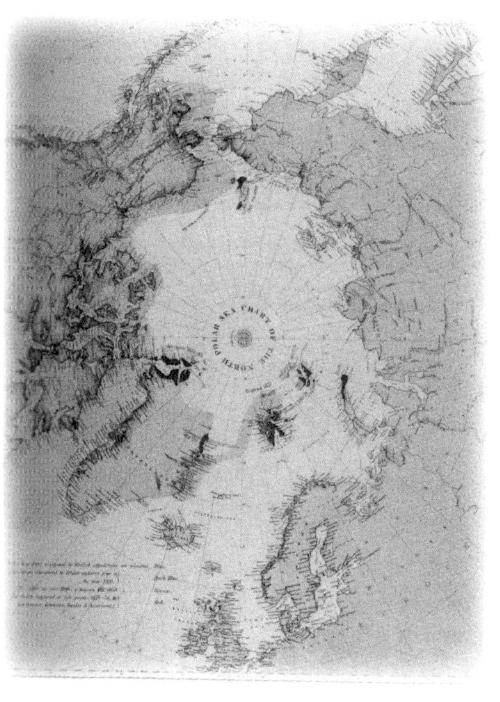

046.JPG

047.JPG

From Frederiksen's book: EM had gradually learned that newspapers and books are two different things. What is possible in one media does not have to be possible in the other.

048.JPG

049.JPG

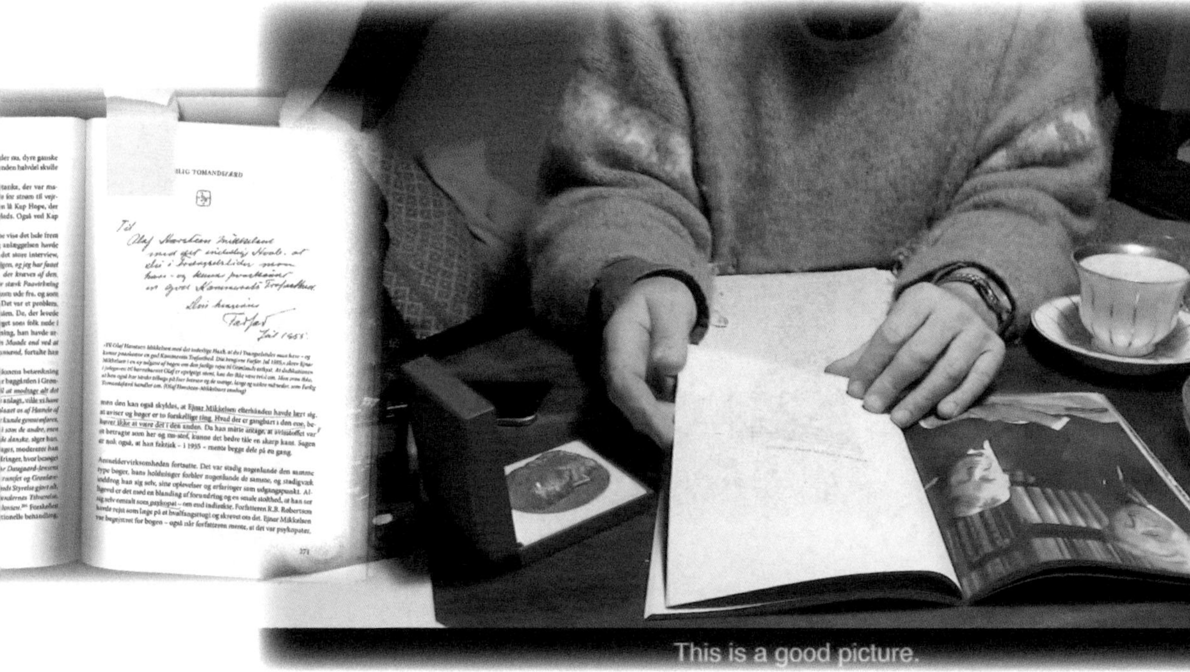

In February 2020 in the moving image *Aftermath: Narratives on EM* Father said: "This is a good picture."

050.JPG

051.JPG

052.jpg

EM was an official in the colony Scoresbysund. He used his son's savings to buy an old ship's bell from a French warship to the new establish church in Scoresbysund. EM was my great-grandfather (source from Frederiksen's book).

053.JPG 054.JPG

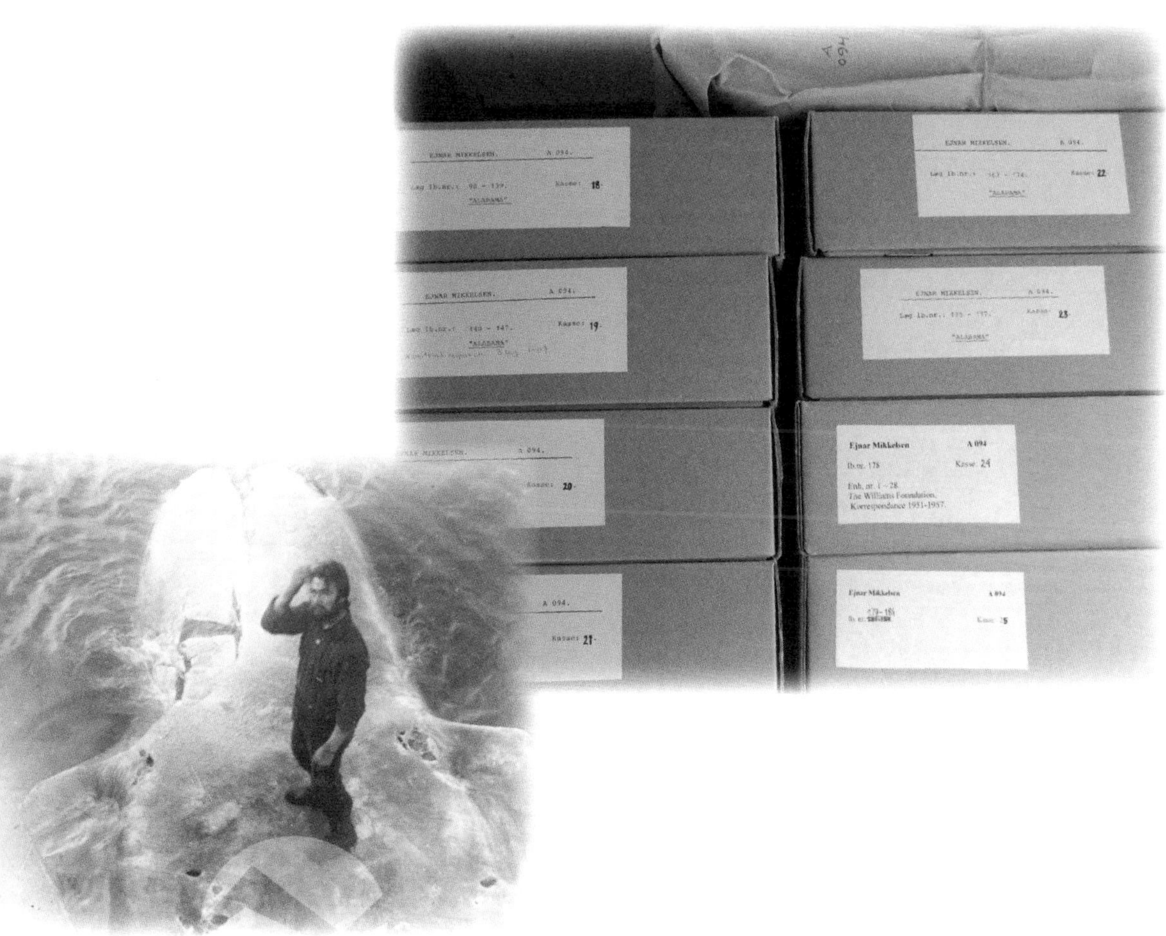

EM was a Danish captain and investor. He owned a whaling hunter station in the Faroe Islands. He sold the intestines of whales to the perfume industry, before his whaling hunter station went bankrupt. EM was my great-grandfather (source from Frederiksen's book).

In February 2020, Father wrote: Lopra, the Faroe Islands (station).

In April 2020, Father wrote: Suderø. The southernmost island in the Faroe Islands. Lopra (city located on the southeast coast).

055.JPG 056.JPG

QUESTIONS TO FATHER

Questions asked when filming for a short mockumentary 'mockumentary' is a pseudo-documentary genre characterised by being designed and presented as documentarism, although it is fiction. translation *Aftermath: Narratives on EM.*

Act 1:

Formal setting. Father and I are in the living room. Camera and audio are recording. Conversation in English, February 2020.

Father, tell me about EM.
What kind of character was he?
In what way was he a role model to you?

What do you see of him in yourself?
Also in relation to what he taught and told you?
ere something you have brought down to me which you inherited from him?
What did he do in Greenland, the first and later encounters?
nd New Year we discussed his motivation volve and engage with the Greenlanders giving them a better livelihood. Can you elaborate on this?
In what way was it good that Greenland became a Danish colony?
would you understand his reputation after his death?
would you understand the myths/histories that surround him?
How do you remember him?

Act 2

A less formal setting. Father and I are in the living room. Camera and audio are recording. Conversation in English, February 2020.

Tell Father about the booklet *Narratives on EM* page by page (or however he wants to read and go through it). Tell Father about the different myths and narrations I have found regarding EM's character and position presented on every page.
Show the moving image *Dialogue w. EM through Father*. Gudrun Havsteen-Mikkelsen, 'Dialogue w. EM through Father', mix of found footage and own footage, 01:35 min. Tell Father about the concept of my research, and how the project, *Snowblindness*, has also evolved to a research into what my design practice emphasises regarding the inclusion of collaborators when being in conflict with 'collective memory'. Tell how it is very much a matter of methodology, connected with some of the research topics like myth-making and history writing (which are aligned with practising contemporary design, when using the same mechanism in myth-making to sell an idea or concept by creating a new 'reality').
Tell about the people I have been in contact with regarding collecting information and memories.
Tell about all the different narratives I have contextualised – some are narratives from Greenland and Denmark.
Tell Father about the struggles I have had with

being presented with the stories from some Greenlanders, where EM is accused of killing and harassment.

Tell how I am interested in the aspect of myth-making/history-writing (again in relation to my own practice and understanding of my own position and background).

Tell how I am a product of colonial heritage, because I also see a lot of myself in the character EM – engaged in Greenland/the Arctic, but also share how I find it problematic due to the colonial legacy. Is this something Father also can relate to? Reference to an earlier talk we had in January 2020 on Father's consultant work for the Red Cross in Ethiopia and Indonesia.

LETTER TO FATHER

Dear Father, Imaginary, fictional letter to Father in March 2020.
ately I have felt a bit out of place here in nsterdam. Living here in the Netherlands ade me think about their colonies. What it es to be a coloniser, and the odd influence it has caused in society and in human (mis)behaviour.

This made me think of Greenland too, Denmark's former colony.

You went with your grandfather to East enland in 1958 to see the colony he established in 1923/1924.

What does that mean for you?

ve hardly heard you tell stories other than ones known in public about your grandfather's deeds and experiences in Greenland. be there is not more to tell, or maybe you did not know what happened during the Danish presence in Greenland?

o you want to avoid certain topics regarding Danish colonialism?

We never really discussed the difficulties ween the oppressor and the oppressed, did Or did we never really discuss the memo- he Greenlanders had of your grandfather and father?

I started to research your grandfather's atives in Greenland in public and private ives. I came across unwritten stories from landers, which were not always in favour of your grandfather.

Apparently, the rumours about him imply ual harassment of Greenlandic women in land. But, also that he killed thirty-eight ndigenous people, before his colony was lished. July 2021, in conversation with Father after the latest reading of the *Shorteblindness*. Father says: "He would never kill anyone. It is a myth that has been created for whatever reason I do not know."

st time we spoke, you told me about how he was to you as a grandfather, and about the sailing dingy he gave you, which you amed after him and which you won many medals with.

family gained a lot of admiration because r grandfather's role in Greenland, mainly ecause of his initiatives from 1924 to 1931, h ended in the Eastern Greenland case in Hague, that made East Greenland Danish territory and property.

You said you were glad that Denmark got ntrol over all of Greenland since Norway d not have been a better coloniser, In July 2020, I discussed Danish colonialism vs. Norwegian colonialism in relation to how

Greenland would have evolved, and even how Greenland would have evolved if it became a Dutch colony (since the Dutch whalers for centuries had regarded the Greenlandic waters and resources as their territory and property). as the Norwegians were mostly interested in the capital they could gain from it.

In my research I came across the fact that the indigenous people of Greenland never believed that they were entitled to own land, nor the waters or resources, so why should the Danes?

Every summer you spent time with your grandfather in his summerhouse on Bornholm, and you even lived in their house during the war in the upper-class neighbourhood Charlottenlund, north of Copenhagen. There is also a bust of your grandfather there and one in Greenland, Ittoqqortoormiit/Scoresbysund.

110.JPG

You told me that your grandfather was establishing the colony to create better livelihoods for the indigenous people in East Greenland and did everything in his power to maintain an argument for the Danish state to keep the colony. The colony in East Greenland had twelve good years after it was established, but ever since it has suffered from hunger, high suicide rates, and misuse of alcohol.

Do you believe it was a good idea the colony was established at all?

I am observing the discussions that are taking place here. There is an odd mixture of embarrassment and ignorance from the Netherlands about their colonial past as a superpower – a position Denmark once shared, and maybe to some extent still holds.

You yourself have worked as a consultant in the Global South; Indonesia, Ethiopia, Brazil, Tanzania etc., and you know more than many others what it means for a people not to have access to basic needs; food, water, and medicine. I hardly heard any stories from your time in these countries.

In the following years Greenlandic adults and the younger generation stood up and talked openly about their mistreatment and the oppressors in Greenland during the 300 years of being a colony under Danish diplomacy and governance.

You hope that Greenland will continue to be a part of the Danish Kingdom, July 2020, correction by Father: *'Rigsfaellesskabet'* since you believe that Denmark can protect Greenland from being bought or controlled by the USA, Russia, or China. Still you do understand and do not deny their wish

for and right to independence.
Can you understand the hate that many
enlanders feel towards Denmark? And do
understand why some poured black paint
the bust of your grandfather in Ittoqqor-
ormiit/Scoresbysund? Certainly, in July 2020, Father said that
another person's work and artwork in relation to the debate on what had
in Greenland, when some people poured red paint over the statue of Hans
Egede and wrote 'decolonise' at his feet.
It seems to me that I have gained a blurred
in my research, since I do not know how
ntinue anymore. I am, after all, a product
the Danish deeds in Greenland, and have
en advantage of my position as the polar
explorer's great-granddaughter – as if the
es of the famous protagonist from the last
ntury were passed down to me, though not
even by blood.
ank you for sharing your archive with the
various articles and artefacts on and by
grandfather, and his initiatives in Green-
nd. It is touching to see, to share with you,
and to follow.
Love, your daughter

CONVERSATION WITH ANONYMOUS FAMILY MEMBERS

Email conversations with anonymous family members after I ask them to look through the booklet, *Narratives on EM.*

Anonymous, January 13, 2020, 13.18:

Dear Gudrun

Before we can give you feedback on your
consider the following five things:

1 Have you asked yourself, why you are
doing this work? The overly
interpretation would be, 'Okay, the
obviously mad at her father,' which after,
will be her with the 'father-murder'. Since
is seen many times before, we do not see
very innovative.

2 If what you are trying to be is critical,
it is rather a journalist's job you are trying
take upon yourself by reviving an old
from a book. We don't know as much
artistic practice as you do (not at all!).
we can see, nothing but the text's content
carries the critical element - as opposed
contrast to the form. It was of our understanding that the artist's foremost task
develop the form-language. But of course,
may be us who misunderstands.

3 You risk tocompletely ruin your great-grandfather's reputation, thus making your father very sad. In these times (metoo, etc.), nothing is needed before rumours spreads and nothing is needed before an accusation escalates. We have seen several cases where suspicions and assumptions have fired people (or give them a bad reputation). This contradicts the legal principle that 'one is innocent until proven otherwise'. But you can't tell this to a population that is more prone to violation than ever before. So, unless you really want to give your own name a bad reputation, it's a really bad idea to work with this topic.
If we were artists, we would instead criticise the tendency to always judge others. It's bad style, a populist and a proletarian practice, in our opinion.
4 It is a bit hypocritical to draw that picture of your great-grandfather when you use him as an actor in your own work and profit from something, he (maybe) has done wrong.
5 This thing about criticising the past, by telling them how they should have done things differently is, in our opinion, anachronism. You take some standards from today (how to treat women, Inuit, etc.) and apply it to the past (EM in this case), to reprimand them, and those who pay tribute to them (your father).
It is weak to do this for a number of reasons:
1) They do not have the opportunity to defend themselves, so you will never reach the explanation of why they did as they did. This will also be a very one-way criticism. 2) Those who pay homage to the past, do not do it for everything they have conducted. Despite EM's shortcomings, your father is still proud of many other things his grandfather did for him and his family.
In other words: Humans are never perfect, nor should they be judged like that, and not at all the people from the past.
We hope you will think about it. And even if you choose to do it anyway, would love to hear your answer to the above.

January 13, 2020, 13.30-14.00:

Anonymous and I in phone conversation: Heavy discussion on the concept of the text, the artistic critique, and the ethics around it. Conversation unfortunately not recorded nor in other forms documented.

Anonymous, January 13, 2020, 14.05:

Dear Gudrun

We trust you have thought about it. But just allow us to be critical. The microscopic risk of it escaping the academy realm is just not one we would ever take.

It's ok that we disagree on what needs to be done. We just mean you're better than that.

Anonyms, January 13, 2020, 17.49: ...

We are not going to censor you. But we would prefer if you showed the text to your father before, and talked more openly about it with him, so that there is no risk of him being surprised by a possible conflict.

And then remember to state where you have the stories from, so people do not think it is something you bring to light.

Me, January 13, 2020, 20.29:

Dear Anonymous,

Thank you for your honesty. I wish you could understand what I am working on and what I am doing, and how it is connected to a design critique. Nothing will escape the academy without my consent and Father's consent. And there is nothing that is not already known by the individuals who have dived into the various stories I represent in the text and images. But delete what I sent to you.

Anonymous, January 15, 2020, 15.24:

Maybe we don't understand your art, we can just read texts. If you don't want to read the texts literally, you might want to take care calling your methods something akin to anthropological.

In relation to a possible conflict, we recommend you to share the texts with others in our family, to hear their opinions. Although, of course, it's up to you who you want to listen

Anonymous, January 20, 2020, 13:38:

We came across an article's passage that might help you to emphasise the fictitious in the text. The article is about the particular form, 'performative biography,' in which one can challenge what is real, based on the lives of real people.

Me, January 20, 2020, 18.08:

Thank you, Anonymous. Auto-fictional writing is something I know already.

Anonymous, January 21, 2020, 10.01:
When writing fictional about other than oneself, we would say it goes beyond the auto-fictional.

Me, January 22, 2020, 20.34:
To return to our earlier discussion. May I ask what it is specifically I mean what I can't write in the text, if you can recall the passages?

Anonymous, January 22, 2020, 20.48:
We can't go into a formulation study, but we think we wanted, if we were you, to clarify with your father what he thinks is fair to say. Either that, or leave out the controversial part, like the part with the women, or rumours of the Inuit killings.

Me, January 22, 2020, 20.34:
Yes, I thought that was what caused the turmoil. I myself want to talk to Father about the rumours, but it is not rumours that are unknown (not saying they are true)!

Anonymous, January 22, 2020, 20.48:
We know that this is not new, but that does not mean that everyone knows it. And furthermore, it is new that you, as a great-granddaughter, pronounce it!
If you are talking to your father, listening to him, and respecting him as a source, for then to bring up a story in the booklet he is not interested in, then what you have made, is deeply unethical.
We do not want to comment on the artistic quality for the text.
You may not say directly that the rumours are true, but you risk contributing to their truth-value if you mention them at all. That is why it would be best not to treat EM at all.

Anonymous, January 23, 2020, 15.58:
We trust you are good, Gudrun.

EM was a polar explorer. In the Amdrup-expedition he went to the east coast of Greenland and shot 38 Inuits in Taiilaq. There were bullet holes in their skulls. EM was my great-grandfather, but not by blood (source from local Greenlanders and told in Pia Arke's book *Stories from Scoresbysund* and Nikolajsen's film *Scoresbysund – kolonien er mit eget barn*).

In April 2020, Father wrote: This is a myth?

In May 2020, I added the subtitles from Nikolajsen's film: "That's why they suspected that EM and them had killed Greenlanders on their trip."

In July 2021, Father wrote: That's why they suspected that EM ~~and them~~ or others had killed Greenlanders on their trip.

057.JPG

In April 2020, Father wrote: Else (1914-1933) because of an accident from the boat.

In February 2020, Father wrote: This dingy was given to me at my confirmation in 1955. The boat was named, 'Miki' and I won many races with it in Svendborg Sund and Lunkebugten.

:M was a sailor. He gave his only daugh-er, Else, a boat. Else, 19 years old, later lied because of an accident in the boat. :M never recovered from his loss. EM vas my great-grandfather (source from Frederiksen's ook).

ki liaaer snekladt.

g vestkyst.

ar KNK's første års rekognoscering langs den samme tstrækning, der som nævnt betragtedes som kendt, der kortlagt 6 lokaliteter med tilsammen 37 husru-r, 37 teltringe, foruden 10 grave og et større al køddepoter og rævefælder.

o-historisk baggrund

coresbysund fjordkompleks, der med sit areal på ca. 38.000 km², er verdens største, var ubeboet da kolonien Scoresbysund i 1925 blev oprettet. Der havde tidligere levet en eskimoisk befolkning i området, men i lighed med resten af nordøstgrønland var befolkningen her uddød. Muligvis har området været menneske-tomt i 1822 da Scoresby fandt og navngav fjorden. (Scoresby 1823:186.)

I 1911 fremkom Harald Olrik, assistent under Styrelsen af Kolonier i Grønland, med planer om at bebygge Scoresby Sund området. (H. Olrik: Forslag om at bebygge Scoresby Sund Egnen i Østgrønland ved Vestgrønlandske Sælfangere.) Olriks oprindelige forslag blev dog ikke iværksat.

I 1919 udsendte det danske Østgrønlandske kompagni fangstfolk til Nordøstgrønland for at drive jagt på kommerciel basis. På samme tid var der stor fangstaktivitet af norske fangstmænd i Østgrønland, så da det danske monopolområde i 1921 udvidedes til at omfatte hele Grønland, følte normændene, at monopol-

DDRUP KIRKE

8.JPG 059.JPG 060.JPG

[illegible]
5. maj 1971
Ordrup kirkegårdskapel

se til langfredag, dagen for Jesu lidelse
e lade være med at kigge efter Ejnar Mikkelsen
ur først og fremmest den dag, han gik i kirke.
dag, ved jeg naturligvis ikke bestemt.
to klædte hinanden i deres - skal vi sige -
rdet barsk hverken passer på langfredagen eller
r tale om barskhed, men også om så meget andet.
og dog er langfredagen så helt forskelligt
dag går på den indre linjes kamp, - som E. M
mand.
med Gud, er så naturligt, det kunne ikke være
d, der står over for naturens vælde og udfordring
denne vælde. "Gør Jer til Herrer over jorden"
esfortællingen, og det var jo det, han ville,
et var hans natur, han kunne slet ikke andet.
n vældig livskraft, og denne livskraft forlod ham
seneste år. Han havde - som vi sang - svært ved a
og det var svært for os at sige farvel til en mand
r det først og fremmest for Jer, der har delt
så for os, der fik den lykke at møde ham, -
sig et stykke af jorden underdanig, og som fik

kraft ebber ud, også manden, der gør sig
undergivet de dødeliges vilkår, og over for
- den afmagt, der føles livet igennem, gør vi
ham, der førte livskampen på den indre linje m
r ydre fælder.
en høre ~~til~~ langfredagsteksten, (Esajas 53, vers 2
om i et syn Guds og menneskers tjener, der en-
gøre sig til herre over menneskesindet og

et til at drage vort blik, uden ydre, ringeagtet,
n man skjuler sit ansigt for, agtet ringe, vi reg-
og: vore sygdomme bar han, tog vore smerter på
e han bytte.
fortæller om den stærke, der bevogter sin borg,
ler, på alle onde magter, der holder os
så fortælles der også om en, der er stærkere, og
nder den stærke, og uddeler hans
døden binder os med sorg og afmagt, trænger herre
livets håb, han åbner vejen til Gud, afdækker
land, hvor "ingen, der mødes skal skilles igen".
vend.

or at tage afsked med en af vort lands stormænd,
ig til Herre over en del af jorden, en mand
dere.
der ved sin lidelse og død gjorde sig til herre
og forløste os tværs igennem døden til [illegible]

[illegible]

Til fru Mikkelsen
med kærlig hilsen
Deres hengivne
Mogens Zeuthen

EM was a fisherman. He piled cod along Greenland's West Coast. EM was my great-grandfather (source from Frederiksen's book).

In April 2020, Father wrote: Gudrun, are you sure it was the West Coast and not the East Coast?

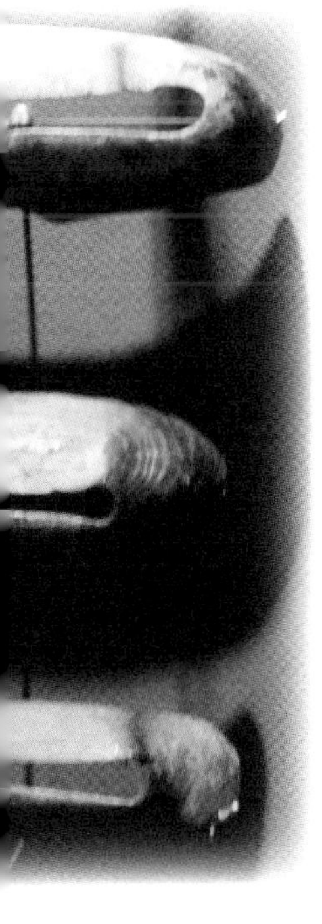

063.JPG

064.JPG

In April 2020, Father wrote: I studied agriculture and visited them during the summer holiday.

EM was a member of the Freemason Society. He was part of the European upper class and lived in Charlottenlund. He had a summerhouse in Bornholm. My father lived with them during the summers and would polish EM's shoes. EM was my great-grandfather (source from Father).

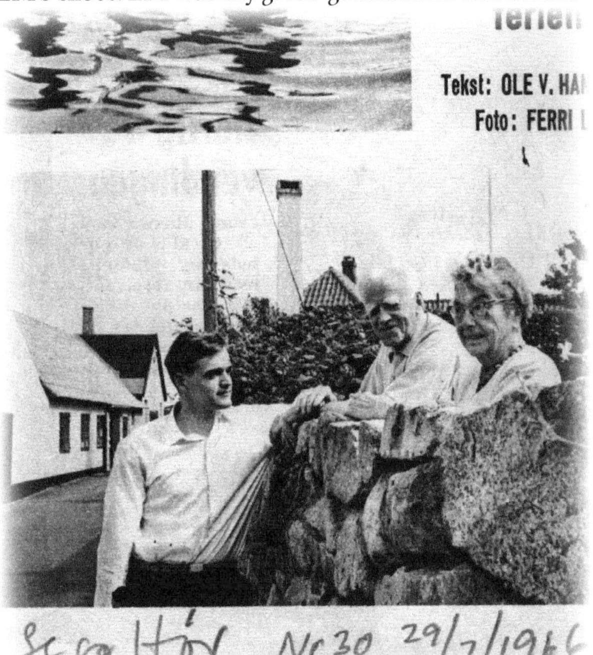

065.JPG

066.JPG

067.JPG

THOUGHTS ON METHODOLOGY

'"The more we know the more we see" implies that we can multiply the meanings we can make from our visual impressions, and what is not seen is as important as what is seen.' Cramerotti, *Aesthetic Journalism*, 71.

In the making of *Snowblindness* I became familiar with the methods of 'Aesthetic Journalism', also referred to as 'artistic journalism' or 'designalism'. Previously, I was accustomed to explaining that I borrowed methods from journalism and combined its methodologies with other disciplines from either arts or soft sciences into my work. However, that explanation never satisfied my urgency, nor what I wanted to communicate, in my practice. As for classical journalism, it does not allow the same amount of freedom by combining documents, events, and imagination as Aesthetic Journalism does.

In the book *Aesthetic Journalism – How to Inform Without Informing,* Cramerotti formulates that the journalistic attitude is the bearer of linguistic and visual documents of reality – it is an instrument for reading the world that provides a certain 'security', by establishing an order for the things *out there*. Cramerotti, *Aesthetic Journalism*, 23. Aesthetic Journalism offers another format; it provides instructions for building new realities, which allows space for experimentation and speculation towards what can be imagined, which includes the spectator (and the protagonist) in a completely different way.

These spaces of experimental approaches to storytelling speak to approaches in design that are 'speculative', 'critical' or even 'fiction', which 'allows us to think and imagine other realities, explore new perspectives on the future, or represent something that is hard or even impossible to represent otherwise' Wynants, ed., *When Fact is Fiction*, 10., as Nele Wynants writes in the book *When Fact is Fiction.* I find it relevant to the urgency with which I make this research, as well as to the role of the designer today.

Now more than ever we experience information and opinion blended, often uncaringly, into one another. The documentary form is blurring the distinction between actuality and fiction, that may no longer be accurate through the traditional means of the documentary genre Cramerotti, *Aesthetic Journalism*, 14. and the constant accessibility through the news-media's platforms. The interaction between visuals and written journalism is a widespread cultural phenomenon (very present in current popular media), which appears in many different forms. The approach of Aesthetic Journalism can articulate and contribute critical knowledge and tangible experiences with the mere use of aesthetic 'regimes' and domains, with the effect of raising doubts about the 'truth'-value Cramerotti, *Aesthetic Journalism*, 22. of 'collective memory', where other strategies and traditional disciplines are failing. It is these moments that allow designers to work both investigatively, communicating a story, and to visualise the narration and 'truth' of the world, both of today and in the future.

Adopting techniques from Aesthetic Journalism I have used archive and field research, surveys, and interviews. I have been making use of narrative analysis, post- and decolonial theory, and source criticism. I have worked with archival footage and moving image; novels; art and historical essays; writing and analysing e-mail correspondences and phone calls; and doing close readings of diaries, letters, news articles, and historical documents, to eventually be able to sketch out a scene of my own background's colonial influence in Greenland, and to explore how to leave space for new stories visualised in a design translation. In my collaborative work I have displayed formats in a documentary style through graphic visualisation, moving image, radio broadcasting (podcasting), text- and photo-reportage, and, finally, I applied certain semi-fictional narratives onto three-dimensional objects (furniture, engraved maps, booklets, jewellery, and glasses).

Collecting and documenting material on the narratives surrounding EM in relation to Nordic colonialism enabled Anna and I, in collaboration, to combine historical documents with imagination. By connecting aesthetics and information in translations of displacements – or re-contextualising – we were able to construct various new stories that occasionally resonated with some local Greenlander's stories of EM. This made it possible for us to create research and design interventions in relation to the case study by using myths, facts, and narratives with EM as the main character at the centre of the research. At the same time, it allowed me to no longer depend on the cultural determinisms, the visual and mental reflexes of the background I am born into, but to make translations in both directions Nicolas Bourriaud, *The Radicand* (New York: Lukas & Sternberg, 2009), 56. – by researching rhizomatic writing and including fictional components. This way of working, carrying out investigative research while writing fictional texts, can also be experienced in the following chapters;

TOP VIEW & INFORMATION CARRIER, 174.JPG

NOTIONS ON CANNIBALISM, 137.JPG

SHRIMP PARADOX, 048.JPG

I THINK I GOT IT, *SNOWBLINDNESS,* 044.JPG

and ANOTHER SILVA RERUM? 001. JPG, 040.JPG, 161.JPG

as they determined the aesthetic language when making both this book and physical design objects.

Scepticism is essential when dealing with various truths and narratives, as it brings a constant questioning of the past and the status quo. I have been in some kind of position of flux or nomadic bias, where at a certain point I found it necessary to construct a self-reflective position, to keep asking myself questions. This will hopefully encourage the readers of this book to ask questions of themselves too, to 'stay' with these questions, and to use the blank space in the book to write their own comments and thoughts. The texts in *Snowblindness,* nor the objects, podcast, or moving image translations, don't seek to give answers.

'The very debate on the responsibility towards "truth" is better framed in terms of what kind of "truth" we feel most responsible for.' Cramerotti, *Aesthetic Journalism*, 28. Some 'truths' are recognised as myths or rumours by some, while the same content for others are, with 'security', articulating a 'truth'. Some myths are born anonymously, which leaves space for other myths to be multiplied and ramified without fear of controlling the myth-teller. Trinh T. Minh-ha, *Woman, Native, Other: Writing Postcoloniality and Feminism* (Bloomington: Indiana University Press, 1989), 61. This became an interesting and challenging point in my research, since through conducting interviews concerning some taboo matters, the interviewer (myself) had to create a common understanding Kirsten Hastrup et al. *Ind i verden – en grundbog i antropologisk metode* (Copenhagen: Reitzels Forlag, 2003), 235. with the interviewee (Father, archivists, artists, local Greenlanders, etc.) in order for the conversation to evolve; at times into a common understanding or narrative that I did not necessarily agree with.

The approach of Aesthetic Journalism clearly also borrows methods from ethnography, just like many different branches of journalism (and design). However, in my work I tried not to interact with the interviewed as the 'exotic other', as has been done previously in anthropological practices as an imperialist act. Instead, I tried to reach an understanding of another perspective, negotiating abstract and concrete meanings, connected to human experience Kirsten Hastrup et al. *Ind i verden*, 242. and memory. In the interviews, especially in the conversation with Father, I had to move within the same paradigm as the interviewees in order to grasp the depth of the subject of discussion. Since I could never assume a complete understanding of the articulated narratives of EM, I allowed the opportunity for miscommunication to be open, while approaching the subject with an autoethnographic approach, as a 'domestic ethnographer'. This autoethnographic approached allowed me to write in a personalised style, as I was drawing on my own, and my Father's, experiences in order to widen my social knowledge and cultural critique, both for myself and the reader. The autoethnographic approach is a patchwork of experiences and feelings that can be used as a research method, as theorist Sarah Wall writes in her text 'An Autoethnography on Learning about Autoethnography', Sarah Wall, "An Autoethnography on Learning about Autoethnography" in *International Journal of Qualitative Methods 5* (June 2006): 5. as well as the understanding that 'knowledge does not have to result from [academic] research to be worthwhile, and personal stories should have their place alongside research in contribution to what we know about the world in which we live.' Wall, "An Autoethnography on Learning," 11.

The miscommunications and misunderstandings that occurred through the conversational research allowed for interpretation that produced modes of indeterminacy, which generated new readings of contexts. Barbara Neves Alves, "Relocations: The Idiot as a Figure of Miscommunication," *Parse Journal Issue 3* (2016): 85. This was implied in the design choices for the translations in both the moving image and book forms when editing and recontextualising material. It led me to understand that the distinction between fiction and nonfiction is false; that 'there is only narrative.' Cramerotti, *Aesthetic Journalism*, 17.

Source criticism as a method also played a crucial part in dealing with the collected archived material, as it led to difficulties when dealing with family stories; who has the right to what sources and narratives and under what conditions? This question can also be applied to journalism practices today, since source criticism is implicated in a constant struggle between its ethical vision and its question of power. Which story, whose side, what ethical responsibility do we feel accountable to and for? There is simply no easy solution. This is also treated in the chapter

REFLECTION ON 'TRUTH' & THE 'COLLECTIVE MEMORY'.

I do not see it as my goal in *Snowblindness* to argue that there is only one way of telling the story, or neglect that other stories exist. The very point with making *Snowblindness* is to present other ways of reading, hearing, and seeing a multiplicity of narratives, since there is no singular way of perceiving. I see it as an opportunity to translate and reveal various narratives by giving them a platform in this 'complex' story through means of opacity, trust, and honesty. I am not claiming to reveal the 'truth', since, as treated above, 'truth' is something that is constructed in the interpretations of both the author and the receiver. Instead, I am trying to approach the 'real', by constructing a model of it; by always questioning a 'truth' and its discourse, and by suggesting plural realities and perspectives through the book's stream of images and graphics. I am not trying to strip down my research into bare facts, but instead I am collaboratively making a patchwork of layers that embodies notions of many myths, many agendas, and many narratives, and am trying to notice, to pay attention to, what that reveals within me and in other spectators. On this matter, I already know that I should have included many more voices and collaborated with many more people, and for this reason this book is, at this stage, incomplete.

Aesthetic Journalism as a methodology welcomes the idea of playing with fiction and thereby challenging the way that narratives from the past are read. As a strategy it has helped me to understand what it means to imply and construct aesthetics in processes of documenting, editing, and sharing, and how these affect writing, while reflecting upon visual languages and graphics. In recent years we have seen that traditional journalism seems to fail, due to the production of subjective beliefs and counter-stories – in other terms also named *fake news* (which seems to be an accusation from political oppositions) – where critical objective journalism is being categorised as lies. There is now an opportunity for designers and other artistic practitioners to keep asking questions, investigating, speculating, and leaving space for other narratives to be heard, for other perceptions of the past and the present to be communicated, shared, and connected. There is a possibility of engaging with – and shaping – a future through the means of Aesthetic Journalism, which should stay critical while revealing a transparent agenda. This is also treated briefly in the chapter

EDITING & SHARING.

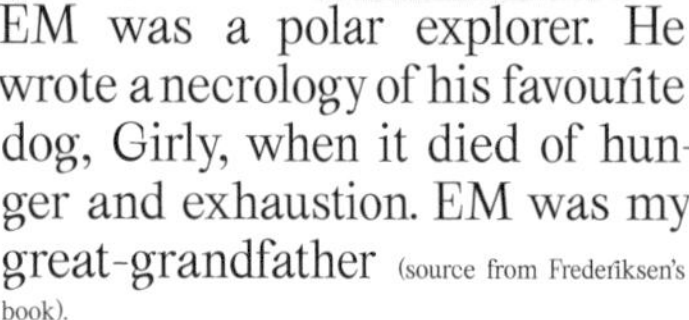

EM was a polar explorer. He wrote a necrology of his favourite dog, Girly, when it died of hunger and exhaustion. EM was my great-grandfather (source from Frederiksen's book).

In April 2020, Father wrote: Sledge dog.

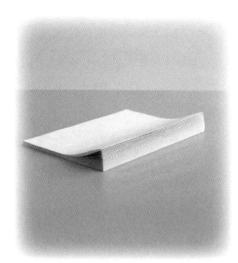

Fra den 17. og frem t
distriktet, blev der
giske informationer i
opfordring blev der g
til Stewart Ø, for de
Forsøget måtte desvær
ene.

RENLAND
MILNES LAND
GÅSELAND

⊡: vinterhuse og teltrin
□: vinterhuse
^: teltringe
-: grave
-: rævefælder og kødd

Resultaterne af feltund
i rapportform i KNK's a

068.JPG 069.JPG 070.JPG

st, hvor vi forlod
ogiske og arkæolo-
og på kommunal
på at komme ned
et ruinkompleks.
rund af isforhold-

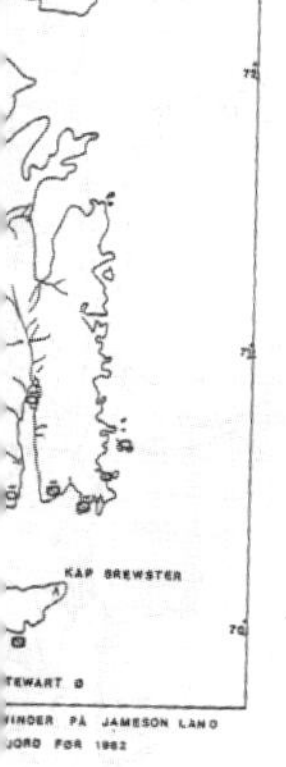

82 foreligger
t over Grønlands

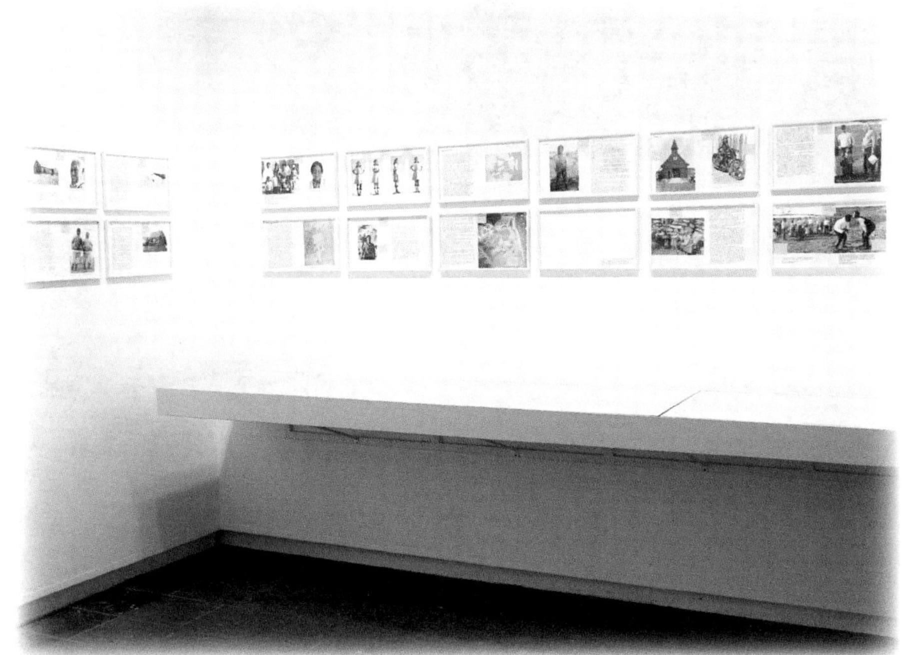

071.JPG

EM was a Danish inspector in an East Greenlandic colony. He loved the Greenlanders – especially the Greenlandic women. He could not keep his fingers off them. He mostly visited them when the men were out hunting. The women were afraid of him. EM was my great-grandfather, but not by blood (source from local Greenlanders and people interviewed in Nikolajsen's film *Scoresbysund – kolonien er mit eget barn*).

In April 2020, Father wrote: It is a myth.

072.JPG

073.JPG

EM was a Danish captain and an inspector. He banned alcohol in Greenland. He forced the sailors to throw strong liquor overboard before sailing. EM was my great-grandfather (source from Frederiksen's book).

74.JPG 075.JPG

EM was a writer, storyteller, and a fantasist. He wrote severa books on his explorations and adventures in Greenland anc in the Arctic. He wrote several articles on how Greenlanc should evolve. EM was my great-grandfather (source from Frederiksen's book

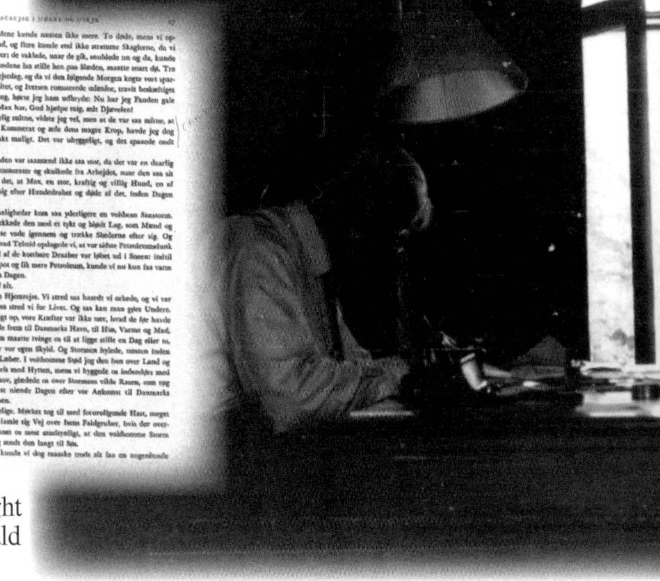

In EM's *Farlig Tomandsfaerd*: I never experienced or thought of the possibility that they (himself and his mate Iver) would assail one another.

In April 2020, Gudrun wrote: Notions of cannibalism.

076.JPG 077.JPG

EM was a journalist. He was a foreign correspondent in Finland during World War I. EM was my great-grand-father (source from Frederiksen's book).

In February 2020, Father wrote: Reykjavik in 1958 on our way to Green-land. At his desk in Vilhelmshåbsvej 6, Charlottenlund.

078.JPG

079.JPG

TOP VIEW & INFORMATION CARRIER

Definition Cartography is the study and practice of making maps. Combining science, aesthetics, and technique, cartography builds on the premise that reality can be modelled in ways that communicate spatial information effectively. Wikipedia, "Cartography," accessed May 29, 2020, https://en.wikipedia.org/wiki/Cartography.

Act 1

At Greenland's National Museum and Archive in Nuuk, Inuit maps are exhibited. The Inuit maps are made out of wood, and have a three-dimensional form. It is possible to perceive the coast by letting your fingers stroke the material. You can read the engravings in the three-dimensional forms.

153.JPG

Archivist: These maps were acquired in Ammassalik in East Greenland during the 'Konebaads Expedition'/'Umiak Expedition' in 1883–85, led by the Danish polar explorer Gustav Holm. Gustav Holm (1849-1940), Danish polar explorer and EM's first father-in-law. The map on the left shows the coastline between Sermiligak and Kangerdlugsuatsiak (seven to eight miles long). Kalaallit Nunaata Katersugaaivia, *Gustav Holm Samlingen* (Nuuk: Kalaalit Nanatta Katersugaasivia/Grønlands Landsmuseum, 1985), 47. The map on the right accompanies the other map and shows the offshore islands by the aforementioned coast. The lengths of the artefacts are 14 and c. 24 centimetres. G. Malcolm Lewis, *Maps, Mapmaking, and Map Use by Native North Americans,* vol. 2, book 3, (Chicago: University of Chicago Press,1998), 169.

Me: Why did the Inuit make these maps, which almost look like ancient artefacts rather than functional objects?

Archivist: Research tells us that the maps were not designed for practical navigational use but rather as storytelling aids. Daniel Weiss, "Wooden Inuit Maps," accessed May 30, 2020, https://www.archaeology.org/issues/337-1905/features/7550-maps-greenland-wooden-inuit-maps.

Me: The maps do not contain any information of reality?

Archivist: By showing the Inuit map, the others who were listening to the story could get an understanding of the contours of the coast, and the relationship between the islands and the coastline. Weiss, "Wooden Inuit Maps".

Me: Then why all these details?

Archivist: The details indicated where a traveller would have to carry their kayak overland to get to the next fjord. We assume that it brought a value to the storytelling, since there is no evidence that the Greenland Inuit commonly produced such wooden maps. Weiss, "Wooden Inuit Maps".

Act 2

Tonnes of stone blocks are being quarried every year from mining locations in Greenland. The stones are transported with cargo all over the world, but they only cover 1.7% of the total export income in Greenland. OEC, accessed May 31, 2020, https://oec.world/en/profile/country/grl/. This stone sheet comes from quarries outside of the Netherlands.

Me: I want to laser-cut in stone, in order to make an engraving of a map.

Technical support: OK, what rock type is it?

Me: Greenlandic granite, dark.

Technical support: It should be fine. You have had experience with this before?

Me: Yes. I need the engraving to be deep, in order

to get the right texture. I need the temperature to melt the granite surface slightly.

Technical support: OK, if the temperature and the speed are set on the maximum capacity it should work, without losing any details. Though we might need to re-trace the drawing's trajectory if the granite does not melt at first try. What does the map show – a shoreline?

Me: Yes, it is a slightly manipulated shoreline of an eastern coast in Greenland – a shoreline my great-grandfather drew.

Act 3

100.JPG, 174.JPG

The roads stop outside the city. The Greenlandic towns are separated from each other. A closed system. Impassable for automobiles. Impassable for miners?

Exploration manager 1: The mine is located in Fiskenæsset, where we have two licenses. We have invested many millions in the gemstone project, and we have a great interest in continuing the work in the mine and its infrastructure. Act 3 is an extract of an interview I made in Nuuk, Greenland, in 2017 with the mining company LNS Greenland.

Exploration manager 2: Right now we are drilling and exploding, and we are planning new explorations in the same area.

Exploration manager 1: After years of core-drilling, years of mapping in the area, and big investments, we finally got licenses to mine for the gemstones.

Me: What kinds of gemstone are you mining for?

Exploration manager 1: Ruby. We have the whole colour spectrum there.

Me: Do you have any by-products?

Exploration manager 2: Yes, there is gold. But the cost is too big to extract the gold, so it can't pay off. It sinks in the nearby lake along with the rest of the ore.

Me: I have been in dialogue with your director who says that you are visiting the mine every Tuesday?

Exploration manager 2: No, Wednesdays and Fridays.

Me: Ok. Would it be possible for me to join you and see your production in Fiskenæsset?

Exploration manager 1: We do not have the resources for it. It is a very inaccessible location. The only way to access it is with helicopter. We cannot risk taking you there, and besides that, the helicopter transport is very expensive.

Me: I have insurance. And I am willing to pay for the costs.

Exploration manager 2: No, it is not possible. We cannot have you running around there.

Me: Do you then have any stone material here in Nuuk I can have or buy?

Exploration manager 2: No, it is not something we just hand out.

Exploration manager 1: We neither can nor must give it away. Such a piece of stone is almost worth nothing, but we must not spread it out. First, we will need an export permit, and it can take about three months.

Me: And this is something the Greenlandic Government has decided?

Exploration manager 1: Yes. You would not even be able to get the stone through customs in the airport. You cannot just take rubies out of the country – otherwise you get into a trap – even if the stone is not valuable.

Me: And you have access to the mine all year round?

Exploration manager 2: We are frozen in from mid-January to mid-May. The rest of the year we can access the mine by boat.

Exploration manager 1: We only bring the concentrate of the rubies to our deposits in Nuuk, since we extract the rubies in the mine.

Exploration manager 2: We have a whole floor in the Greenlandic Bank for our rubies. It is a little sum we extract, 50 kilograms per 100 tons maybe. I do not know. After all, it is not much.

Me: Would it be possible to see your deposits in the bank?

Exploration manager 1: Yes, we could arrange a visit, but after lunch.

Me: Thank you! That would be very much appreciated! And when do you think you can start selling your products?

Exploration manager 1: No date has been set yet, but we have to start a sale this year.

Exploration manager 2: It is also about branding and marketing. We will not flood the market. We are able to blast and extract the entire mine in six months, but we stretch it out for nine years.

Exploration manager 1: It is also about which market you want to encounter first. For example in Las Vegas there is a gemstone sale fair at the end of June. In China it is in October. And it is the colour of the stones that tells where there is the greatest demand. Right now we are trying to prepare ourselves for the entire market.

Exploration manager 2: In Russia, there is great demand.

Exploration manager 1: We are very much interested in getting our giant investments back.

Me: I am also very much interested in mining minerals. Do you have any suggestions for an accessible location, where I can collect something other than granite, quartz, or gneiss?

Exploration manager 1: I do not know if the river runs now at this time of year, but outside the city near Qinngorput, there you can wash gold. There are gold sediments in the riverbed.

063.JPG

Exploration manager 2: You can drive out there by bus. It is where the road ends.

Act 4

In Ancient Greece it was believed that the Arctic was populated by pygmies. And the Zeno brothers from Venice invented imaginary places of the North that future map-makers copied into Greenland's eastern coast, including Mercator. Pia Arke, *Scoresbysundhistorier* (Copenhagen: Borgen, 2003), 26. As the number of expeditions grew, the white surfaces on the maps became covered with names of monarchs, businessmen, scientists, and cultural figures and celebrities from Europe. Arke, *Scoresbysundhistorier,* 110. However the mapmakers were forced to rely on second-hand knowledge and individual observations. Arke, *Scoresbysundhistorier,* 24. Still, only one tenth of Greenland's eastern coast was mapped today until quite recently, which means that many Greenlanders are still using maps based on aerial photographs from the 1970s and 1980s. Martin Breum, "Grønland kortlagt," Weekendavisen, accessed June 3, 2020, https://www.weekendavisen.dk/2019-11/samfund/groenland-kortlagt.

Me: Why did you draw this map over East Greenland?

EM: I became sensitive and intolerable to my surroundings, impossible to be with. I wanted to go out again, away from the twinkling bonds of civilisation. I wanted to go far North where you could live fully and be yourself enough. Ejnar Mikkelsen, *Farlig Tomandsfaerd* (Copenhagen: Gyldendal, 1962), 9. And everyday pursuits and small incidents compel one to seek knowledge of land for their self, where colleagues and friends put their lives to the test in order to wrest the wilderness and some of its well-guarded secrets. Mikkelsen, *Farlig Tomandsfaerd,* 10.

Me: Did you make any discoveries?

EM: As we dragged along the coast, our eyes were on the land we passed, watching carefully to decipher everything that we could not immediately define. Nothing could avoid our scary looks, nothing edible nor that which we had travelled so far to find: the traces of those who disappeared. Mikkelsen, *Farlig Tomandsfaerd,* 66.

Me. And did you find them?

EM: The search on the ice was hopeless, given

that the three men's last camp had been on the icy sea, as Jørgen Brønlund wrote in his diary of the last days of his fellow travellers. Their corpses had either been driven away with the old ice or sunk in the sea as the ice burst for the fall storms and swells or melted in the summer sun. Mikkelsen, *Farlig Tomandsfaerd*, 26.

Me: How did you map the landscape?

EM: I spent a lot of time on drawing maps and marking dots where we were, and comparing our progress with the itinerary I had prepared. Mikkelsen, *Farlig Tomandsfaerd*, 45.

Me: What was your impression of the landscape when drawing the map?

EM: To the south I could see a dull and low coast stretched out with a rocky foreshore, to the north the eye followed a somewhat higher but monotonous coast to 'Kap Rigsdagen', an extremely sad and godforsaken land. And far behind 'Kap Rigsdagen', 'Eastern Peary Land' faded beyond the horizon. Mikkelsen, *Farlig Tomandsfaerd*, 71.

Me: Was it not difficult to survive in the big wilderness?

EM: We could not survive without any provisions. We needed all the provisions we could carry with us, and more. First we were going to 'Denmark's Fjord' and from there we would try to get back to the ship, a journey of roughly 1500 kilometres – in addition to the countless detours that are inevitable on the long journey. Mikkelsen, *Farlig Tomandsfaerd*, 34.

Me: Did you not sense the isolation?

EM: We were cut off from the planet's crowd of humans, as if we were miraculously thrown out into space and dumped into the largest crater of the moon, bordered by an unbroken ring-wall of unbelievably high mountains, beyond which we could not find our way – to an equally desolate region outside. Mikkelsen, *Farlig Tomandsfaerd*, 38.

Me: What was your plan for the future in Greenland?

EM: A repopulation of the deserted coastal areas where we [Iver Iversen and I] had lived for a few years. Mikkelsen, *Farlig Tomandsfaerd*, 130. We looked at a map and tried to determine where the best opportunities for an Eskimo immigration were to be found. And we finally settled on the fact that Scoresbysund was probably the most suitable place for a new colony. Mikkelsen, *Farlig Tomandsfaerd*, 130.

ANOTHER STORY ON EM

Explorers, scientists, and the general public have questioned whether EM demonstrated superpowers or other invincible forces. Others have questioned his discoveries. And some have questioned his intentions with the establishment of the colony Scoresbysund (later named Ittoqqortoormiit). One of them is the artist Pia Arke. Arke claimed that the narrative of the establishment of the colony had fooled us, and that the argument and narrative of the colony, the history, was more sublime and boundless, which seemed to separate the Greenlanders from the Danes Arke, *Scoresbysundhistorier*, 10. and their perceptions of the events that took place. The narrative propelled by the 'collective memory' explains that Ittoqqortoormiit/Scoresbysund was colonised/established to relieve famine and disease in Ammassalik. Arke, *Scoresbysundhistorier*, 10. Arke believed that it was a misunderstanding that the colony was established, since the inhabitants of Ammassalik have a long tradition of 'moving' south with their European progenitors, Arke, *Scoresbysundhistorier*, 10. to trade at the coast and at sea. In her reflections and her work she highlighted the lack of narratives from Greenlanders, since the 'collective memory' was almost exclusively relayed by Danish narrators. The same happened with the photographs taken at that time, mostly composed through the camera viewfinders belonging to the Danes; the Greenlandic faces were only recognised, preserved, and documented by Danish photographs in Denmark.

Through the reading of Arke's book *Stories from Scoresbysund: Photographs, Colonisation and Mapping*, I became aware of her own personal history and connection with Ittoqqortoormiit/Scoresbysund, and her engagements in cultural critique from a colonial, personal perspective. The personal perspective was situated within the notion of being the 'other', and always placed in relation to Europeans. Or, as Arke expressed herself: 'I make the history of colonialism part of my history in the only way I know, namely by taking it personally.' Arke, *Scoresbysundhistorier*, 11. *Stories from Scoresbysund* pointed out to me the already-known problematic colonial activity in Greenland in the 1900s up to this day, but also stories regarding my great-grandfather EM that were not familiar to me. These unknown stories, of quite a disturbing character, brought troubling information to the surface.

Immediately, I started to pin down the narratives, which I was convinced were not *truly* represented in Arke's work, in relation to the facts of the events that happened in East Greenland. I disappeared into a critical dialogue with her work, that was left behind in books, moving images, photography, and articles, all by or about Arke, and related its content to matters of my concern. At that moment, investigating her work, I started to enter a space where I felt the need to protect the legacy of EM. In *Stories from Scoresbysund* she criticised EM and connected him with all the unhappy moments in East Greenland. I noticed that I started to defend EM instead of trying to understand the perspective that Arke was speaking from, even though her work occurred to me sometimes to display a narrow-sighted narrator. But the real struggle was to be situated as the purveyor of 'truth'. Both Arke and EM seemed to have moved from the absolute to the relative and assumed the role of purveyor of 'certain truths', pursuing a 'perspectivistic knowledge'. Minh-ha, *Woman, Native, Other*, 55. EM might have maintained 'scientific objectivity' as a methodological approach in his expeditions, as many other explorers did at that time, Here also referring to the 'Danmarks Ekspedition' (1906-1908) whose goal was to explore and map in Northeast Greenland, and rebut Robert Peary's (American polar explorer) claim that a canal separated North Greenland from South Greenland. as an argument for their deeds, while Arke had the perspective of an artist and a 'mongrel woman', as she described herself, who is 'neither we or they, I or you'. Kuratorisk Aktion, *Tupilakosaurus* (Copenhagen: Kuratorisk Aktion, 2012), 9.

Arke's work promoted her cause by demonstrating knowledge of how to distinguish the 'real' from the 'false' through her medium and her artistic practice. EM did the same. And I promoted mine, which over time has fluctuated between different positions, which later brought me into a discussion with myself around preserved myths and colonial stories in relation to generating a reflective design practice. How can I ever create work with a 'certainty' of what is true and what is false?

Arke had an agenda and produced a large and multifaceted body of work with her agenda in mind. She devoted her artistic practice to breaking the 'silence' of Danish colonial domination and tried to visualise the cause of the effect of the long Greenland-Denmark relations – and in a larger sense she looked to break the 'silence' in the relation between the 'West and the rest'. Kuratorisk Aktion, *Tupilakosaurus*, 8. For that reason I admire her and I am inspired by her work.

Arke claimed that the Danes' narrative, 'the collective memory', was full of self-congratulation, and saw the East Greenlanders as Danish minions. Anne Knudsen, "Øm om hjertet," Weekendavisen, accessed July 22, 2020, https://www.weekendavisen.dk/2018-7/boeger/oem-om-hjertet. From my own experience being in Greenland, collaborating with people form the North Atlantic, and after observing relations between people in this region, I understand Arke's perspective very well. I have seen the presence of arrogance in the Danes towards Greenlanders and their perspectives – something that is both historical and something that, unfortunately, still happens today. This arrogance seems to be born from the same mechanisms that caused so many unhappy moments and failures in Greenland's modern history; nuclear waste and explosions in Thule in 1968 at the US airbase, Blok P (an apartment building in Nuuk, 1965–2012, as an act to modernise and centralise the Greenlandic society in Nuuk), the forced relocation of Greenlandic children to Denmark in 1951, and the forced closure of the coal mining town Qullissat in 1972, to mention just a few.

When encountering Arke's work there is no doubt as to who she believes is to blame for Danish colonialism in East Greenland: EM (a name she rarely used, instead favouring 'the colony inspector' or 'the colony inventor'). It seems that Arke was trying to understand neither the context of the time in which Ittoqqortoormiit/Scoresbysund was established, nor the geopolitical consequences probable if other countries would have conquered and colonised Greenland (or even split the country into two – a West and East side). EM was aware of this, and fought for this 'unwanted' colony in East Greenland, Referring to the title of the book EM published in 1964, *Den Uønskede By* (English title: 'The Unwanted Town') which Father read for me while filming him in July 2021. against the Danish Government, who seemed to not understand the consequences of a poor catch in that area for the Greenlanders further south on the east coast. Regardless of the reasons why Ittoqqortoormiit/Scoresbysund was established, whether for a larger Danish Kingdom (more territory thus more power), for the Greenlanders themselves, or for EM's legacy, Arke used EM as a character to promote her own position. Arke developed work around the narratives of Denmark as a colonial power conquering East Greenland, which used to be a 'conflict-free' region, as she describes it. If Arke was still alive I would be very curious to hear her thoughts on the matter of positionality, and on using other individuals' achievements and failures to develop artistic work. I would be very interested to hear her ethical considerations towards EM's work, photographs, and writings, too.

I reiterate: I am not trying to defend any colonial actions in Greenland, in Ittoqqortoormiit/Scoresbysund, or indeed any colonial action, nor am I trying to defend EM. What I am questioning are the formats in which myths and narratives are communicated, and to whom. Arke's work is still exhibited both in Denmark and internationally – most recently in 2021 in a solo exhibition in Denmark at Louisiana Museum of Modern Art, Louisiana, "Pia Arke," accessed July 21, 2021, https://louisiana.dk/en/exhibition/pia-arke/. and in 2017 at Charlottenborg Kunsthal, during the group exhibition *Slow Violence*. Kunsthal Charlottenborg, "Slow Violence," accessed July 22, 2020, https://kunsthalcharlottenborg.dk/en/exhibitions/charlottenborg-art-research-slow-violence/. In both exhibitions, text and photography by and about EM on the newly established colony Ittoqqortoormiit/Scoresbysund were presented in frames. The frames showed the selected pages/spreads of the dummy of her book *Stories from Scoresbysund* before it was sent to print with sticky notes. What do these works represent and generate?

A growing interest in colonialism and coloniality amongst academic and artistic circles is mirrored in its increasing prevalence as a public concern, and now it is slowly being presented as a politically urgent matter through discussions in parliaments – this includes also the matter of Nordic colonialism. Ideas about the much needed yet seemingly endless task of re-writing Danish colonial history have been debated heavily over the last years. This, as well as the mechanisms of post-colonialism and coloniality, are finally critically discussed in the public domain, and taken seriously in relation to how coloniality is located in current social structures. I fully support the need to discuss and challenge the dominant production of history and the need to transform violent and exclusive structures away from coloniality and the colonial past, and encourage the educational institutions to take responsibility for working towards that, too. Though I also believe that debates around narratives and judgement need to be treated carefully, without accusations or judgements themselves. I advocate for a critical and reflective discussion on the origin, content, and agenda of dominant narratives. I advocate for narratives being heard, listened to, and discussed, yet still I advocate for more opacity and less accessibility when information appears as harmful material, or generates violence or separation. But who has the clause on what information – the 'collective'?

The narrative in which EM supposedly shot thirty-eight Greenlanders A statement and a narrative both Father and I believe must be constructed and false, which is also why we see a need to make this footnote. and sexually harassed Greenlandic women – as it stands alone today without being followed up by any counter-positions – does in my opinion not contribute with inclusitivity, nor the care of nuance in storytelling and opacity. Read also the chapter

NOTIONS ON CANNIBALISM.

Engagement in dialogue and sharing stories in opposition to 'collective memory' can be a tool to heal a post-colonial society such as the Greenlandic-Danish relation, while respecting wishes for opacity and insisting on a wide variety of stories to be heard. I am not claiming that the narrators of those stories about EM are telling lies, but that these narratives must also be seen under the light of source criticism if they are claiming to be 'true'. What is the underlying reason for the story to be heard? What are the ethical roles of the artist, journalist, and historian? Is it really all about the narrative; is there nothing but the narrative?

I am not trying to dismiss Arke's position or work, since I too find it important to perceive history differently than as a singular, linear timeline of actions and events. I too find it relevant to connect stories across the conventional logics of time Kuratorisk Aktion: *Tupilakosaurus*, 115. and subjectivity. What I would be curious to hear are her thoughts on accessibility, opacity, and editing when creating artworks; published work. I would be curious to hear her position on legitimation when using pre-existing material. Under the conditions now, in which she is no longer around, I have written a fictional dialogue where I am in conversation with Arke through her own written work and her cultural critique.

In this chapter however I would like to add a reflection on the media Arke used most consistently in her work. Arke promoted her narrative with photography, as EM and other explorers did almost a century before her. The familiarity of certain people in her photographs builds a sense of the present and immediate past. As a medium, photography is often used to lay down routes of reference, and serves to help us construct and revise our senses of a more distant past. Susan Sontag, *Regarding the Pain of Others* (London: Penguin Books Ltd, 2019), 74. Photography was and is such an important medium for civilisation (through it, we have seen the farthest reaches of the earth), especially during the period of high colonialism and nationalist conflict in Europe at the end of the 19th century and the beginning and the 20th century. Wekker, *White Innocence*, 98. It recorded and documented the progress of civilisational missions, of which it became an integral part: the project of the future, the conquest of the Earth to the last square centimetres. Photography was at that time efficient to produce the subject as a mass subject, available to be viewed at all times. Kathryn Yusoff, "Configuring the field," 71. Photography depicted this irreversible process, but it also did something more: it helped to conquer, to occupy territory, to take possession, Arke, *Scoresbysundhistorier*, 9. and therefore photography played a crucial part in colonisation. Arke used photography to switch the roles of the observed to the observer, where the viewfinder's frame was switched around, and instead pointed towards the colonisers and their deeds. Even though Arke used footage from the EM, Even footage she borrowed from EM's relatives' private archive, which is unfortunately not known to the public nor something Arke ever communicated. the photographs reveal the contexts that we talk in and from – both colonial purposes (the things that made Greenland Danish territory, by stating it was 'good', and that the alternative would have been worse), and a de-colonial purpose (by stating that the colonial moments were violent, unnecessary, and inhumane).

Photo albums have become the perfect medium for telling complex and layered visual stories that push the ideas and boundaries of the documentary genre. Stefan Vanthuyne, "Fiction as a Visual Strategy in the Photobook" in Wynants, *When Fact is Fiction*, 97. For that reason, Father's family albums have been an important source of information in this research on being 'snow-blinded'. Arke uses photography to communicate her narrative. EM did the same. This can also be said of my design practice.

From: Me Sent: April 26, 2020, 07:59

...sense of privacy, I give the person I have been in contact with regarding EM the cover name XM) Subject: EM

Dear XM,

...te to you because I have the last half year ...tigated EM's deeds and doings in Green-...d and in the Arctic, as a part of my project ...in my master education in Design (about myth-making and history-writing). ...ve dived into all kinds of source material ...the small documentary *I Farfars fodspor*) ...nd myth stories on and by EM, and in this ...tion, I came across the artist Pia Arke. Are ...ou familiar with her, and her book/artistic ...ject *Stories from Scoresbysund?* Pia Arke ...id not try to hide that she was unsatisfied ...th EM and the initiatives he implemented in East Greenland. Father did not know of ...r, but he discovered that she had named an ...own woman in the attached photo as Ella Mikkelsen. If you have time, can I then ask you about this topic, Greenland and EM?

Kind regards from Gudrun

Unfortunately, it is not possible to share the response of the email correspondence due to reasons of privacy. However, the email contains information to the effect that Pia Arke obtained material from a descendant of EM to use in her work without crediting EM's descendant, apart from calling him an 'old man in Lyngby'. The correspondence also contains the confirmation that it is neither Ella Mikkelsen nor Gustav Holm in the image.

From: Me Sent: April 27, 2020, 23:03 To: XM. Subject: SV: EM

Dear XM,

Thank you for your mail and good to hear from you. Though I am sad bringing up an uncomfortable memory regarding Pia Arke. I hope Aksel was not affected by Arke's agenda. I was also a bit worried and not at least surprised by Arke's stories. I cannot remember if it appears in *Stories from Scoresbysund* or *Tupilakosaurus* that she mentions, and possibly also thanks Aksel for his help (but she does not connect the two actors; EM and Aksel).

But yes, I have also encountered her narrative, that she found pictures in an attic of an "old man" ... It is quite sad that her sources do not match reality, and that she is thus writing a constructed "holistic narrative" which is supposed to be perceived as the 'truth'.

This is also something I am trying to investigate further, which agendas play a part in the contemporary writing of history and the myths about Greenland and EM.

When I visited Greenland in 2017, I had conversations with some locals in Nuuk, who some stories about EM with me. But this fall when I tried to reach out to some the locals, there was an uncertainty as to the stories were about Lauge Koch Lauge (1892–1964) was another Danish polar explorer and geologist. or EM ... Arctic is still a great interest of mine, and far as possible to combine that interest my design education. There is a tendency designers to do a self-critical analysis own background, position, and origin. my project I try to deal with and discuss the conflicting stories, and I have been in with Father about EM (even though grandfather was not EM's biological son). through a photo album and saw some of you cousins as children, probably EM and Ella's home in Charlottenlund around a Christmas tree.

007.JPG

Father told me about Gyldendal who will publish EM's books and that a feature about EM probably also will be made collaboration with Netflix. I am curious how it came to be? Who got the idea? what story or expedition do they want reproduce? Hope you are doing well, and you clarifying that it is not Gustav Holm sitting next to the woman.
Best regards, Gudrun

Unfortunately, it is not possible to share the response of the email correspondence due to reasons of privacy. The response includes the rumour of EM being a murderer during the Amdrup Expedition, a short description of Nikolajsen's work (with which XM helped), and at last a reflection on a family conflict connected to EM.

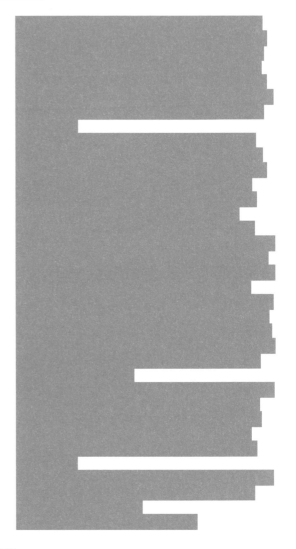

From: Me Sent: August 6, 2020, 09:44 To: XM Subject: SV: EM

Dear XM,

Thank you very much for your email – I am really sorry for this late reply! It was such a fun coincidence at Danish Arctic Institute earlier this summer when we met. I'm glad I could meet you in person, since it has now been months since you wrote your reply. I was at Danish Arctic Institute and had an interesting conversation and tour by Trondhjem, together with an architect friend from the Sandberg Institute, in relation to a project we are about to develop in relation to Arctic artefacts. Danish Arctic Institute was a good help for us to understand the context of their collection, and with what backgrounds on why, who and how the various ethnographies have been

ved from the Arctic and Greenland and
brought to Denmark.

r email you mentioned that a few years
there was a young Greenlandic student
ade a video project in Ittoqqortoormiit/
esbysund, where she took a 1:1 cardboard
of EM to Ittoqqortoormiit/Scoresbysund
few people who knew him. I have been
contact with the student and now gradu-
d visual artist, Nikolajsen, about her film
bysundkolnien er mit eget barn. She was
nough to open the links to her film for a
while for me to see her work.

It was quite interesting to hear about the
us myths and stories about EM from the
Greenlanders themselves, even though
ne of the stories seemed absurd – that he
was to murder an Inuit settlement.

, it is exciting to think what the film and
ollaboration Gyldendal has with Netflix
will result in.

o you think about *Farlig Tomandsfaerd*
filmed and then produced through the
r streaming service Netflix? And do you
how far they are in the negotiations? Do
think they will film other books of EM's
well? And what do you think it means, if
will be a renewed focus and interest in
polar expeditions in Greenland? Or on
ark's deeds in Greenland at the time, in
ion to Greenland being former a Danish
colony?

hank you for your reflections. It is never
when families split or reunite in another
nstellation. I understand that it may have
d wounds and I do not wish to intervene
ing these memories back. Father did not
ish to talk about it either, and of course I
ect that. But yes, it is a good side-note to
e in relation to a self-critical analysis of
one's own background.

y project is soon taking shape, as a book,
hopefully, if I manage to scrape funding
gether, will be printed in a small edition.
has been and it is an exciting rewarding
rocess that touches on many dilemmas,
complications, and opportunities.
Kind regards from Gudrun

As the artistic research developed, new narratives and agendas followed, often at such a pace that my inbox encountered a lack of storage. The research included multiple views on EM's legacy, while being in conversation with EM's descendants, museums, publishing institutions, local Greenlanders, etc. As EM is a known figure in Greenland and a part of the 'collective memory' in Danish historical writing on Greenland, the Greenlandic population have been educated about EM's work in East Greenland. In Denmark, though, it seems only to be the older generation that is aware of these Danish actions and actors. A few Greenlandic/Danish artists have worked with these narratives about EM in East Greenland. Pia Arke was one of them. Another artist was Nikolajsen Nanna Ánike Nikolajsen (1984) was an artist working with the relationship between language, materials, and craft, often in relation to Greenland-Denmark. Throughout this book she is referred to as Nikolajsen, since she has articulated to me that she does not make art anymore. Still I believe her work is important and should be recognised as that, meanwhile respecting her wish to not include any of her work or communication in this book. who went to Ittoqqortoormiit/ Scoresbysund, the colony EM established, and recorded several locals' memories of EM. Nikolajsen shared her films with me for a brief moment in 2019. The films contained stories from both Greenlanders and Danes, which were told into and recorded by Nikolajsen's viewfinder.

Me, December 5, 2019, 14.30:

Dear Nikolajsen,
From several acquaintances in Greenland and Denmark I have been recommended to contact you and get familiar with your work, *Scoresbysund kolonien er mit eget barn* [*Scoresbysund colony is my own child*], which you exhibited in April 2011 at the Museum of Contemporary Art in Roskilde, *Inuit Live: the Performative Greenland in Motion, Words, Sound and Images*.
I am studying Design at Sandberg Institute, where I am developing a research on myth-making and Nordic colonialism in relation to a design practice.
Since I am the great-granddaughter of polar explorer EM, I have a great interest in dealing more with his experiences, intentions, and actions in Greenland.
It is particularly important for me to get an insight into the locals' view of EM in East Greenland, as the 'story' is often told from EM's own perspective.
From what I could read about from the press material, which the Museum of Contemporary Art in Roskilde has shared with me, this is precisely also what you investigate in the work *Scoresbysund kolonien er mit eget barn*.
In this regard, I would like to hear if there is an opportunity for me to see your film that was shown during the exhibition?

It is my intention to develop my project rther with a critical approach to my own ound, in the form of a small publication/ let. Being able to see your work will give a better understanding of the local voices, eriences, and history in Ittoqqortoormiit/ esbysund. Thus, a better understanding colonial rule that set the agenda in East Greenland right up to the present day. pe to hear from you and will be available time if you require further information.
Kind regards, Gudrun

Unfortunately, it is not possible to share the response of the conversation due to reasons of privacy. In Nikolajsen's reply, she sent me links to her film and told me about a book that was inaccessible for her to see, something about trading in East Greenland, which she found odd and secretive, also in relation to some of the topics and myths in her film. When Nikolajsen made the film, it came as a surprise that people in Ittoqqortoormiit/Scoresbysund were not as negative towards EM as she previously thought, due to the colonial conflict between Greenlanders and Danes. At last in the email, she confirmed that the skulls with bullets in the heads had never been investigated, nor has how these people died.

Me, December 14, 2019, 15.50:

Dear Nikolajsen
ank you ever so much for sending me the links to your film! And thank you for the

description about your background on your work. It is very impressive – and important – work and research you have done. Thank you for sharing it with me. I have just seen them all, and I can understand that you would like to cherish your work and keep the link closed. It has really been interesting to watch, especially because I have met some of the same stories around EM from Greenlanders in Nuuk. I could also imagine that they would be a bit more upset. Because yes, it has undoubtedly not been a painless process for the indigenous population, to be moved around or to be a Danish colony etc. When you say you could not find the book on the East Greenlandic trade, is it because there was a connection with EM's time as an inspector and the missing book on the trade? It's a wild story the one with the skulls, and I wonder why the case has never been investigated to the bottom... Worrying indeed. Do you have a family in Ittoqqortoormiit? And did you have a special goal with the work?
Kind regards, Gudrun

Unfortunately, it is not possible to share the response of the conversation due to reasons of privacy. What I can reveal is that Nikolajsen's research question when making the film was; 'what was the Greenlander's view of Danes?' with the very specific entry point of EM in Ittoqqortoormiit. And in the end of her email, something about the rumour of the skulls, in connection to the archaeological work done by Sandell.

Me, December 14, 2019, 15.50:

Dear Nikolajsen
It is remarkable that they are retaining material from that time. It was the museum director at the Ammassalik Museum, Lars Rasmussen, who recommended that I contacted you. The Museum of Contemporary Art in Roskilde had only one article and press-release lying around. I am sorry to ask you about the rumour again

M had killed people at the peat cabins; but
Sandell? And do you know if anyone has
vestigated it? I hope you will have a Merry
Christmas!
Best regards, Gudrun

Unfortunately, it is not possible to share the response of the conversation due to reasons of privacy. What I can reveal is that Sandell is two archaeologists who have worked in the area where the skulls with the bullet holes were to be found.

Me, February 1, 2020, 13.50:
Dear Nikolajsen
If I come in contact with the books, I will
rm you :) Thank you for your help and your
nces. Knowing yours and Pia Arke's works
ped me a lot in the process of my research.
Best regards, Gudrun

In February 2020 in the moving image *Aftermath: Narratives on EM* Father said: "So, maybe we should go through this together."

So, maybe we should go through this together.
as eyes.
rubies?!
reenland. I smuggled them out and am now trying to fulfil
OW BLINDNESS
is a painful eye condition caused by overexposure to
much ultraviolet light hits the transparent outer layer of
urn. Snow blindness symptoms can be disorienting, and
headache, blurred vision and temporary loss of vision. [86]
approve of smugg
out of Greenlan

Me: Are these glasses functional?

Researcher: Yes, when the strong and intense sunlight is reflected on the bright snow surface it can cause snow blindness.
To prevent the very painful eye dieses, the Inuit made snow goggles, which only allow the light to enter through the narrow viewing slit. It restricted the field of vision and reduced the amount of light that reached the optic nerve. [87]

Me: They look so futuristic and almost alien to me.

Researcher: However they were extremely important for the Inuit and their possibility to survive in the wild wilderness of the Arctic.

In the sketch of the manuscript *Snowblindness*, Gudrun wrote: Me: Ye rubies from Greenland. I smuggled the out and am now trying to fulfil my promis

In July 2020, Father corrects the manuscript: Your gran father and great-grandfather woul not approve of smuggling things o of Greenland.

080.JPG

081.JPG

082.JPG

083.JPG

In April 2020, Father wrote: This is Lady Mollie Butler, your grandmother's sister. She was married to Lord Butler who was Foreign Secretary for Great Britain.

EM was a polar explorer. He got into a conflict with the Queen of England, because he told her that if he would run out of food, he would eat the sled dogs. The Queen of England was a patron for the protection of animals. EM was my great-grandfather (source from Frederiksen's book).

Well, the Government, Danish Government,
where not so keen on him, doing what he was doing.

EM was a polar scientist and captain. He convinced president Theodore Roosevelt to finance the expedition and transport equipment on one of his expeditions in Alaska. EM was my great-grandfather (source from Frederiksen's book).

January 2020 in the moving image *Dialouge w. EM through my ther* EM/Father said: "Well, the Government, Danish Government, were not so keen on him, doing what he was doing."

35.JPG

086.JPG

REFLECTION ON 'TRUTH' & THE 'COLLECTIVE MEMORY'

'...Colonial history is made up of awkward encounters and turning points in social relations; these are the colonial moments, often protracted, and always affecting both colonised and colonisers in the process.' Hastrup, "Colonial Moments in Greenland," 243.

Recently, Danish historians published a new publication about Danish colonialism titled *Grønland – Den Arktiske Koloni* translated; *Greenland – The Arctic Colony. Danmark og kolonierne* by Niels H. Frandsen, Hans Christian Gulløv, ed., and more (English translation: *Denmark and the Colonies: Greenland - the Arctic Colony*), 5 volumes, published in 2017 by Gads Forlag. Greenlandic historians and voices, however, have had a very narrow platform through which to communicate their own history. That 'the pen is mightier than the sword' (Edward Bulwer-Lytton, 1839) still seems to ring true. Danish history-writing, foreign and security policymaking, finance, and language – in higher education and professions – still seem to have a tight grip on the Greenlandic past, present, and possibly also the Greenlandic future. These elements seem to keep the colonial relationship between Greenland and Denmark alive. As mentioned earlier in

MY STRUGGLE WITH SEEING CLEARLY,

it could be argued that there still is a disturbing collective arrogance that comes with Danish history-writing – especially regarding moments of Danish colonialism in Greenland. Many Danes have deep feelings of guilt when considering the troubles the Danish colonial effort inflicted on locals in Greenland, but still it is worth noting that most Danish (and published) writings on colonialism in Greenland and Greenlandic history are marked by 'an almost flagellantic glee with which the sins of the government as well as individuals committed in Greenland have been depicted in every detail.' Hastrup, "Colonial Moments in Greenland," 255. It is only through a radical challenge of the gatekeepers of colonial discourses that the power relations between Greenland and Denmark can change. Were the first polar explorers and colonisers in Greenland all responsible for this arrogant interpretation of the history and for the colonial discourse? Or is EM an exception?

The myths and narratives that circle around what happened outside the polar explorers' expedition goals in the Arctic seem not to be described nor treated critically in literature I have until quite recently encountered a few critical writings on Danish colonisers' imprints on Greenland. These critical voices of colonial moments in Greenland are mostly represented in the young generation in Greenland such as by Julie Edel Hardenberg and Niviaq Korneliussens among many others. Newer works by Danish researchers, Kirsten Thisted's *Stemmer fra Grønland* (English title: *Voices from Greenland*) from 2021 and Anne Kirstine Hermann's *Imperiets Børn* (English title: *Children of the Empire*) from 2021 are critical towards the Danish history-writing on Greenland. It seems like there is a 'shared' consensus that the polar explorers are heroes, A notion expressed frequently by Danish Arctic Institute through their podcast series: "Arktiske Historier," accessed May 12, 2020, https://arktiskinstitut.dk/index.php?id=102. and the heroic narratives are still dominating the 'collective memory'. As the Louisiana Revy publication from 2013 states: 'The polar heroes moved in the borderland between myth and reality, between the living and the dead.' Monica Kristensen, "Noget om helte" in *Arktis Louisiana Revy* (September, 2013): 56. From the perspectives of the polar explorers, they believed fully that they lived up to the stories they dictated themselves as polar explorers,

Kurt Frederiksen, *Ejnar Mikkelsen – En biografi* (Copenhagen: Gyldendal, 2015), 111. as if it was their 'printed word that created the ascription of heroism', Elizabeth Baigent, "'Deeds not words'? Life writing and early twentieth-century British polar exploration," in *New Spaces of Exploration*, eds. Simon Naylor and James R. Ryan (London: I.B. Tauris, 2010), 24. almost as a part of the food chain or the survival of the fittest; who could overcome the extreme and the sublime and then later preserve that story?

The stories told by the polar explorers conveyed meanings of their experiences that extended beyond the narrative itself. There was a tendency to embellish; often what the polar explorers claimed to have experienced in the 'sublime North' did not fully correspond to their actual experiences and actions. Their narratives therefore repeatedly extended and reproduced previous narrations of polar explorers and Danish colonial memory. It is a well-known fact that history is written by the victors. What we tend to forget is that the narration comes from the victor's position and their completely totalising perspective. Claus Bryld and Anette Warring, *Besaettelsestiden som kollektiverindring* (Roskilde: Roskilde Universitetsforlag bind 5, 1998), 65. The preserved polar explorer narrative is both reduced and appears as an open story, almost a tale of the 'sublime North', which romanticises the heroes in myths. Their mythical origin and ideal goal are both rooted in the narrative of the hero. Bourriaud, *The Radicand*, 45.

It is said that 'collective memory' is a political compromise, and at the same time is part of the overall production of memory. Bryld and Warring, *Besaettelsestiden som kollektiverindring*, 55. It can be both realistic and mythical. Bryld and Warring, *Besaettelsestiden som kollektiverindring*, 69. One could argue that the polar explorers' narratives did not have a documentary function but an illustrative one. Meaning that it is the narrative's structure and content that are in focus, not the interests of the narrators. These narratives, structurally and through content, contributed in producing memories for the 'collective'. Bryld and Warring, *Besaettelsestiden som kollektiv erindring*, 56. Still, I would like to maintain that the interests of the narrators were very present and an essential part of the overall 'collective memory' production, since it was vital for the polar explorers to gain and collect enough capital and publicity to finance their next expedition, as it was the rich and influential businessmen and newspapers in Western world that financed these adventures. However, these adventure narratives were something the international public were also demanding. The Western public were expecting to be entertained by the polar explorers' life-threatening expeditions. The illustrative narratives the polar explorers produced were very popular among new consumers during the late 19th and early 20th century, which Arke as an example also mentions in her work on the explorers' documentations and mapping practice; 'The extent of the amateur photographic material from Scoresbysund [Ittoqqortoormiit] shows in its indirect way how "far out" the Europeans have moved through Greenland's roadless geography and that only royals have been photographed as much as the Greenlanders.' Arke, *Stories from Scoresbysund*, 12. This also refers to the Danish national interest in Greenland and its people, however the Greenlanders are often almost referred to as 'the other'.

'Collective memory', or 'collective tradition', is as an expression that is understood as the total memory production, the dominant and archived history, which is kept alive by one or several communities of remembrance Bryld and Warring, *Besaettelsestiden som kollektiverindring*, 56. (communities that cherish the historical events and memories), as Bryld and Warring write, which can appear as historically factual but presented in an 'unusual storytelling'. Thus, when unpacking colonialism in this sense, a consideration of the actual relationships between old and new inhabitants (and stories) in Greenland and Denmark is implied. It points us towards the notion of contact zones; the idea that colonialism is both practised and located in space and time, which affects both parties. Hastrup, "Colonial Moments in Greenland," 243. But colonial history-writing is still an unfinished matter. Cultural understanding on a global scale still seems to be marked by colonial discourses produced by the Western world, and sees them as universal. I wonder why two of the biggest publishers in Denmark have secured contracts with EM's descendants to re-publish EM's books without questioning any implications of what a re-telling of the colonial past could mean, especially when decolonisation movements are globally – and rightfully so – winning time and space in news and social media. Why does Netflix Netflix, together with the Danish publishing company Gyldendal and the closest descendants of EM, signed a contract to make a feature film about EM's expedition in 1909-1912. not show the story from the perspectives of the Inuit? Why another glorification of another white man's deeds in the 'wilderness'?

Unfortunately, it is not possible to share the details of the conversations between the descendants and heirs of EM in this publication, due to reasons of privacy and due to agency contracts between the descendants and the publishers. However, the information that I can share is that the descendants are discussing copyright and a re-publishing of EM's work in more languages, in tandem with the upcoming Netflix film, *Against the Ice*.

Unfortunately, it is not possible to share the details of the conversation between the descendants and heirs of EM and the publisher Gyldendal in this publication due to reasons of privacy and due to agency contracts. The conversation contains information regarding a re-release of EM's work in the US and terms of copyright, sales, and deadlines. The conversation ends with "It's the big machine that's going to work behind the release."

The secondary system of languages ('second-order semiological systems' – a theory developed in Roland Barthes' work *Mythologies* from 1957) recognises the existence of a meta-language, and that in many cases is translated into a form. Barthes calls this form a 'myth'. Bryld and Warring, *Besættelsestiden som kollektiv erindring*, 62. The myth 'steals' meaning or significance from the object language; it becomes a 'de-politicised speech'. The myth 'neutralises' what is created in society; Bryld and Warring, *Besaettelsestiden som kollektiv erindring*, 62. a sentiment that can be applied to Danish history-writing regarding the deeds of the Danish polar explorers in the Arctic. Once again, 'the pen is mightier than the sword'.

According to Barthes the myth is rhetorically ahistorical, categorical, reductive, identifying, and repetitive; 'there is no longer anything to choose from, you just have to sign.' Bryld and Warring, *Besaettelsestiden som kollektiv erindring*, 62. Or, as Kirsten Thisted writes about the two partners involved in the colonial mishmash; it is as if 'a conspiracy of silence [has] enveloped - as if Danes and Greenlanders have agreed upon letting these histories rest.' Kirsten Thisted, "De-Framing the Indigenous Body: Ethnography, Landscape and Cultural Belonging in the Art of Pia Arke" in *Tupilakosaurus* (Copenhagen: Kuratorisk Aktion, 2012), 291-292. However, at this moment in time, this notion of letting stories rest is about to change. Traditional or colonial storytelling of Danish colonialism in Greenland is clashing with current reactions against structural racism, where the Black Lives Matter movement and movements calling for decolonisation, among a whole array of activists, are contributing opinions by painting or tearing down the busts and sculptures of their previous oppressors all over the Western world. In Greenland it is especially the younger generation who are stating their argument against coloniality, colonial monuments, and colonial policies, as they want to tell their own stories and decide their own futures. Young Greenlanders painted monuments of Hans Egede in Nuuk, a bust of Knud Rasmussen in Hundested, and, a few years back, a bust of EM in Ittoqqortoormiit with red and black paint. There is a tendency for the older generation to show a certain arrogance, and to declare the younger generation a disgrace for their critique of the past, and the way they make their criticism heard. The criticism from the younger generation, though, is advocating for a new set of values in public spaces such as street names and monuments related to imperialism and colonialism. This has set the 'collective memory' up for debate, so to speak, which will hopefully affect the way the 'collective Danish – and international – memory' perceives Greenland, causing it to shift. This would allow for reflections on how future stories and myths, or even 'truths', are narrated, archived, and reproduced. It might also enable us as a society to question hidden structures and to allow more pluriversal agendas to contribute to the production of 'collective memory'.

The structure of 'collective memory' itself is diffuse, as anything can be absorbed and choreographed, as long as it is accepted by the majority of a 'community'. This speaks to the ideas of 'fake news' and maybe more so the 'reality' genre as in the dominant fiction in popular culture, where one can only experience reality as a particular version of the 'real'. The 'real' is a catalogue of images that provides us with possibilities and limitations by which to understand the world in the postmodern era. Depending on which facts and news we consume, we are all constructing our own realities and 'truths', 'We now live in a "post-truth" society. A world in which truth no longer matters, where facts are countered by "alternative facts", and reality is more about your media diet than about the world as it is.' From Rob Wijnberg's article "How the truth became whatever makes you click," accessed May 3, 2020, https://thecorrespondent.com/410/how-the-truth-became-whatever-makes-you-click/9567807150-326405ae. precisely by virtue of the tension between realism and mythologising, as well as the reductionist and the diffuse nature of 'collective memory', which can be used as a hegemonic force, collective traction, or community of remembrance, Bryld and Warring, *Besaettelsestiden som kollektiv erindring*, 72. as Bryld and Warring problematise. This can be applied to the colonial moments in Greenland throughout history writing.

The way EM wrote seems to me to be in close connection to how the realistic and mythic features of narratives are linked. It is like when realism is acting as a kind of 'raw material' for the myth. Bryld and Warring, *Besaettelsestiden som kollektiv erindring*, 69. From several sources I have heard that EM was a brilliant storyteller, but in reading his books it became even more clear to me that the writing of his memoir becomes sort of history-writing that contributes to the 'collective memory'. The notion of history-writing is also treated by filmmaker and literature theorist, Trinh T. Minh-ha, who writes in *Woman, Native, Other;* 'history-writing quickly sets itself apart, consigning story to the realm of tale, legend, myth, fiction, literature'. In EM's writing – and in the writing of other polar explorers – it seems as though the 'fictional and factual come to a point where they mutually exclude each other, when fiction, not infrequently, means lies, and when fact means truth.' Minh-ha, *Woman, Native, Other*, 120.

As mentioned previously, I am not trying to reveal what is true or false, instead I would like to consider how EM's writings influenced the 'collective memory' in Denmark and Greenland, as in the rest of the Western world. EM had, as did many other explorers and scientists, the advantage of being supported by scientism and professionalism, as coming from 'civilised' Europe. Minh-ha, *Woman, Native, Other*, 49. What I find interesting in EM's writings is the link between the professionalism of his diary notes and the imaginative perceptions of his achievements. To get a sense of these writings, I recommend reading EM's own books and the chapter in this book

TOP VIEW & INFORMATION CARRIER.

What is central to understand regarding myths, and mythical meaning, is the willingness to sacrifice everything else in order to create a simplification of historical diversity. It is in these moments where new myths arise. Bryld and Warring, *Besaettelsestiden som kollektiv erindring*, 69. I am wondering if EM took any precautions on this matter, to benefit the myths around his expeditions and his achievements. One could argue that this was something that happened in newspapers in the early 20th century, and that it was expected of EM and other polar explorers to create excitement and mythical meanings, since expeditions were often funded by newspapers so that the stories (told by the explorers) could generate public interest and therefore capital. The 'truth'-value in these stories by the explorers therefore also relied upon a shared set of values between the idea, the author, the production, the audience, and the distribution. Cramerotti, *Aesthetic Journalism*, 41. Or as Frederiksen also writes in his email to me on May 2, 2020 in relation to *Danmark-Ekspeditionen:*

> "All the previous Northeast explorers created myths when writing about their experiences. This also applies to EM. It can hardly be different – and is probably okay too."

I feel an urge to answer this with a critical remark, since as the visual and cultural theorist Daniela Agostino writes; 'narratives of colonial innocence and benevolent exceptionalism are often enabled by the logics of colonial archives, which tend to subsume the violence of the colonial experience within narratives of state reasons and progress.' Daniela Agostinho, "Archival encounters - rethinking access and care in digital colonial archives" in *Archival Science*, vol. 19, no. 2 (2019): 145. However, the one 'who represents his [/her] own discourse on myths as a myth is acutely aware of the illusion of all reference to a subject as absolute centre. The packaging of myths must somehow bear the form of which it attempts to enclose, if it wishes to come closest to its object.' Minh-ha, *Woman, Native, Other*, 61. Was EM aware of the mythical character in his writings in diaries and later in books and articles, and for what reasons? To come closer to what object? Greenland?

Maybe the same counts for many artistic practices, regarding creating stories around the profession. Designers or artists often draw on historical sources, oral testimonies, and archived material, to then translate the empirical sources into an artistic universe and thereby also deliberately blur the boundaries between what is generally known as 'fiction' and 'reality', Wynants, *When Fact is Fiction*, 13. or simply with the intention to work with 'material' in order to create a visual language and form. It seems that my own role in my design practice can be just as confused as EM's genre writing (which one could categorise as memoir, free epic form, docudrama, or docu-fiction), since a free narration presents human nature in its bold outlines; 'history in its individual details'. Minh-ha, *Woman, Native, Other*, 120. In my practice I too create narratives. I too claim that I communicate a trustworthy 'truth' on how the world is situated, and even that I as a designer have solutions to problems (which seems to be expected by society of their designers). But also, as it is written in "Between realities # Athens" by Sigrid Merx; 'Designers are expected to prove their social value by using their imagination for real solutions to real problems, which reduces imagination to a tool', in Wynants, *When Fact is Fiction*, 165. It is unfortunately also a very Western logic to be convinced that one could articulate 'truth' and generate solutions for the world, and that the designers of today are entitled to do so (as the Western imperialists have done for generations).

In the process of dealing with material from my own background, I noticed that my role and perspective were constantly shifting. I kept asking myself questions on sources, myths, and collaborative interaction throughout the research. I was in a constant dialogue with myself as to whether an actual rupture with the 'collective memory' in its national and mythical state could happen, and if that rupture would result in a shift in roles between 'hero' and 'villain'. Bryld and Warring, *Besaettelsestiden som kollektiv erindring*, 71.

In fiction, one adds to reality in order to construct a possible 'truth'. Whereas journalism (and often the documentary genre, too) extracts from reality to *'rep-resent'* 'truth', and only by a particular fragment of it. Cramerotti, *Aesthetic Journalism*, 74. I would claim that the same counts for the designer's method: dealing with different archives and sources of narrative, and later de- or re-contextualising these narratives into a new form – both real and fictional – that can shape our understanding of the present and open up to possible imaginations of the future. Still, as a designer I can never claim what is true and what is false. It is also simply not in my interest, but what I aim to do instead is to work towards a speculation Jonas Rutgeerts and Nienke Scholts, "TALOS/Talos – What Sort of Future Do We Want to See Performed?" in Wynants, *When Fact is Fiction*, 187. by staging, writing, and making space for other voices. Working with speculation, fiction, and myth in storytelling has become necessary for my design practice as a product of a colonial legacy. It has become necessary to question and re-contextualise moments from the past by gaining access to information and material to debate in the present.

In this process of making the book with Anna, we have used the layout in the book to try to deconstruct the barrier between the designer as the creator and the spectator as the consumer. Cramerotti, *Aesthetic Journalism*, 56. We are convinced that this is possible by engaging and inviting other narratives, both into the medium of the book and in the *Snowblindness Podcast Series*. Through moments of collaboration in the editing, sharing, and consuming phases, the creator is no longer in control of the spectator. The readers, the spectators, of this book are, as mentioned in the

PRELUDE

EDITING & SHARING

chapters, free to leave edits, comments, and corrections on the stories and reflections. There are spaces for comments and other stories in the wide margins on the pages.

When designers and editors are acting as both the creator and the spectator of their own work, by constantly discussing its content, form, and communication in the process of the development and in the final work's appearance, it can allow for other interventions. This dualistic position, being the creator and the spectator, while being personally invested in the research, can create space for new experiments, misunderstandings, and thereby unforeseen directions and collaborations. In the text

ANOTHER STORY ON EM

the Danish/Greenlandic visual artist Pia Arke's work is discussed. Arke's work draws parallels to the above. In my attempt to understand Arke's work and methodology, I noticed that the material and sources she used are missing links to their origin. In her book *Stories from Scoresbysund: Photographs, Colonisation and Mapping,* Arke criticises EM and all his doings in Greenland without paying attention to, as it seems, the context of the time he was operating in and the potential consequences if he did not act or establish Ittoqqortoormiit/Scoresbysund. Is the attention towards the context of the time necessary at the time the colonial action happened? When reading Arke's texts,

I could not avoid a moment of fear, since her influence and her interpretation of EM reaches an audience – an international art scene – who could regard her work as the only 'truth', because her work is presented in that way, or I interpreted her work in that way, that EM, in Arke's opinion, represents all deeds of Danish colonialism in Greenland in the 20th century. However, I acknowledge that we cannot speak about a 'whole truth', but only moments of a truth, throughout a variety of means in time and space, Cramerotti, *Aesthetic Journalism*, 42. and for that reason I can and will not neglect her position nor her work. Instead, I would advocate for the designer or artist to be aware of ethical implications when communicating narratives as 'truths'. This is especially important when the designer or artist is an embedded actor in the work and narrative themselves, as well as the discourse they unfold. Still, there must be space for (counter-)narratives and those narratives' qualities, when questioning 'truth' and history writing – and thereby also a 'snow-blindness'. Or as it is phrased by Isaac Julien in *Essays on the Essay Film:* 'By inserting into the film images, characters, and places that were not necessarily part of what the official story tells us, [it enables us] to extrapolate notions of reality and truth. History is something that must be rewritten as time goes by. It can and should be contested, so that new narratives emerge, and this way we are able to create new forms of identification, while learning to relate differently with our past and memory'. Isaac Julien, "From 'Ten Thousand Waves' to Lina Bo Bardi, via 'Kapital' (2016)" in *Essays on the Essay Film*, eds. Nora M. Alter and Timothy Corrigan (New York: Columbia University Press, 2017), 342.

For the *Snowblindness Podcast Series*, Anna and I were in conversation with the Greenlandic photographer Inuuteq Storch to discuss myth-making and storytelling as tools in an artistic practice. *Snowblindness Podcast Series*, "Let's talk about what it means to find something and use it" in conversation with Inuuteq Storch. We talked about how some narratives do not represent reality, but instead how these narratives create a world and new content to delve into, as a way to communicate other narratives Minh-ha, *Woman, Native, Other*, 62. and cultures. Below is an extract from the podcast.

098.JPG

Storch: Let me start with how I started using other people's photos, because that's another story. One of my best friends was working in a dumpster in my hometown. I would spend some time in his work at night when I had nothing to do. We would look for things and, yeah, just being us. And at some point, I found films [negatives], like five or six films in the dumpster, and I was like 'wow I found some films.' So, I took them and developed them.

Were you already a photographer back then, or was this more like a hobby? Or you kind of already knew what you were looking for also?

Storch: Yes, at that point I was strictly working only on my own photos, I wouldn't touch any other people's photos ... Those photos I found in a dumpster, they were actually taken in the end of 90s and beginning of 2000s in m hometown.

Gudrun: Did you recognise people in the photos then?

Storch: Some of them. But I could not recogni the guy who took the photos. When I scann the photos, I already started to be that guy w took the photos. I named him, and wrote hi life story. So at the time I was not taking photos, I was 'taking photos'.

Anna: I'm not sure if I understood completely, when you say you named him, do you then mean you made a fictional story?

Storch: Yeah, I made it up, being that guy that t the photos. It worked out in a good way, so t then I figured out that I don't need to take photos to make them mine, to make them m story.

These narratives presented in Arke's, Storch's, EM's, or my own work might not be the most 'realistic' in representing reality directly, but as mentioned previously, they are narratives that use the world and mechanisms of language to (trans-)form other narratives as they reach the receiver, which calls for new interpretations, or misunderstandings, and possibly new voices between the two; Greenland and Denmark.

On another level, taking other people's work or narrative and using it in one's own artistic practice does not only concern matters of ethics, but also speaks to a much broader and complicated concept of copyright. In the chapter

this is discussed in relation to the *Snowblindness* book and its preceding research; who has the right to what stories? I will not try to investigate who found what first in the Arctic region, or the competition between polar explorers. I will rather treat what it means in a design practice to use the same methods and media as the polar explorers did in investigation, map-making, and storytelling in the attempt to make *Snowblindness*.

From: Me Sent: Wednesday, April 29, 2020, 13:25 To: Frederiksen Subject: SV: Scrapbooks

Hi Frederiksen,

Thank you very much for your help earlier in clarifying where EM's scrapbooks are kept, and how the material around EM is filed at Danish Arctic Institute.

I am still developing a small publication about myth creations and history-writing in relation to Greenland – where I use EM as a reference/actor, as part of my final research at Sandberg Instituut. There are some rumours and obscurities I would like to have confirmed rebutted, which I thought you would be to help me with. I am re-reading *Farlig andsfaerd* (Gyldendal, 1962 edition) and page 25 EM reports that he miraculously finds Jørgen Brønlund's corpse and a bag with a calendar and wallet, with a few etches by Mylius-Erichsen, Høeg-Hagen, and Landtonings from Denmark's Fjord Danmark-Ekspeditionen (1906–1908). now that there has been some discussion ever since, whether EM actually found nlund's belongings with calendar, notes, records of territory. Some sources say he Mylius-Erichsen's diaries, other sources say the opposite or at least question EM's dibility in that context. In EM's own tale *rlig Tomandsfaerd,* it seems that he does clearly state *what* he actually found. And later, as you write in your book on pages -100, led to another harsh criticism from Rasmussen. Knud Rasmussen (1879-1933) was a famous Danish polar connected to the findings of the diaries, however it is still discussed how another myth in North Pole. Who actually found Erichsen's diaries? And where does the mour come from that EM must have shot eight Inuit during the Amdrup-Expedi- A rumour I first got familiar with in your ok, and later in Nikolajsen's video work, *resbysund colony is my own child.* I hope will have time to answer my questions.

Kind regards, Gudrun

From: Frederiksen Sent: Saturday, May 2, 2020, 14:54 To: Me Subject: SV: Scrapbooks

Dear Gudrun

By reading Vagn Lundbye: *Omkom 79'fjorden* (Brøndum 1984, Borgen 2006), I think, you will get a better overview and control over who found what, when they did it, what they later told, how and why. That book gives in short form the whole story while the book at the same time relates a lot to the mythology. All the previous Northeast explorers in Greenland created myths when writing about their expe- riences. This also applies to EM. It can hardly be different – and is probably also okay too. What I include on pages 99–100 in my book is that EM removed a cairn report without putting in a new one explaining what he had done, when, why, etc. He broke a common code of that kind, which Knud Rasmussen blamed him for – and rightfully so. But everything like that has to be judged all the time based on how the situation was in that particular time.

There are many conspiracy guesses – which
also comes from the fact that not everyone w
constantly interested in wrîting everything
down. Read Lundbye and get back to me, if
you do not find what you are looking for. Th
rumour of the 38 dead Inuit people is related
to the fact that they have died of natural
causes (hunger, disease). When the member
of the Amdrup expedition came to inhabited
areas close to the incident of the 38 dead Inu
people, and tell them about their discovery, t
rumour arîses. EM has also shown no objec-
tion to wrîting about it, this rumour and the
discovery. This counts for most of the Arctic
literature ever wrîtten that one should not le
the truth destroy a good story. On the other
hand, much of what they experîenced was so
amazing and unlikely – although true – tha
is almost is unbelievable.
Kind regards, Frederîksen

In April 2020, Father wrote: Here EM is not discussing with Knud Rasmussen. EM (born 1880, died 1971) was a polar explorer. He and the other polar explorer Knud Rasmussen (born 1879, died 1933) had an argument because of a missing note in the middle of Greenland's icecap. This missing note almost costs Knud's life. EM was my great-grandfather (source from Eriksen).

087.JPG

Fakturadato	21-03-2017
Forfaldsdato	21-03-2018
At betale DKK	**100,00**

Beskrivelse	Antal	Enhed	Pris	Beløb
Non-gem corundum	94	gram		100,00
		stk.		0,00
		stk.		0,00
		stk.		0,00
		stk.		0,00
		stk.		0,00
		stk.		0,00
		stk.		0,00
		stk.		0,00
		stk.		0,00

Betalt kontant

Subtotal	100,00
	0,00
Total DKK	**100,00**

088.JPG

EM was a Danish polar explorer. He promised to occupy land in the name of the United States, North of Alaska. EM was my great-grandfather, but not by blood (source from Frederiksen's book).

089.JPG

090.JPG

EM was a polar explorer. He was so adapted to getting funds to his voyages of discovery that the very wealthy people fled from him when they met him on the streets. EM was my great-grandfather (source from Father).

EM (born 1880, died 1907) was a captain. He wen
to Alaska to find new land. His ship sank
The whole crew drowned. EM was m
great-grandfather (source from Alaskan natives).

091.JPG

092.JPG

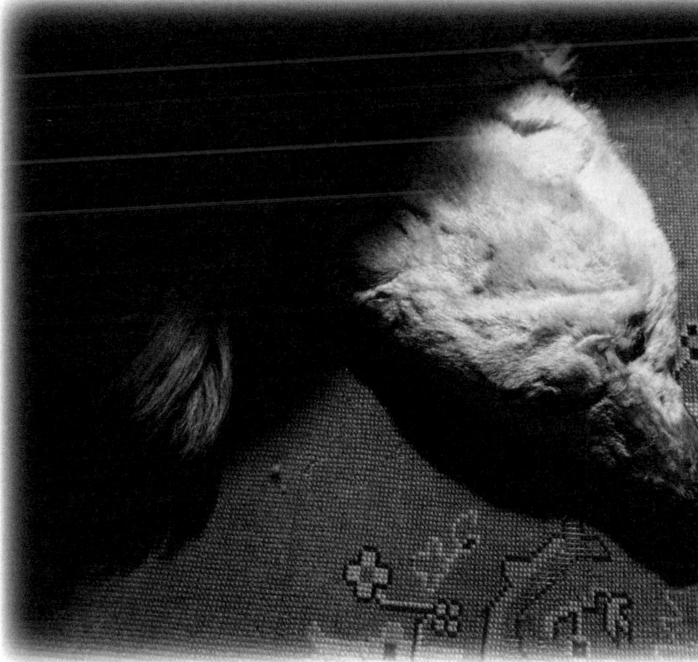

EM was a polar explorer. He shot a polar bear, while he was captured in Greenland's northeast coast. The stuffed polar bear now belongs to my brother, who is named after him. EM was my great-grandfather (source from Father).

In April 2020, Father wrote: Polar bear on carpet that once belonged to EM. Photo taken in Borgnæsdal.

093.JPG

094.JPG

EM was a Danish inspector in Greenland. He saw it as Denmark's responsibility to take care of the Greenlanders. He became one of the most influential persons in the relation between Greenland and Denmark. EM was my great-grandfather (source from Father).

095.JPG

096.JPG

EM was a polar explorer. He got a Danish Arctic warship named after him. That ship was recently in Syria under Danish Command during the war against IS. EM was my great-grandfather (source from Father).

097.JPG

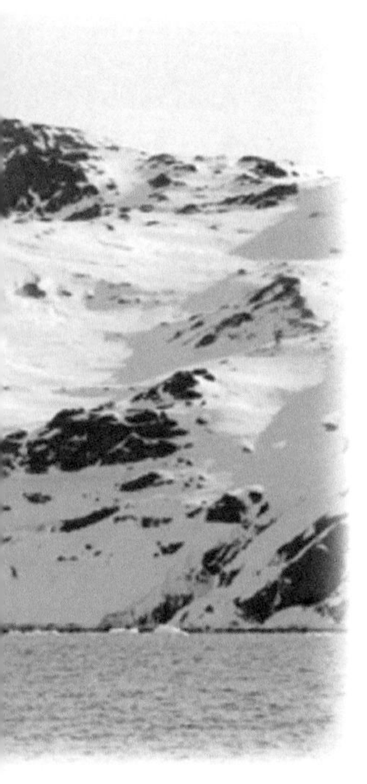

2
Let's talk about what it means to find something and use it
Snowblindness
30.4.2021 18:00 CEST, 14:00 GMT-2
x
Working with archives and photography to highlight forgotten narratives.
Inuuteq
tune in!
Storch
https:// alonetogether.pub
funded by the student council
Student Council

EM was a polar scientis He was the first to deman a wireless connection be tween Greenland and Den mark (1921). Today there is sti a part of Greenland, whicl does not have an Interne connection. EM was m great-grandfather (source fro Frederiksen's book).

098.JPG

099.JPG

EM was an inspector. He got a fjord named after him in Greenland. Miki's Fjord it is called. EM was my great-grandfather (source from Father).

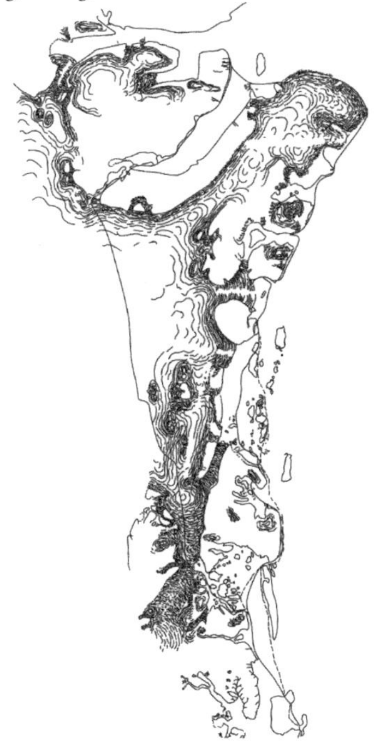

100.JPG

101.JPG

EM was a polar explorer. He named an island on Greenland's east coast after his first wife, Naja. EM was my great-grand-father, but not by blood (source from Frederiksen's book).

EM was not a gold digger. H experienced the Gold Rush i Alaska and Canada in the 190C I would have done differenti EM was my great-grandfath but not by blood (source from Frederiks book).

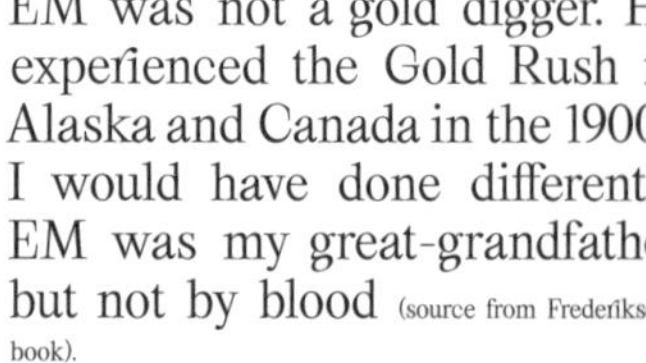

102.JPG

103.JPG

104.JPG

105.JPG

NOTIONS ON CANNIBALISM

Definition Cannibalism is the act of consuming another individual of the same species as food. The rate of cannibalism increases in nutritionally poor environments as individuals turn to conspecifics as an additional food source. Cannibalism regulates population numbers, whereby resources such as food, shelter, and territory become more readily available with the decrease of potential competition. Wikipedia, "Cannibalism," accessed June 1, 2020, https://en.wikipedia.org/wiki/Cannibalism.

Act 1

The fact that sledge dogs can eat each other on a polar expedition due to extreme exhaustion and hunger is a call for bad luck. However, EM never experienced nor thought of the possibility that they (himself and his comrade Iver Iversen) would assail one another. Mikkelsen, *Farlig Tomandsfaerd*, 27.

EM: I remember Iver throwing the wildly howling Bjørn [Iver's sledgedog] out into the roaring storm and cold snow, without even knowing his error. Iver cursed 'cannibal, get lost!' Mikkelsen, *Farlig Tomandsfaerd*, 49.

Me: Were you and Iver ever so hungry that you would eat your precious sledge dogs?

EM: I had no idea what these strange cuddles meant, and was a little more puzzled when my question was answered. Mikkelsen, *Farlig Tomandsfaerd*, 88.

Me: Iver wanted to eat his sledge dog?

EM: At first I wanted to scold him [Iver], for being a cannibal Mikkelsen, *Farlig Tomandsfaerd*, 88.

Me: But what about the thought of eating Iver - did that thought ever appear?

EM: We had food half a hundred miles further on, in the Danmarkshavn [North East Greenland], and before that there was no chance of anything edible. Unless we would run into a bear and shoot it. I looked sadly at Iver carrying the rifle and a thought jogged through my brain and I asked him: 'Honestly tell me Iver, is that the rifle you are afraid of?' Iver nodded reluctantly, looked at me with faithful eyes, handed me the rifle and said: 'Take it and let me have something of yours to carry! I no longer want to go with the rifle – it's dangerous!' At that moment I knew, and refused to carry the rifle. I said to him: 'Keep it, Iver, carry it, as you have done so far, do not think too much, but if it can give you peace of mind, you can be in front of me all the time. And when hunger extinguishes pain, fatigue, and sense, just be aware, I think the same as you do.' Now if he falls and dies, what then? Will you, or will you not eat it – that no longer is Iver? Mikkelsen, *Farlig Tomandsfaerd*, 113.

Me: Would you, or would you not have tried to save your own life by eating the body of the deceased mate?

EM: Neither of us knew, but what we know for sure is that the question appeared in our brains as the hunger attacks became too violent and we saw how difficult it was for the companion to make it through to the life-saving supply in the cabin at Danmarkshavn.

Mikkelsen, *Farlig Tomandsfaerd*, 140.

Me: Do you believe Iver could have eaten you?

EM: He claims that he couldn't have touched me without first removing my hands, fingers. He thought that hands separated a human from the animals. With their hands, most people can do everything the animal cannot. For him, the 'human' is in the hands. Mikkelsen, *Farlig Tomandsfaerd*, 140.

Me: When you were close to dying, what did you then do?

EM: Every night I wrote in my journal about the ravages of the disease in my body [one of these diseases was snow-blindness]. And Iver had promised me to take that diary home with him even if he couldn't carry anything else. After all, the diary's description of illness would be his only evidence that my death had a natural cause.

Mikkelsen, *Farlig Tomandsfaerd*, 82.

Act 2

The photograph has been a central element in magazines to visualise the explorations of the world and has contributed to its extension into and throughout the 20th century. Photography is one of the tools by which civilisation has penetrated back and forth between the farthest reaches of the earth. It has recorded and documented the five steps of the civilian mission and, as such, is an integral part of that process, of the future project, the conquest of the Earth to the last square centimetre. The photograph depicts this irreversible process, but it does something more: it helps conquer, invade territory, and take possession of it. Arke, *Scoresbysundhistorier*, 9.

Me: What makes you think that EM killed thirty-eight Inuit people?

Pia Arke: EM was very young at the time, and when they [EM and the rest of the Amdrup-Expedition] arrived in the Tasiilaq area, the crew took out their rifles and aimed at the locals.
Later EM was Inspector here [Ittoqqortoormiit/ Scoresbysund] in the 1930s, perhaps in 1934, but at least in the 1930s. He told the hunters not to touch the peat huts, not a single one of them. Usually they did not touch the peat huts. It was because

he had killed the people in there that he did not want the hunters to touch the peat huts. There is evidence of this in Tsulitsuuligai, the place is called 'a place with peat huts'. By the river of this stone lie many skeletons of children, young and old. There are many peat huts all over the island. It must have been a large community at that time. At that time there were some of the elders who could not accept that they were getting extinct. They had therefore said to the Inspector of the colony [EM]: 'It is you who has killed our ancestors!' Of course, no one really answered that. 'It is you who is killing the Greenlandic people here!' Of course, they had a suspicion, but it ended in no result. I think that's true. I've seen the bones on Tsulitsuuligai myself. The skeletons are so new that the teeth still sit intact on the jaws. If scientists examined the skeletons, they could probably find out how old they are and how they died. Sources from Nikolajsen's film, *Scoresbysundkolonien er mit eget barn* (2010).

Me: Why do you think it was a misunderstanding that the colony Ittoqqortoormiit/Scoresbysund was established? Based on the data from the population in Angmagssalik/Ammassalik, it is very clear that the population suffered from famine and diseases, and that this was precisely the motivation for EM to establish a colony with a national (Danish) interest, too.

Pia Arke: The inhabitants of Angmagssalik have a long tradition of 'moving' south with their European progenitors. Arke, *Scoresbysundhistorier*, 10. The colony, Scoresbysund, is one of the only three inhabited places on the 3,000 kilometres of the drift of ice-ravaged east coast. And it was populated with 100 Greenlanders from Angmagssalik. Arke, *Stories from Scoresbysund*, 11.

Me: After I read your book *Stories from Scoresbysund,* it seemed strange to me that you also construct your own reality or perception of the 'truth'. Here I am thinking of your approach to the sources.

Pia Arke: I include a lot of stories that family and friends [in and outside of Scoresbysund], Greenlanders, and Danes have opened up for me; a confused cluster of memories attached to and released by these photographs taken in Scoresbysund and spread by the north wind. Arke, *Stories from Scoresbysund*, 13

Me: You said that you found four photo albums in a big villa in Lyngby belonging to a kind old man that show the colonisation of

Scoresbysund/Ittoqqortoormiit in 1924 and the first ten to fifteen years of the existence of the town. Arke, *Scoresbysundhistorier*, 18 That kind old man was EM's son. Why not acknowledge that you got the help with the conviction that you will remain true to the sources?

Pia Arke: I make the history of colonialism part of 'my' history in the only way I know, namely by taking it personally. Arke, *Scoresbysundhistorier*, 11

Act 3

Me: I need to make a frame, where both sides of the document are visible.

Wood workshop manager: Do you have a drawing of it and the dimensions?

Me: Yes. I imagine a wooden structure, a frame with outside measurements of 590x840mm, which holds two pieces of 2mm glass together. In between the two pieces of glass the documents, photography, and an envelope will be exhibited.

Wood workshop manager: Do you have the wood material the glass at hand?

Me: Yes. 12mm for each side of the wooden frame, all birch plywood. The concept is that you can see what is on the other side of the documents, in order to not lose any details or information of origin.

Wood workshop manager: And the glass and documents are squished and placed in between the wooden frames in the engraved wooden grooves with dowels?

Me: Correct. The photograph is a top-view of East Greenland, Scoresbysund/Ittoqqortoormiit and its fjords with peat huts, islands, and icebergs around it. Behind you can see the sign 'AP'.

Act 4

Interview with EM in 1960 by Karl Bjarnhof, I Farfars Fodspor, Danmarks Radio.

Interviewer: Can one become a cannibal? Can one get the thought of ...

EM: That is a damned question to bring up!

Interviewer: Yes, but one has heard ...

EM: Yes, I can understand that. I can understand that.

137.JPG

AUTOETHNOGRAPHIC QUESTIONING

By using the same mechanisms as the big media companies and news platforms it is possible to convince spectators – consumers – of a story's plot and message on another level. Cramerotti, *Aesthetic Journalism*, 29. Artists, filmmakers, and designers who are adopting an archival research method, documenting and experimenting aligned with the mechanisms practised by aesthetic journalists, are able to counter-balance and interrogate the effect of media manipulation and discovery of new territory.

> 'Maps, charts and the names of places [named by the polar explorers] stand out as geographical material for recording explorers' lives and deeds. Narratives, sketches, and photographs, with their accessibility and the relative affordable photographic material, were central to geography as rational entertainment and central to the business of exploration'. Baigent, "'Deeds not words'?", 29.

Photographs, narratives, and geographical locations – staging – were an important trade-value in the information industry during the time EM was exploring and reporting on his explorations and businesses in the Arctic region (Alaska, Canada, Greenland, Iceland, and the Faroe Islands). I am curious if EM actively used an aesthetic approach to promote his narrative as a national hero, adventurer, author, and scientist. If that was the case, EM was quite contemporary and forward-thinking for his time.
EM brought his Leica camera everywhere on expeditions, not only for purposes of posterity via photographic documentation, but as a way to generate legitimacy. Frederiksen, *Ejnar Mikkelsen*, 185. The photographic documentation was the evidence of his expeditions and explorations. But was it also a way to visualise territorial control and sovereignty? EM must have known that the act of archiving and communicating visual data was crucial in order to keep the visual 'collective memory' alive. Özge Çelikaslan, "Autonomous Archiving" in *Lost and Living (in) Archives: Collectively Shaping New Memories*, ed. Annet Dekker (Amsterdam: Valiz, 2017), 231. Furthermore, EM must have found it necessary to document with his camera and through his writing, since there were many arguments and conflicts between the explorers regarding who discovered what, first, when, and how. This is also something that was discussed during a conversation with Trondhjem in June 2020 at Danish Arctic Institute in Copenhagen in the development of the ongoing project *Tracing Kalaallit Nunaat:* *Tracing Kalaallit Nunaat* is an ongoing project in collaboration with Mathilde Stubmark and Silke Xenia Juul focused on Greenlandic artefacts in private Danish collections.

> "For example, we have a lot of diaries and photographs from expeditions and so on, where the submitters of these diaries say that they would like to have a clause on the material for the next forty years, because the polar explorers did not write so nicely about each other. And some of them have had temperament and so on. And when they

> were all alone in the wilderness, the only place they could endure their madness was by writing it down. Then it is obvious that sometimes some personally sensitive things came up, which the submitter believes should not be passed on."

The notion of passing down specific chosen narratives and information through generations in text format is not something new. *'Silva rerum'* (practised from the 16th through to the 18th century in mostly noble families, especially in Poland) Wikipedia, "Silva rerum," accessed July 28, 2020, https://en.wikipedia.org/wiki/Silva_rerum. was a specific type of book, a multi-generational chronicle, where a wealth of information was staged, and where everyone who was given permission could contribute to the story of the specific family. The 'silva rerum' contained anything that the authors wished to record and preserve for future generations. The concept of 'silva rerum' is also discussed in the chapter ANOTHER SILVA RERUM?

By documenting events, EM was engaged in the preservation of his own image, existence, and importance in the region. A staging seemed to be crucial to gain influence and co-determination in the developments in Greenland at that time. And through staging, one is also creating a 'reality' – one kind of 'reality' – for oneself and for other spectators. This re-contextualisation of reality could then generate new meanings over time, when and if relocated. Is that Netflix's goal with *Against the Ice,* to re-contextualise EM in a specific discourse? Is what I am doing not also closely connected to what EM did regarding self-promotion by making this work? I too am drawn to the North Pole. I too am eager to contribute with something good for the Arctic people. Did I also go to Greenland to explore and conquer? Am I copying EM? And am I entitled to do so? Am I staging or 'branding' myself as the great-granddaughter of a polar explorer and coloniser by making a design project around the stories, where I am a character in my own narrative? Am I making use of the same mechanisms as EM in another way by practising Aesthetic Journalism or continuing a 'silva rerum'? Am I too revealing my findings in the form of a book, photos, maps, graphics, artefacts, text, and interviews, as EM did? Am I too trying to convince spectators to read and believe in my (various) narratives? Am I also making a route on a territory in Greenland I claim to operate in? Am I creating an exclusive work by placing the spectator in the position of an ethnographer, and thereby creating a distinctive manner of value by sharing a process of reflection on the project and my practice?

Through the questions above, different notions of (self-)reflection are situated in another perspective, situated between subject and object. When practising an autoethnographic approach to the work, the authorial subjectivity is explicitly in question or on display in the work, Renov: "Domestic Ethnography," 4. as is also treated in MY STRUGGLE WITH SEEING CLEARLY.

It could seem that when dealing with this history, using autoethnographic methods and implementing EM in Greenland as a case study, the entire investigation, artistic research, and its reliability are at stake, as I am embedded in my own work, involving my family while I still try to maintain a professional approach and a certain design quality. However, despite the distance to the subject, there is a mutual play of determination, a condition of consubstantiality, since I treat the story while still questioning the level of what embeddedness in the story I reveal.

The autoethnographic questions above often arise in design and editorial practices; where is the legitimacy when dealing with this subject, and what is my position? For whom am I making this project? At what stages does my position change, and under what conditions?

At this point, regardless of my continued interest in and concern for the Arctic and its futures, as a designer and as an individual, it is clear that I am making this project for myself.

EM (born 1880, died 1971) was a polar explorer. He was one of the only few who experienced how the Inuit people lived and hunted. EM was my great-grandfather (source from Frederiksen's book).

106.JPG

107.JPG

In April 2020, Father wrote: He crossed the north Atlantic as captain with no rudder on the vessel.

EM was a captain. He was known for always surviving after expeditions, but never returning with his ships. EM was my great-grandfather (source from Danish newspapers and Frederiksen's book).

108.JPG

109.JPG

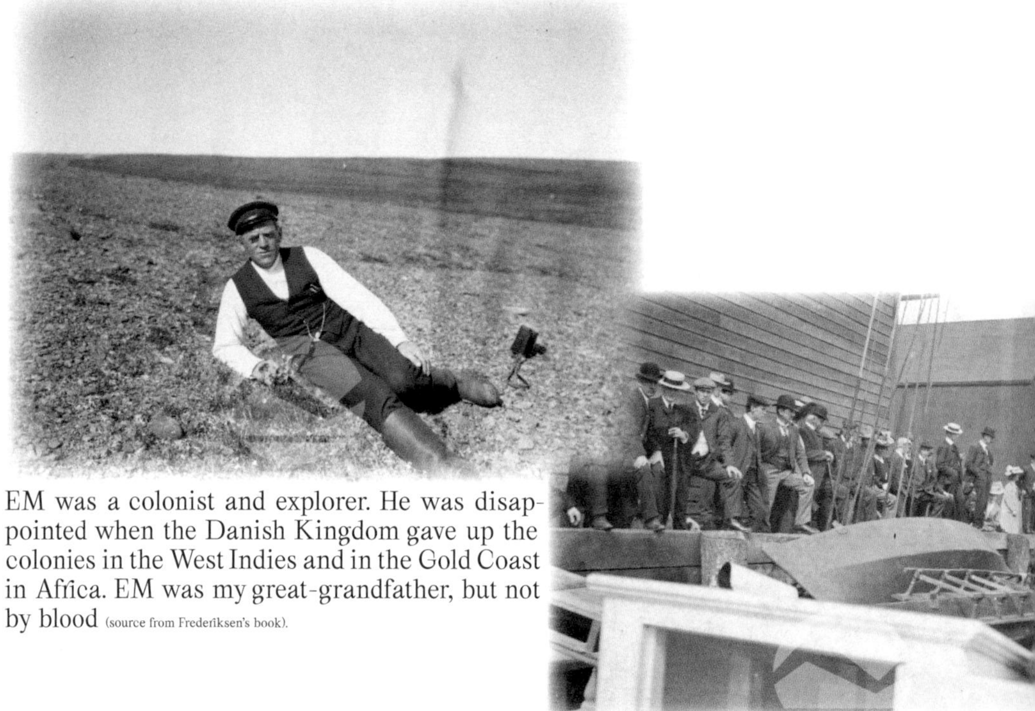

EM was a colonist and explorer. He was disappointed when the Danish Kingdom gave up the colonies in the West Indies and in the Gold Coast in Africa. EM was my great-grandfather, but not by blood (source from Frederiksen's book).

EM was a Danish investor. He wanted to create businesses in Greenland, which were intended to benefit the Greenlanders, and prevent other nations' interference on Greenlandic waters and resources. EM was my great-grandfather (source from Frederiksen's book).

110.JPG

111.JPG

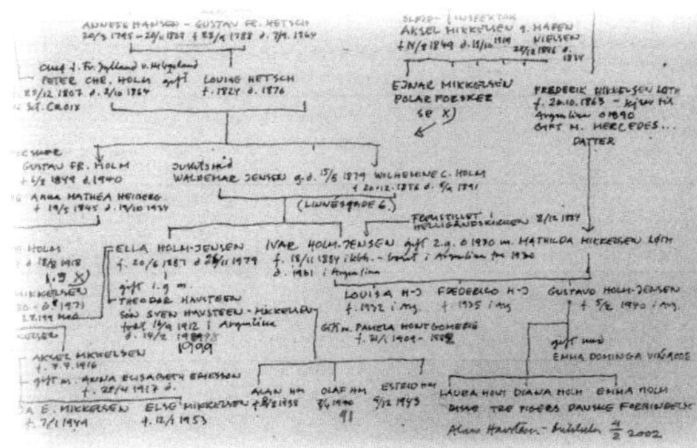

112.JPG

113.JPG

EXTRACT FROM DIARY IN GREENLAND

The wind is coldest. Without paying tion to non-covered skin you will start to feel the pain of thousands of needles.
The camera is not always working – also affected by the cold.
ter seeing the reindeer skin being thrown to a container, my heart started to beat so fast that I thought my right hand, the one I write with, would fall off.
The cold scares me.
re are two worlds in the Arctic: the visible world *'Sila'* and the invisible world *'Silap Aappaa'*.

Greenland sustains all the elements in the periodic system.
Interview with GEUS (Geological Survey nmark and Greenland) was unfortunately t recorded. Their argument was that the conversation should run freely and in an n dialogue, because it is an independent isation that prioritises science. They offer to companies and to the government in land based on facts, not political direc- or emotions, which many Greenlanders nd to do regarding the mining industry. romantic thought about not mining is an illusion.
Where there is science there must also be elings and passion – the power to protect and find.

If Greenland sustains everything why is it not possible for me to collect just a bit?
enland is traditionally a mining nation.
n the coal mine in Qullissat was closed own in 1972 by the Danish Government r forty years of mining exportation, the ng culture in Greenland was destroyed.
knowledge and the know-how around ning was suddenly, from one day to the next, of no importance, and many people lost labour value.
ning company has drilled around 70km where in the Kvanefjeld, in the interest of exploitation and exportation.
It is the mining companies' intention to create a new industrialisation and make Greenland grow!
enland's underground is the baptismal certificate of life on planet Earth (quote Minik Rosing, Professor in Geology, on photosynthesis).

From the Resource Department in Nalaakkersuisut: 'Mineral Resources Act, Paragraph 45e. (1) Non-residents, see section 45(1), may not collect or extract minerals; but see section 33(6). (2) Only non-residents who have obtained a relevant export license may export minerals; but see subsection (3). (3) Non-residents may for non-commercial purposes export minerals from Greenland without an export license being required, provided that the minerals have been purchased by a permanent resident and the purchase can be documented.'

March 10, 2017 Dreamed that I found a ruby mountainside in Nuuk. The snow was gone, and the ruby mountainside was shining red. I woke up and decided not to pulverise stones as the mining-industry does.
I wish to grasp the sound of Greenland. Make it resonate!
The mountain rock is solid. Can a rock be frozen?
All the days I have been here I have seen trucks carrying stones from A to B. But there are no roads in between the towns. No road infrastructure!
Greenland is a huge country and there must be places untouched.
Again I feel limited by the weather, the Danish mentality is haunting me.
The local granite mine – the mountain already has a scar from earlier extractions to feed the world population with new kitchen-table surfaces.
Again today it was in the local newspaper, Sermitsiaq, where the mining industry was in focus: 'Lost confidence worldwide.' From Greenland being the seventh most attractive mine country to being the fifty-fifth. The news claims that Greenland needs a success story around the mine-industry to improve its reputation.

March 11, 2017 What will the stone tell if I cut through it? The stones around Nuuk are gneiss, some of the Earth's oldest rocks. Gneisses are a metamorphic rock, which exhibit foliation (mineral grain summarised in layers or oriented in linear structures).
Mining was prohibited in early Greek antiquity because it was thought to be mining the Earth's womb.
The quarry is like a stamp on the Earth's

…ce. Should I create such a stamp-sign as well?

Again, I dreamed I was mining. I found semi–precious gemstones!
…inking of shapes and immaterial things.
…e is a factor; the geological development has continued for 3800 million years.
…move something from earth (territories)
…s then possible to re-establish it? Or give something back? A monument or sign?

Dreamed of stone and old travels.
…ill speculating if I should go to the south
…ry and get in contact with a person called
…rsen from LNS Greenland (mining com-
…ny). It will cost me around 800 euros. Can
…ut that kind of financial responsibility on your project?
…something I can deposit my longings into.
…mmaterial thing as value – can it be put into an object sincerely?
…deadly serious when they talk about the weather.
What are the promises outside the text?

The politicians are investing with their own capital in mining explorations.
…ed with a local who recommended me to
…o the suburb Qinngorput, where gold has
…n found in the river. With old gold-digger methods, I will be washing gold.
…mbarrassing to be a Dane in Greenland sometimes – clumsy and greedy.
…st and Rosing were planning Greenland's
…e 'To the Benefit of Greenland'. The plan
…o divide the land into zones: zones where
…here should be mining industries. Zones
…re nature should be left alone. And zones where tourists could come and visit.
'As long as it [natural resources] is in the
…it has no value' (said Kuupik Kleist in an interview I conducted on March 14, 2017, in Nuuk's culture house).

Dreamed again of valuable stones,
…ollected in Greenland. The ruby miner
…lsen's story also started as a gold-fever, a
…ildhood dream that he could not let go. A
…onging to use the potential in Greenland,
…ing after rubies in order to create capital
…d value for the country as a whole. A part
…e feels a bit sad by disappointing him for

not being Icelandic (lied about my nationality), but being a Dane, recalling so many moments of suppression of the Greenlandic nation.

March 16, 2017 Earlier today I was in Qinngorput, where I was told I could find gold. Unfortunately, the river was frozen and covered with at least one metre of snow.
Most of the Greenlandic mining industries are focusing on selling the minerals and precious stones to the jewellery market. They use the argument that it is for the women of rich men. I believe men just as much as women have the longing to transform themselves into something precious, covered in jewels.
It was really easy to sense some kind of snobbish approach from the Danish officials to the Greenlandic officials in the Tower (where the Greenlandic Government, Nalaakersuisut, operates). I wonder how my great-grandfather would act there.
Who is the narrator?

March 17, 2017 I love the dead life in stones. Mining is a difficult profession to feel trust. Will mining end in a dystopia? Has Michael Houellebecq a prediction on this?

March 18, 2017 Fable animals, magic animals, and spirits are essential for Greenlandic form-language.

March 19, 2017 On the boat: the captain, Palo, and his helper, plus five other passengers – all hunters. At this time of year, they are after rubies and rabbits. All with guns, rifles, and other equipment with which to kill something.

March 20, 2017 Materials, not materials. Access, no access. Political limitation, no political limitation. People think I am a geologist.

March 21, 2017 I got a receipt: 94g rubies for thirteen euros from ruby miner Olsen's company.

March 23, 2017 It is an old saying that none of the Greenlanders thought that they could claim the land. I have made a promise. I will be back in Greenland. I have made a promise to the mining industry in Greenland, a real handshake promise, to help them promote their agency. I also promised I would give back the ten Danish kroner [Danish currency] to the bus driver uuk, because my ticket was wet and I did not have any cash on me. We talked about hardness – catalyst and physical, chemical impacts on rocks. We talked about the anthropocentric impact. After all, everything is just an illusion. Mining is digging deep.

24, 2017 Helicopters are flying around to asure the quality of the wind and weather. he wind is making the plane jump. Flying ver the clouds – it reminds me of Andrei rkovsky's film *Solaris*. It flickers in the sun and the land under me disappears.

EM was a polar explorer. He was on the front cover of The New York Times in 1912 and 1913. EM was my great-grandfather

(source from several encyclopedias and Frederiksen's book).

The New York Times.

CAPT. EJNAR MIKKELSEN'S OWN STORY OF TWO YEARS OF ARCTIC TORTURE

Disease, Hunger, and Cold Fought for Lives of Danish Explorer and His Comrade.

CAPT. EJNAR MIKKELSEN

EM was a polar explorer. He wanted to find land, a paradise, in the North Pole, where the women were 'nice and fat'. EM was my great-grandfather

(source from Frederiksen's book).

15.JPG

117.JPG

EM was a sailor. He saw gold-diggers cutting up a stomach of a dead Italian man, who in his greed had swallowed gold nuggets during the Gold Rush. There were about 3000 dollars in his stomach. EM was my great-grandfather (source from Frederiksen's book).

EM (born 1880, died 1971) was a polar sci
entist and colonist. He receive
gold and silver medals from th
Danish King and the Militar
together with several Geograph
ical Societies from all over th
world. EM was my great-grand
father (source from several encyclopaedias and Freder
sen's book).

In April 2020, Father wrote: He was highl
decorated.

117.JPG 118.JPG 119.JPG

EM was a polar explorer. For eight months EM and his fellow explorer, Iver, were walking from Danmarks-fjord over the icecap to the Shannon Island (app. 1,900 kilometres). They were so hungry that they wanted to eat each other. While hunting, they decided that Iver should hold the riffle and EM would have to walk behind him. EM was my great-grandfather (source from Father).

120.JPG

121.JPG

122.JPG

In February 2020 in the moving image *Aftermath: Narratives on EM*:

[1960] Interviewer: "Can one become cannibal? Can one ..."

EM replies: "That's a damn question to come up with!"

Interviewer: "Yes yes, but one has heard ..."

EM replies: "Yes, I can understand that. I can understand that."

Can one become cannibal?

123.JPG

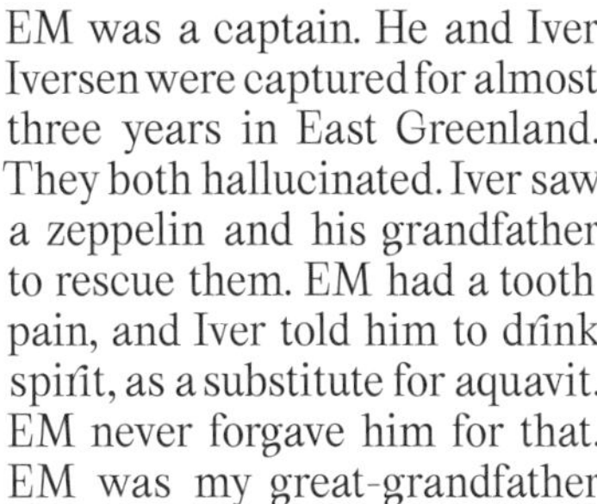

EM was a captain. He and Iver Iversen were captured for almost three years in East Greenland. They both hallucinated. Iver saw a zeppelin and his grandfather to rescue them. EM had a tooth pain, and Iver told him to drink spirit, as a substitute for aquavit. EM never forgave him for that. EM was my great-grandfather

(source from Denmark's Radio and Television Archive).

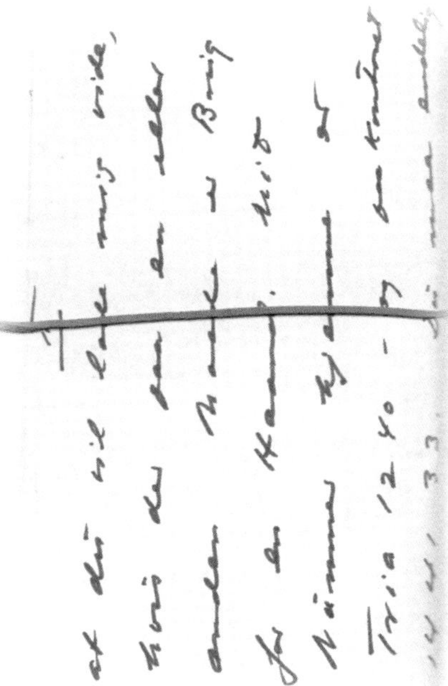

124.JPG

125.JPG

THE SHRIMP PARADOX

Definition The paradox of plenty refers to the paradox that countries with an abundance of natural resources tend to have less economic growth, less democracy, and worse development outcomes than countries with fewer natural resources.

The amount of shrimp is controlled every season by officials. Every day the Greenlandic fishermen have to collect data on the shrimp population on the seabed, to avoid unsustainable over-fishing, but also to avoid value inflation.
The country, Greenland, lives off selling shrimp to the rest of the world – around half of all Greenlandic export consists of this shrimp production. However, the export value is not high enough for the country to sustain itself. Martin Breum, *Hvis Grønland river sig løs* (Copenhagen: Gyldendal, 2018), 45. Greenland is not an independent country, but still a part of the Danish Kingdom, and is tightly held together by the Block Grants Economic support provided every year by the Danish State to the Greenlandic Government. (providing one quarter of Greenland's GDP, and more than half of the public budget). The International Trade Administration, "Denmark Doing Business in Greenland," accessed April 30, 2020, https://www.export.gov/apex/article2?id=Denmark-Doing-Business-in-Greenland Though there is a high demand for shrimp on the global market, officials (who are mainly Danish) keep the exports moderately low to prevent large economic growth in Greenland – and thereby also preventing independence. I wonder if this affects democracy? Democracy for whom? The shrimp is an unforgettable resource – and a promise!

Act 1

Me: Can you help me scan this shrimp with your 3D-scanner? I would like to have some data on the shrimp.

3D-programmer: Yes, but first you have to fix the shrimp's surface. It is too shiny and the 3D-scanner will not be able to read its data. Let's spray-paint the shrimp white.

The 3D-scanner starts to read the material through 360-degree analysis on a computer-controlled spinning wheel. There are lines in the studio room that separate and connect the shrimp's data. In the 3D-scanner's program, behind a screen of liquid crystals, I can see the shrimp take shape.

Me: Thank you. This is exactly what I had wished for. Is it now possible to manipulate the data of the shrimp in another program?

3D-programmer: Yes, in another software you are able to remove and reshape its form.
What do you want to do with this data of a shrimp?

Me: I made a promise. I want to make a ring out of this data in the shape of a shrimp.

3D-programmer: So you will need the 3D-printer as well?

Me: Yes, I know how to progress from now on.

In the 3D-modelling software I can see the shrimp floating in space. I have captured it and I can manipulate it here. I can close and open its surfaces. I can reshape it and remove unnecessary material. I can transform the shrimp into a ring. I prepare the file and preview how it will look after it has been 3D-printed in a grey resin. There are pillars that support the shrimp through the printing, almost like a scaffolding structure.

053.JPG

Act 2

I once made a promise; a promise to a ruby hunter, a Greenlandic miner, that I would help Greenland to detach themselves from the Danish state (here comes the point to reveal myself: I am a Danish woman, the great-granddaughter of a coloniser and inspector of East Greenland. I convinced the Greenlanders that I was an Icelandic citizen and activist – which to some extent is true) by collaborating with his gemstone business ...

Ruby hunter: Me and my business partner have fought for the last ten years to get permission to collect rubies. After a long and difficult process with the Ministry of Mineral Resources we finally got a small-scale license to collect rubies at Fiskenæsset. Fiskenæsset is an area south of Nuuk (Greenland's capital) a few hours away by boat, with promising prospects for mining explorations and gemstones.

Me: How come it has been so difficult for you to get a license to mine gems?

Ruby hunter: Because of the Danish officials, they do not want us Greenlanders to create value with the resources that are available in our mountains. And in the long-run the Danish officials do not want us to become independent.

Me: This is also what I experienced in Nuuk; that the Danish authority works in the interests of Denmark and not to benefit the Greenlanders.

Ruby hunter: Yes! That is why it is so very useful for us to make business deals with other countries – like with Iceland.

Me: Sure, I will introduce your gemstone company to my network in Iceland. And we can make a strategy so you can create extra value and sell your ruby products in other countries.

Ruby hunter: Yes, sounds good! I can make you an offer: 94 grams of purple rubies for 100 Danish kroner. The Danish currency is also Greenland's currency. 100

Danish kroner is about 13,4 Euros. How is that?

Me: Deal! I promise, I will help your business find prospects in a Greenlandic-Icelandic gemstone collaboration.

148.JPG

Years later. Contact with the Ruby hunter is lost. No collaboration happened after all. Interest and investment in gemstone jewellery are declining worldwide. I would have focused on using rubies for new technologies, rather than jewellery-making. Greenland is still a part of the Danish Kingdom.

Act 3

Me: Can you help me with casting this shrimp in a valuable metal?

Jewellery maker: Yes, your shrimp has the slip-form and seems to be in a solid material. We will use the sand-casting method, but first you need to decide what material you want your shrimp to be in.

Me: The closest that comes to the aesthetics of gold.

Jewellery maker: Okay, brass is probably the choice then. It is an alloy of copper and zinc.

The sand-casting method is an ancient method of making objects in metal or glass. The jewellery maker is creating an empty space in the sand, made in two halves. Rob Thompson, *Manufacturing Processes for Design Professionals* (London: Thames & Hudson, 2012), 121. The force from a hammer compresses the sand. The hammer and the jeweller maker have merged into a fluid movement of force. The two halves are held together and only a 'runner' and tiny air channels separate them. Inside there is a negative form of the shrimp.

074.JPG

Jewellery maker: We will need to melt the brass at 940°C, and when you can see the chicken-eye effect in the melted brass, we will then start to pour the metal into the 'runner' in the sand-casting mould. Do you follow me?

Me: Can I touch the shrimp now?

Jewellery maker: First cool the shrimp in cold running water. I can see you will need to remove some material from the shrimp. With a file and a metal-saw you can clean up its shape.

Me: Thank you, but I would also like to make space to give the shrimp eyes as well. I have rubies from Greenland I would like to add as eyes

Jewellery maker: Actual rubies?!

Me: Yes, rubies from Greenland. I 'smuggled'

July 2020, Father wrote: "Your grandfather and great-grandfather would not approve of something taken out of Greenland." them out and am now trying to fulfil my promise.

048.JPG

COMMENT TO THE READER

If it seems to you, dear reader, that this book is an endless stream of truths and reflections, I will strike a blow for fiction. In an understanding of the past and how it is relevant to a design discipline, fiction is, as Albert Camus phrases it; 'the lie through which we tell the truth.'

'[Fiction] allows us to imagine other realities, explore new perspectives on the future, or represent something that is hard or even impossible to represent otherwise.' Wynants, *When Fact is Fiction*, 10.

Fiction can open up the world for sensing a better understanding or a certain clarification, but also for questioning. In the making of *Snowblindness* I see fiction as a crucial part in the design process for the book and research, since fiction offers different perspectives and narratives, and a wide range of other possibilities. This is also something described in the chapter THOUGHTS ON METHODOLOGY.

Fiction is honest, since it does not claim to be telling the 'truth'. But apart from being honest, what can we gain from employing fiction in design? By rearranging and reshuffling facts into narratives, stories, and made-up events, we can enable ourselves to imagine future realities, and in that regard, fiction *benefits* a design practice. In the making of *Snowblindness,* design is also about storytelling.

'[I]n all fiction, there is room enough to keep even Man where he belongs, in his place in the scheme of things; there is time enough [...] still there are seeds to be gathered, and room in the bag of stars,' as Ursula K. Le Guin writes in her *Carrier Bag Theory of Fiction* (1986).

It is not only in design practice that fiction and memory can make a substantial contribution to historical discussion. Peter Van Goethem, "Screening the City" in Wynants, *When Fact is Fiction*, 44. The media that deals with fiction recognises and reveals that history is always partial, and that personal, socioeconomic, and political contexts also determine the interpretation of the past. But through imagining and engaging with fiction I see it as a valuable tool in challenging the commonly known and shared perception of 'collective memory'. Therefore, dear reader, rest in the semi-fictional texts, as they deliberately blur the line between fact and fiction, just as EM's writings maybe also do from time to time – for the sake of a good story!

EM was a polar scientist. His diary was eaten by a polar bear during an expedition in Greenland. EM was my great-grandfather (source from Father and Frederiksen's book).

126.JPG

EM was an investor. He wanted tourism i Greenland. Tourism is now something Gree land wants to live off. EM was my great-gran father (source from Frederiksen's book).

In April 2020, Father wrote: Tourism is now somethir Greenland wishes to expand to impro their livelihoods.

127.JPG

EM was a polar explorer. He was fantasising more than two winters over an image of a group of girls in white dresses from Sorø's housekeeping school. The only human being around was his engineer friend, Iver Iversen. EM was my great-grandfather (source from Denmark's Radio and Television Archive).

EM was a Danish captain. The Greenlanders called him Miki. Later they called him Mikisauq, which means 'the big small'. Everyone else called him Captain Mikkelsen. EM was my great-grandfather (source from Frederiksen's book).

EM was a Danish colonist. He was proud of the colonial work Denmark had done in Greenland. It was all due to his contribution. EM was my great-grandfather (source from Father and Frederiksen's book).

In April 2020, Father wrote: Ebbe Munck stands at the far right. It was mostly due to his contribution and rapport of good colleagues.

129.JPG

130.JPG

131.JPG

132.JPG

EM was a Danish inspector in Greenland. He organised the internment, a forced displacement, of local Greenlanders in order to create a Danish colony. He was worried that their culture was in danger to become extinct. He moved ten families from South Greenland and moved to Scoresbysund. The people in Scoresbysund were called Miki's people. EM was my great-grandfather (source from Frederiksen's book and Pia Arke's book *Stories from Scoresbysund*).

In April 2020, Father wrote: From Ammassalik to Scoresbysund.

133.JPG

EM was a polar explorer. He supported the resistance movement in Denmark during World War II. He had to flee from the Nazis and move to Sweden during the war with my great-grandmother. EM was my great-grandfather (source from Father and Frederiksen's book).

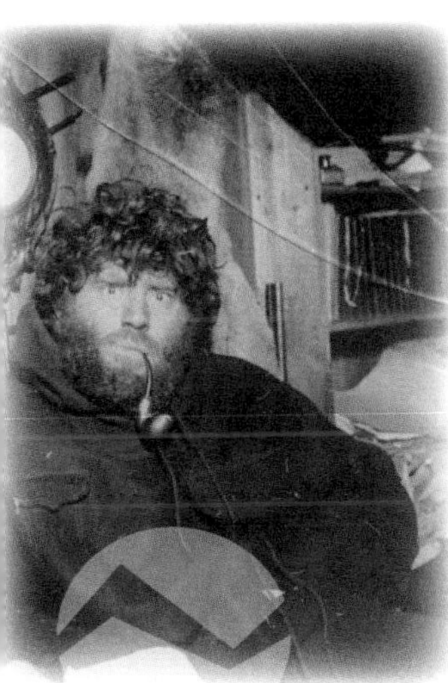

:M was a captain. He used to smoke twenty cigarettes and a couple of cheroots and cigars every day. He stopped smoking from one day to the other. EM was my great-grandfather (source from Frederiksen's book).

34.JPG

135.JPG

EM was a Danish celebrity and inspector. He was not allowed to travel to the United States to negotiate Greenland's survival during World War II with Franklin D. Roosevelt. This was because a German journalist had announced that he was traveling with Hitler's benevolence. EM was my great-grandfather (source from Frederiksen's book).

136.JPG

137.JPG

In April 2020, Father wrote: Is this a ‘myth’.
EM was a captain and a polar explorer. He had experienced a ‘turn-off-the-lamp-game’ in Greenland. He and his son were fascinated by the Greenlandic women. EM was my great-grandfather (source from Frederiksen’s book).

138.JPG

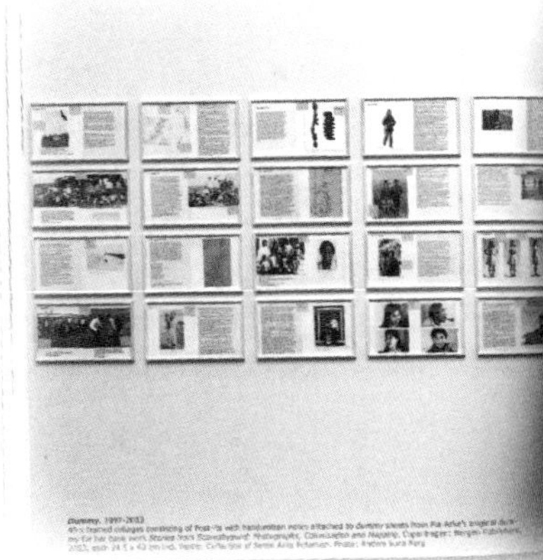

Pia Arke’s work *Dummy* from 1997–2003: Forty-nine framed collages consisting of posits with handwritten notes attached to dummy sheets from Arke’s original dummy for her book and crownwork *Stories from Scoresbysund: Photographs, Colonisation and Mapping.*

139.JPG

140.JPG

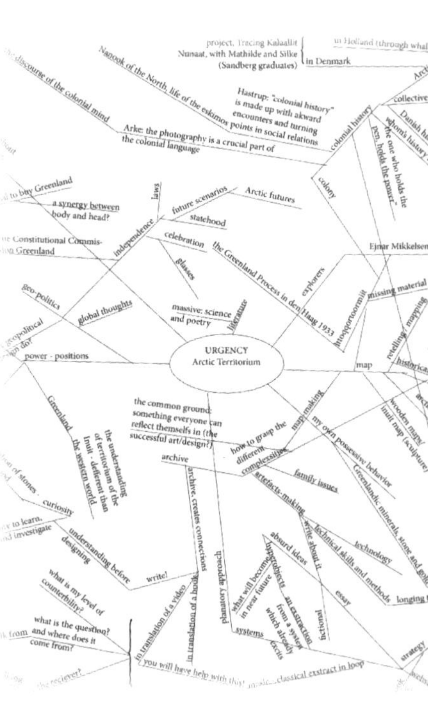

141.JPG

In April 2020, Father wrote: Drum dance in Scoresbysund.
EM was a colonist in East Greenland. He thought that the population from Tasiilaq was childish. EM was my great-grandfather (source from Pia Arke's *Stories from Scoresbysund* and Nikolajsen's film *Scoresbysund – kolonien er mit eget barn).*

142.JPG

143.JPG

In April 2020, Father wrote: I took this photo in 1958 in Scoresbysund.

EM was a polar explorer and an inspector in East Greenland. He was the first person from Denmark who came to Greenland during World War II. Every Greenlander was very happy to see him. EM was my great-grandfather (source from Frederiksen's book).

EM was an inspector in East Greenland. He feared that the Danish Government sold out of Greenland's treasures to the United States, because of the Danish government duties towards NATO. Greenland was an important stepping-stone for Denmark to become part of the Western allies and keep a good strategic position during the Cold War. This is still the geopolitical status. EM was my great-grandfather (sources from several encyclopaedias and Frederiksen's book).

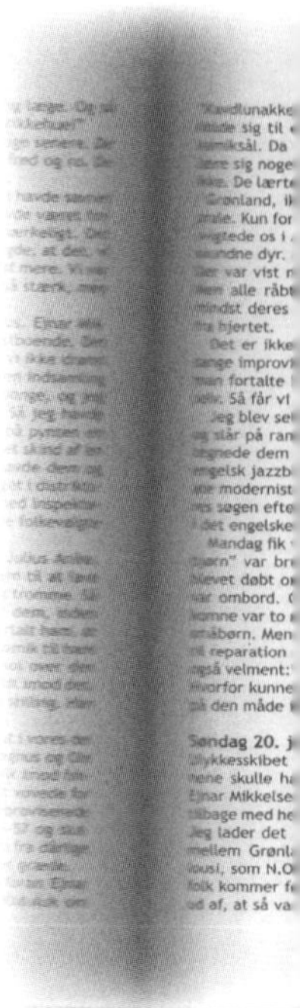

"Kavdlunakke
sig til
Kamiksål. Da
sig noge
De lærte
Grønland, i
Kun for
os i
dyr.
var vist
alle råbt
mindst deres
hjertet.
Det er ikke
improvi
fortalte
Så får vi
Jeg blev se
slår på ran
dem
engelsk jazzb
modernist
søgen efte
det engelske
Mandag fik
var br
døbt o
ombord.
var to
Men
reparation
også velment:
Hvorfor kunne
på den måde

Søndag 20. j
Lykkesskibet
skulle h
Ejnar Mikkelse
tilbage med he
Jeg lader det
mellem Grønl
som N.O
kommer f
af, at så va

EM was an inspector and colonist. He was very critical about the American influence of Greenland. He saw the Americans had ruined the Greenlandic culture – and the Greenlanders' relation to Denmark. He believed that the Americans should pay for all the damages and remove their big boots from Greenlandic ground. This issue is still discussed today. EM was my great-grandfather (source from Frederiksen's book).

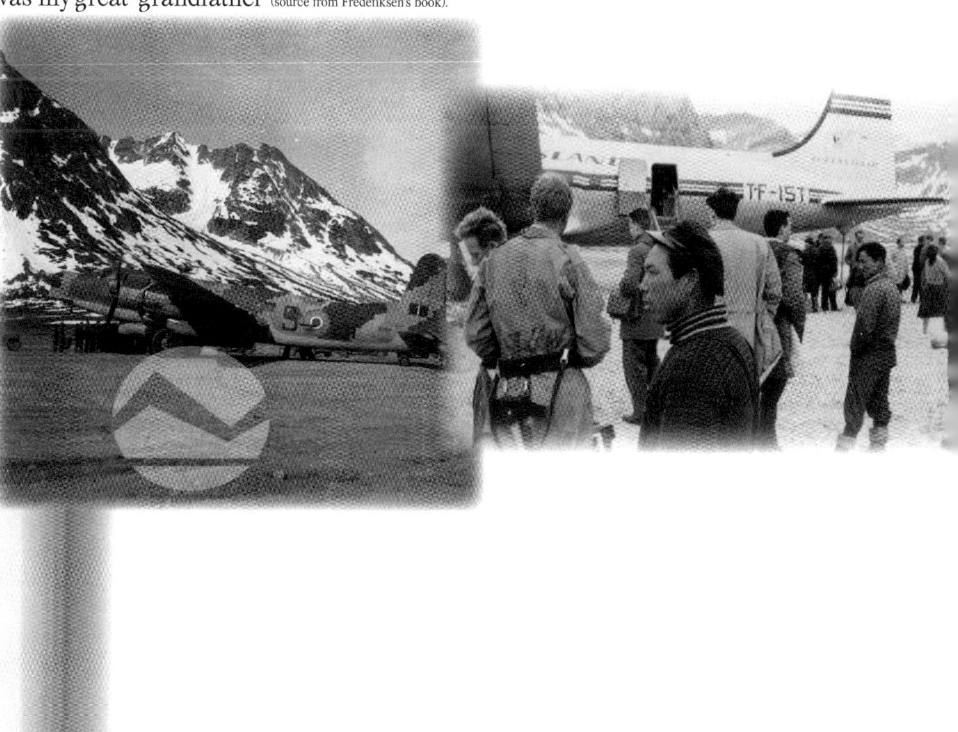

Besøg af "Miki" og farfar · 89

n hund og en kvinde, der ikke kunne
)edstefar og sejlede fra Grønland i en
et, måtte de sydpå kæmpe hårdt for at
fortsatte:" Nogle få af dem glemte os
erden. Men da de hørte, at de, der blev
kom de tilbage. Ikke for at håne eller
svært ved at følge med!). Da fangsten
og viste os, hvor vi kunne finde de for-
for det!" (Det sidste kunne jeg forstå!)
åre af øjenkrogen, da han var færdig.
n glæde for at danse var ægte. Ikke
til både Borchersen og Mikkelsen kom

gte eskimoer i deres trommedanse og
beskrev fra sin 5. Thuleekspedition, at
ord, vi har brug for, skyder op af sig

nmedansen. Hvor de vugger i hofterne
r er lavet af en isbjørnemavesæk. Jeg
oven i købet en af tegningerne til et
hly", hvor jeg ironisk foreslog de rabi-
e skulle optage dette instrument i de-
ing og tekst blev publiceret og udgivet

k telegram om, at sælfangeren "Polar-
s. Det var skibet, "Jopeter", der var
løbig meldtes om 4 omkomne. Min far
meldingen, da man vidste, at de om-
den ene var kaptajn Marøs søn og så to
Skibet ville gå ind til Ålesund i Norge
. Ejnar Mikkelsen sagde lidt tørt, men
om drømt om at stå på et skib i brand.
le mand, der kunne være omkommet
e mennesker?"

hertil næste morgen. Grethe og bør-
den" hjem sammen med Borchersen,
to køjer for lidt, hvorfor de blev holdt
var dem, der ville lave mindst vrøvl!!!"
gså heroppe. Der er en tydelig jalousi
æsenet og Sundhedsvæsenet. En ja-
grint ad, men det er der. KGHs egne
de sidder på. Nå, Grethe og jeg fandt
le farfar.

146.JPG 147.JPG

I THINK I GOT IT, SNOWBLINDNESS

Definition Snow blindness is a painful eye condition caused by overexposure to ultraviolet light; too much overexposed light hits the transparent outer layer of your eyes and gives it sunburn. Snow blindness symptoms can be disorienting, and can cause pain in your eyes, headache, blurred vision, and temporary loss of vision Healthline, "snow-blindness," accessed April 25, 2020, https://www.healthline.com/health/snow-blindness#causes.

Act I

Me: Are these goggles functional?

Researcher: Yes, when the strong and intense sunlight is reflected from the bright snow surface it can cause snow blindness. To prevent this very painful eye disease, the Inuit made snow goggles, which only allow the light to enter through the narrow viewing slit. It restricted the field of vision and reduced the amount of light that reached the optic nerve. The Vancouver Maritime Museum, "Inuit Snow Goggles," accessed April 26, 2020, https://web.archive.org/web/20070314111555/http://www.vancouvermaritimemuseum.com/modules/vmmuseum/treasures/?artifactid=77.

Me: They look so futuristic and almost alien to me.

Researcher: However, they were extremely important for the Inuit and their possibility to survive in the wild wilderness of the Arctic.

Me: What is the material?

Researcher: The first snow goggles were made out of bone – the Inuit worked with what they had to hand in the wood-scarce Arctic. Later, when wood became more plentiful in the early 20th century, wooden goggles began to appear, like with the collection you see in front of us.

Me: I cannot imagine that you can navigate with this narrow viewing slit. Can I try them on?

Researcher: Actually, the width of the slits governs the width of lateral vision. The narrower the slit is, the more the acuity of vision. This simple but ingenious invention is superior to modern high-tech sunglasses.
You cannot touch the museum artefacts, but there is a modern model, a replication, you can try.

062.JPG

The fire-party on the icecap, and the many hours of the shining ice and snow, had probably been too much for my eyes. They were sweating and burning when I laid down to sleep, and were so painful when I woke up. It was almost as if salt and pepper were sprinkled in them. Damn it! Here I had to use my eyes to enjoy God's beautiful nature, and then I was well on my way to snow blindness. I had to be very careful. A blindfold would soon fix it, and cocaine drops could take away the pain. But it was still sad to sit inside the tent in the lovely sunshine without being able to see all the glories around me. Mikkelsen, *Farlig Tomandsfaerd*, 60.

Act 2

Glassblower: Do not look for too long into the kiln. Your eyes can get burned. Just like if you look directly into the sun.

Me: It looks like liquid gold.

Glassblower: Yes, you can become addicted to it. The glass is starting to have the right temperature. You can gently start to blow the pipe in a steady and constant manner while I rotate.

Me: Like a flute?

Glassblower: Yes. Let's hope it works this time.

The glassblower stops the rotation of the glowing object connected to the iron pipe, and moves towards the plaster mould. The plaster mould is a negative form of the snow goggles. He stands on his toes to blow the form into shape.

Glassblower: Quickly, open the oven. The glass object needs to cool down slowly. Tomorrow you can take it out, and start to cut it with a diamanté blade in the cold-room.

Hand blown glass is so sculptural. I decided to make something more modern and user-friendly in plexiglass.

032.JPG

Act 3

Me: I would like to laser-cut this form from transparent plexiglass.

Technician: What is the line in the middle? Is that functional for these glasses?

Me: Yes, you look though the narrow viewing slit.

Technician: But if it is transparent anyway ... ?

Me: It is a translation of Inuit snow goggles. Furthermore, I would like 'celebrating independence' to be engraved on the sides of the glasses

Technician: Which independence do you want to celebrate?

Me: Greenland's independence.

Technician: OK. You will have to use the plastic heater afterward to bend the sides, and form it on a 90-degree edge to make it customised.

044.JPG

Recently in the news I read that the US administration is putting

$12.1 million into projects that benefit business for Greenlanders. The US administration will open an office for the US Agency for International Development in the capital, Nuuk. Olsen, Jan M., "Greenland ready to take US aid but won't accept conditions," accessed May 7, 2020, https://eu.detroitnews.com/story/news/politics/2020/04/23/greenland-ready-take-us-aid-accept-conditions/111588328/.

A GEOPOLITICAL ISSUE

The last years have seen an increasing global interest in the Arctic region. The Arctic has taken an important position worldwide in terms of resources, shipping routes (Northwest Passage), climate changes, and geopolitics. Once a low-tension region, it is now becoming a place where the race between global superpowers unfolds through military, security, and investment activity. Russia's military escalation (that reopened and expanded a number of Soviet-era bases) and China's growing involvement in Greenland (mainly in relation to natural resources), along with the 12.1 million dollar aid-package from the US for the development of the mining sector and infrastructure, indicates that the superpowers' rivalry has entered a new phase (the US is adapting its Arctic policy as a part of their current 'trade war' with China, to make a new strategic reality marked by the 'return of geopolitics', where they in recent years have been relatively absent). Niklas Hessel, "Det højspændte nord," accessed July 29, 2020, https://www.weekendavisen.dk/2020-18/samfund/det-hoejspaendte-nord. And lastly, not to be dismissed, is Russia's attempt to claim the North Pole as Russian territory, by placing the Russian flag on the seabed of the North Pole in 2007. C. J. Chivers, "Russians Plant Flag on the Arctic Seabed," accessed October 13, 2020, https://www.nytimes.com/2007/08/03/world/europe/03arctic.html. Still an unresolved matter of 'ownership'.

Meanwhile, the native population in the Arctic have a voice of their own. ICC is the largest and most influential international non governmental body that represents all the native Inuit inhabitants from Alaska, Canada, Greenland, and Chukotka on matters of international importance. ICC was founded in 1977. They want to have influence on the politics in the region, which should seek to acknowledge and benefit their local economy, cultural heritage, and environment. Depending on where in the Arctic the Inuit populations live (Greenland, Canada, Alaska, and Russia), different urgencies are present. In order to unite these actors by promoting cooperation, coordination, and interaction among the Arctic nations, the Arctic Council The Arctic Council is a high-level intergovernmental forum that addresses issues faced by the Arctic governments (8), with observer states (13), founded in 1996. was established. Its focus is centred in particular on issues of sustainable development and environmental protection, Arctic Council, "About," accessed August 1, 2020, https://arctic-council.org/en/about/. by several other more or less governmental initiatives.

However, in the Arctic region, Greenland is an exception. Greenland is still a part of the Danish Kingdom, and since the majority of the Greenlandic population wants independence, they do not have the same starting point of cooperation as the other Arctic nations. Independence and its polity could take many different forms in Greenland for a population that consists of approximately 55,000 people living on the world's biggest island. Even though all indications demonstrate that Denmark would grant Greenland its independence if it was requested, Phillip E. Steinberg et al, *Contesting the Arctic: Politics and Imaginaries in the Circumpolar North* (London: I.B. Tauris, 2015), 82. it would not be done easily. Denmark has a strong self-interest in maintaining its political (and cultural) ties to Greenland, since it is Denmark's only ticket to the Arctic region, Steinberg et al, *Contesting the Arctic*, 83. as well as the argument for Denmark's unique position in NATO and their tight friendship with their US-American allies.

Questions of who should operate in and with the Arctic region seems to separate the Arctic inhabitants. At least that seems to be the case in Greenland, where lobbyist and neoliberal officials who are being directed by the superpowers are acting and investing in Greenlandic industries. In both the Greenlandic population and at the Danish governmental level this is of high concern. And all this is for a reason; in 2019, then-president of the US Donald Trump made the offer to 'buy' Greenland. Breitenbauch, Henrik. "Et kig ned i afgrunden." accessed July 24, 2020, https://www.weekendavisen.dk/2019-34/samfund/et-kig-ned-i-afgrunden.

It is not hard to imagine the disruptive effect foreign as well as independence policies would have on Inuit society and culture. Steinberg et al, *Contesting the Arctic*, 116. And the effects of a Greenlandic independence would generate significant geopolitical opportunities and implications for the Arctic region. Depending on the eyes that see, this can be used as fuel for Greenlandic political efforts and government, which present themselves as autonomous actors open for business with everyone. Though the political landscape in Greenland has changed since the latest election in April 2021, its goal is still to gain independence on the basis of anti-colonial and separation nationalism, Steinberg et al, *Contesting the Arctic*, 76 but on their terms (meaning no radioactive or petroleum mining activities).

Throughout the 20th century, the political challenges in the Arctic were of great concern to EM, who did not wish for Greenland to be separate from *Rigsfaellesskabet* (the Danish Kingdom). When Greenland do gain independence, will their trading conditions, their currency, their finances, their security, and their language then be tied up in larger global power structures? And will they risk finding themselves in a similar position to many newly independent ex-colonies throughout history? Steinberg et al, *Contesting the Arctic*, 88. My concern for the politics in the Arctic seems to be slightly different from EM's. I support a Greenlandic independence, but fear that a territorial and natural resource race will make the Arctic a high-tension zone with Cold War-like conditions and an expansion of military activity. That my personal background is connected to EM could prevent me in having any say in the debate, since my position could be seen as biased. But I would argue that the design discipline and its toolbox of various methodologies provides my practice with the tools to work with the subject of Arctic futures and geopolitics in a reflective manner that allows for engagements despite a colonial legacy. My intention is not only to create broader awareness of the Arctic, its resources, and its people, but also to debate its politics and its influence. In a collective collaboration with individuals and institutions in Greenland, I wish to suggest visions for the Arctic region – visions that could accommodate the challenges of the Anthropocene, which we are all facing.

I acknowledge that we are left with questions of legitimacy regarding the 'right' to expansion in contemporary political geography when the same spatial practices were the norm at the outset of colonialism. Hastrup, "Colonial

Moments in Greenland," 247. For that reason it is important that these questions are reflected upon, but most of all that space is available for multiple voices to take up. My engagement with the Arctic must be seen in relation to an interest in geopolitical urgencies and future possibilities. With the acknowledgements of the mistakes and the devastating harm of the past, and in contemporary politics, any Danish engagement must practise self-reflection. In my opinion, this self-reflection or self-criticism has been somewhat absent and is still not prevailing in the Danish or Western context of policymaking, debate, history-writing, and 'science to secure'. 'Science to secure' is referring to the need to map territories, and thus gaining territory. It cannot be ignored that this absence leads back to colonial interpretation, misunderstandings, and the misinterpretations of 'terra nullius'. 'Terra nullius' is a latin expression meaning 'nobody's land. Who controls the Arctic? Who has the right to make borders, gain territories? And who owns the North Pole? Can the ownership of these territories be decided by explorers planting flags and drawing maps?

EM was a polar explorer. He wanted to use nuclear energy in order to free the mineral resources in Greenland. This was a suggestion he presented to Niels Bohr. EM was my great-grandfather (source from Frederiksen's book).

In April 2020, Father wrote: Is this a myth?

148.JPG

149.JPG

150.JPG

EM was a polar explorer. He called the Greenlandic citizens 'his children', and they called him 'their father' and 'grandfather'. The Greenlanders loved him. EM was also my great-grandfather (source from Father and Frederiksen's book).

151.JPG

EM was a colonist. However, he did not collect ethnographic artefacts from Greenland. EM was my great-grandfather (source from Frederiksen's book).

In February 2020, Father wrote: With 'narwhale' tooth.

152.JPG

153.JPG

EM was a Danish inspector and a colonist. He made the colony Scoresbysund. He did not like when the inhabitants a few years later changed the name to Ittoqqortoormiit, a Greenlandic name. EM was my great-grandfather, but not by blood (source from Father and Frederiksen's book).

154.JPG

155.JPG

In April 2020, Father wrote: of 972.000 km2.
EM was a polar scientist. He suggested a National park in East Greenland. This idea later became a reality in North Greenland. The National park covers an areal on 972.000 km2. EM was my great-grandfather (source from Frederiksen's book).

156.JPG

ARCHIVES & EVIDENCE

Archives are always confronted with their own agenda regarding what to keep and what to forget. This must also apply to 'collective memory', as being the dominant version of history inside archives. Still, archives should not be seen as threats but as invitations, as Pad.ma suggests in its *Theses on the Archive.* Tina Bastajian, "An Invitation" in *Lost and Living (in) Archives: Collectively Shaping New Memories*, ed. Annet Dekker (Amsterdam: Valiz, 2017), 249. If archival practices and communication would allow for intervention and debate, I would claim that our shared present and its conflicts and conversational fallout would be a lot more constructive and inclusive. Or, as Daniela Agostinho argues; 'the archive is not something which belongs to the past but something which actively shapes us in the present. This is why the colonial archives matter and keep reverberating the colonial past in the present.' Daniela Agostinho, "Archives that Matter - Infrastructures for Sharing Unshared Histories. An Introduction," *Nordisk Tidsskrift for Informationsvidenskab og Kulturformidling vol. 8*, no. 2 (2019): 5. Still, public and private archives are both characterised by relying on the historically constructed concept of property – property of access and property of production. Agustina Andreoletti, "Shadow Publishing: Opacity, Reproduction, Circulation and Legitimation of Knowledges" (Postgraduate Thesis, Academy of Media Arts Cologne, 2019), 3-4. How can we use archives from the past to shape how we wish to see the future when we know that the communities that are excluded from this peculiar logic of cultural preservation and meaning-making (read: the communities that do not support the 'collective memory') are kept outside of authorship and legal copyright (and thus politics of custodianship)? Temi Odumosu, "The Crying Child: On Colonial Archives, Digitization, and Ethics of Care in the Cultural Commons" in *Current Anthropology* vol. 61 supplement 22 (October, 2020): 295.

Through the massive amount of material I have dived into concerned with Greenland-Denmark relations, EM, stories, myths, and conflicts of colonialism, I have interacted with various archives and collections – private, public, digital, physical – in Denmark, Greenland, and elsewhere. The material of privately collected origin in my research is mostly from Father's archive. The public/semi-public sources come primarily from Danish Arctic Institute, Danish Arctic Institute is an archive of documentation and dissemination of the history of Denmark in Greenland and the Arctic (primarily the Danish Expeditions in the Arctic). Established in 1954 by an initiative of Eigil Knuth and EM, Danish Arctic Institute is a private institution and archive, but by appointment it is open to the public. followed by Royal Danish Library, Greenland's National Museum and Archive, Danish Film Institute, and the New York Times Archive. The institutions Ammassalik Museum, Museum for Contemporary Art in Roskilde, CAMP (Center for Art on Migration Politics), Ærø Museum, and Kerteminde Museum have also been helpful in taking my questions further and providing me with references. Unfortunately, I have not been able to study all related archived material fully in-depth, and I have therefore only seen a glimpse of the archives' content. There is a lot more to explore, and for that reason this research is incomplete or unfinished.

During this research I have been looking through a few metres of family albums, photographs, negatives, books, objects, official (political) documents, diaries, interviews, moving image tapes, newspaper articles, personal correspondences, letters, and email correspondences, all in connection to the current geopolitics, post-colonialism, and future possibilities in the Arctic (and in Greenland), and how that can be related to design. Conflicts in the design discipline and the gaps between generational understandings of colonial pasts and histories have been important parts of the research. The research has not only been about creating links, exposing, revealing, and presenting evidence within the book, it has just as much been about a way for me to navigate various archives by trying to understand how they exist, under what conditions, with what gestures, and to understand how the archives relate to a design discipline, for me to move beyond the notion of a too-familiar project when dealing with my own background, which is treated also in the chapter MY STRUGGLE WITH SEEING CLEARLY.

As the art critic Hal Foster phrases the relation between artistic and archival practices; 'the archiving impulse and trend in contemporary art is when artists seek to make historical information, often lost or displaced, psychically present.' Wynants, *When Fact is Fiction*, 13.

The archival impulse works differently from archive to archive, as each has different perceptions of history and different agendas that they wish to communicate and preserve. Many archives are almost identical, which can cause a lack of diversity within what is preserved. As Michel Foucault expresses: 'An archive cannot be described from within or in its totality, rather "it emerges in fragments, regions and levels".' Dekker, *Lost and Living (in) Archives*, 12. The materials I have digested are all subjected to fragmentation, since a document in an archive can change location, be re-contextualised, and at times be destroyed in preference of another document. Dekker, *Lost and Living (in) Archives*, 12. Documents and materials exist within a process of debate and accreditation, Cramerotti, *Aesthetic Journalism*, 30. and for that reason I have tried to treat the materials in the most careful manner, while still seeking access and continuing my questioning. By engaging in a dialogue with archivists, the gatekeepers of memory, I have tried to uphold an open agenda on my motivation to engage with this subject, even though there were controversial moments, where narratives were not to be shared in the public domain. In this interplay between sensibility and systematisation (in archives as well as in design-making), new narratives occurred, which called for further investigation and attentiveness – not only to the content, but also to its origin and placement.

From: Me Sent: June 4, 2020, 16:53 To: Father Subject: No subject

Dear Father, I have scanned the negatives you lent to me from your archive in February. Do you recognise the people? And did you take the pictures in colour? Is the little girl XM? And is the baby EM is holding your nephew Lars Olaf?
Love, Gudrun

From: Father Sent: June 7, 2020, 23:21 To: Me Subject: No subject

Dear Gudrun,

173.JPG

The little girl is not XM. The child on the image I don't know who is. The lady EM holds in his hand might be Sara Helms. But I dare not really say it. Maybe XM or XX knows who it is? July 2020, Father said: "After a bit of thought, I think it could be Mrs. Lidegaard who is the woman on the picture." Take care of yourself.
Love Father xox

'Archival disposal is often an emotionally charged symbolic act that connects to – and ignites – a wide spectrum of cultural connotations from political and oppressive social structures [a coloniality] to question human (im) mortality and inclusion', Nanna Bonde Thylstrup, "What the Archive Can't Contain" in Dekker, *Lost and Living (in) Archives*, 147. writes theorist in Communication and Digital Media Nanna Bonde Thylstrup about archives. On the other hand, as we have all probably encountered, memory can betray us and misrepresent rather than describe the past. 'A deceitful memory can be erased without qualms, for it does not offer an authentic image of the past of which it speaks, but always only a deceptive, fabricated and distorted image.' Robert Sakrowski & Igor Štromajer, "Expunction" in *Lost and Living (in) Archives*, 160. It is not difficult to imagine that selections have been made before arriving to and inside the archives, museums, and libraries, and that in this selection uncomfortable memories and documents in relation to colonisation through the last 300 years of shared Greenlandic-Danish history have been hidden or erased. Does this apply to the inaccessible book Nikolajsen was mentioning, or to the skulls with bullet holes?

From: Hertz Sent: March 6, 2020, 09:55 To: Me Subject: inter-library loan
Dear Gudrun,
You have ordered: Sandell, Birger. *Meddelelser om Grønland: Man & Society* – 1980 SERIES: 1991. – 150 pages, illustrated. – *Meddelelser om Grønland* Idnr: 07226942 ISBN: 87-17-06237-3 Week code: DBF199132 Line-up: 46.7 Part: 15 (1991). Archaeology and environment in the Scoresby Sund fjord: ethno-archaeological investigations of the last Thule culture of Northeast Greenland / Hanne Tuborg Sandell and Birger Sandell.
The material can be found at Nunatta Atuagaateqarfia / The Greenlandic National Library, but for whatever reason we are not allowed to borrow it out for you. Try, if necessary, to contact the library.

The study 'Archival encounters – rethinking access and care in digital colonial archives' (2019) made by Daniela Agostinho indicates that '[a]rchives are not only essential instruments of colonial governance, but they also remain coveted sites of knowledge – and thus of power – after periods of colonial rule.' Daniela Agostinho, "Archival encounters," 149. This means that the powers from colonial times still cause unequal power dynamics and structures in our contemporary time and space through the archive. A widely shared perception of archives is that a few people decide upon and maintain their content and thus the historical value of documents preserved. This idea of archives is slowly changing, as interaction with archive material is slowly changing too. The archive's inherited role and self-understanding as the gatekeeper of history is something Dr. Odumosu also analyses in her research when looking at violent digitally-accessible materials in relation to non-European perspectives, when engaging with the remains from ancestors who were non-European. Dr. Odumosu examines how caretaking can play a role in- and outside of the institution's walls. Odumosu, "The Crying Child," 290.

Newer practices of today's archive (in its very broad sense operating in the internet domain) are generated by everyone (people who have access to the internet and connected devices). These archives of today circulate on the internet and are created and preserved collectively. Dekker, *Lost and Living (in) Archives*, 14-15. They challenge our previous perception of archival practices because their technologies democratise historical archiving, for example through social media, where the user plays an active part in creating content by commenting on the existing, which opens up for different positions and narratives. These attempts can challenge the 'collective memory', but still the public domain and informational commons of today's archives can also just be perceived as another colonial mash-up. A mash-up where cultural materials and knowledge are 'open' for others to profit from, but remain separated from the socio-cultural and economic systems in which they were made meaningful. Christen, "*Does Information Really Want to be Free?*," 2879-2880. This might be the case with the new Netflix film. How can the film *Against the Ice* be meaningful for the people in Greenland too? Or as it is seen in other cases, when institutional archives aim to reproduce everything, the whole scale of the collection (for the sake of the volume in the collection); a colonial past in digitalised format. The big data of the colonial past has at the same time its own forms of erasure, Odumosu, "The Crying Child," 295. as Dr. Odumosu argues. It is even more problematic when studies show that wide-ranging agendas and manifestations of coloniality are situated inside technology itself; such as with cyber racism, colonial algorithms, or the recordings of violence that are stored and shared in digital archives. Odumosu, "The Crying Child," 290. It is urgent to observe and to question how these structures in digital – and physical – archives, unknowingly or knowingly, reproduce a colonial discourse, and how I as a designer and user of archives can challenge this. What would an archive look like, how would it work, if it was able to 'move beyond national economies of guilt and innocence [within 'collective knowledge'], towards a consequent confrontation of colonial legacies that continue to structure the present'? Agostinho, "Archival encounters," 144. Or should the feelings of guilt not be an integrated part of the archive, as guilt or shame can make one learn and reflect emotionally with the past?

When working with archived material from the colonial past, am I then already embedded in the discourse by reusing image material in this publication from colonial moments in Greenland? At what moment do the images become violent or painful? When are archivists aware of how the material in archives, which are for open use, can appear as violent in another sociocultural context? Are the archives of today that contain colonial information aware of the material they make accessible? And what is excluded from ethical consideration when digitising colonial archives? These questions are all important and relevant to ask, however they are questions that I as an individual am not able to fully answer in this book.

From: … Sent: January 10, 2020, 18:09 To: Frederiksen Subject: Scrapbooks

Hi Frederiksen,
ank you very much for your mail - what a
eat coincidence that you were at the Johannes Larsen Museum.
month. I just finished reading your book
A *Biography*. It is really informative and
gative in relation to EM and the time he
s living in. Father gave all of his children
your book as a Christmas gift in 2015.
me relatives handed EM's diaries to the
yal Library several years ago. And they
ember that there were some scrapbooks
ts of my family had inherited which then
later were handed over to Ærø Museum.
se scrapbooks are no longer at Ærø Mu-
. Ærø Museum referred to the Johannes
sen Museum, which could possibly have
material lying around. But unfortunately,
irector of to the Johannes Larsen Museum announced that they were not.
hanks for the references – I have not yet
come across Toft's book about EM. As a
n student I will try to investigate my own
ial background, and critically reflect on
d outside the work, and eventually after
nger research process make either a film
r objects and a publication that visualises
lonial conflicts. For the past four years, I
e been working on the Arctic and the is-
at concern Greenland's movements and
sts. What I am looking for in relation to
EM narrative is more Greenlanders' view
m, what he did of good and evil (probably
best intention) in East Greenland. In my
n, many Greenlanders have not had time
pace to talk about the narratives created
nd by EM and the Danish government's
n Greenland. I have dived into the works
m Arke and Nikolajsen. And have done a

few interviews with people who knew about EM. If you would like to share some information, references, or stories that you think might be useful for my project, then I would be very grateful. And thank you again for your mail.
Kind regards, Gudrun.

From: Frederiksen Sent: January 11, 2020, 14:14 To: Me Subject: Scrapbooks
Dear Gudrun,
Now I think I can help you better with fin
material. First the background: When I wa
working on the book about EM, I visited U
marken where Sven – who must be your un
July 2020, Father said: "Obviously he is misunderstanding. Sven is not your
grandfather! He confused Sven with Alan." – lived and had his st
dio. In the attic, which was a kind of storer
I found some pictures and scrapbooks. Aft
reviewing the material, I figured it would b
shame in all ways if that material disappea
over time. That is why the pictures, which
concerned Sven, should be handed to Johan
Larsen Museum, and the scrapbooks for
Danish Arctic Institute. I did so, so if you g
Danish Arctic Institute's website and search
on "EM", you will find, among other things
the following: The collection consists of th
parts: 1. Private correspondence and diaries
2. Work-related correspondence and work
papers 3. Scrap / scrapbooks. 1. It is private
correspondence and diaries that are prima
from the period 1921-1932 and is between E
and his wife Ella Mikkelsen as well as a m
correspondence between parents of EM an
his three children Sven, Aksel and Else. In
addition, a number of diaries from the same
period. The collection also contains copies
of letters from EM to his parents and siblin
from the period 1885-1900. 2. The work-rel
part of the collection is predominantly abou
Scoresbysundkomiteen. 3. Scrapbooks: 'A
comprehensive collection of newspaper
articles.' NB. Large format. Of this material,
most of the newspaper articles – what I hav
emphasized – you will probably be able to
some of it. However, as far as I remember, i
is quite comprehensive. Here you will be ab
to get help from Hans Toft's bibliography. It
not a book you read from beginning to end
but a listing. Borrow it at the library. If you
think you can use it, buy it at antikvariat.ne
I can see that there is one copy for sale for
130 DKK. That money can quickly be spen
well because they can save you a lot of wor

When I was working on the EM book, I took photocopies of the articles I needed. You can borrow these copies if you are able to swing by. I can't send the material because there is a lot. You also have the option of using Hans Toft's bibliography to find what you think you can use, and then get the library to obtain it. If you think I can help you further, please let me know. I think your particular entry into the material is of a completely different nature than mine was when I wrote my book, but now see what you can find out. At least you must have good luck.
Kind regards, Frederiksen

While the colonial project in East Greenland took shape, EM must have predicted the need to expand and secure evidence, memory, and history in an archival domain. Was this one of the reasons for him to establish Danish Arctic Institute Danish Arctic Institute have been very kind with providing me with image material, contacts, and directions on where to find information about EM. in Copenhagen together with another Danish polar explorer, Eigil Knuth (1903–1996)? I am wondering if the establishment of Danish Arctic Institute was to secure certain narratives; to contribute to the 'collective memory', and to dictate future narrations and explanations. To what extent is the material accessible, and to whom?

As it is written on the website of Danish Arctic Institute's articles of association, its main purpose is to collect Danish expedition history in Greenland and the Arctic region (paragraph 2.1), to file and register material regarding Greenland and the other Arctic regions, and to make this material available to everyone, unless otherwise specified. Danish Arctic Institute, "Vedtægter," accessed June 29, 2021, https://arktiskinstitut.dk/fileadmin/files/arktiskinstitut/pdf/Arktisk_Institut_Vedtaegter_2011_11_09.pdf.

The process of investigating EM and colonial heritage in Greenland has not been without archival difficulties. As Nikolajsen also mentioned in a conversation I had with her, it can be difficult (read: impossible) to get access to certain information, even though digitalisation has led to museums, organisations, libraries, and national archives opening up collections to the public. Gaining access to certain stories is still challenging, and information is not free. I am wondering if there is any clause on certain information about EM and his narratives? Will the reproduction of certain information that corresponds to the 'collective memory' continue for long? These are questions related to matters of copyright. See chapter ANOTHER STORY ON EM.

In dialogue with various museums, libraries, archives, and publishers I came across different policies for the sharing of information. It seems like certain material is often hidden by clause agreements. Who benefits from these agreements that hide information? Will there be moments when institutions see the need to open up for different models of sharing, in which the conservation of content can be accessed publicly while still benefiting from the care of a network of dedicated collectors, Aymeric Mansoux, "How deep is your source?" in Dekker, *Lost and Living (in) Archives*, 97. as Aymeric Mansoux writes in *Lost and Living (in) Archives,* and the care of all the individuals involved in the content? And will these moments of sharing and making public allow other voices and narratives to be communicated, heard, and preserved?

It is stated in Nanna Bonde Thylstrup's article, 'What the Archive can't contain', that no archive will ever achieve a sublime state, but rather function as a representation of different views and values as they change over time. Thylstrup, "What the Archive can't contain," 145. I am wondering if and when different views of Danish colonialism – both lost and living narratives – will ever be widely shared or debated across generations and backgrounds. Will other views on accessibility and openness appear, from which meaningful structures for preserving content will be created? Will there be archival structures that address and regonise historical injustices? What are the levels of opacity? This is something that I as both a designer and a user must critically consider and emphasise when making intersectional engagements and links between memories and archives.

From: Me Sent: Friday, November 8, 2019, 11:33 To: Danish Arctic Institute

Subject: Regarding EM and his deeds in Greenland

Dear Danish Arctic Institute,

With great interest and curiosity for the historical events in the Arctic and for your archive, I write to you in the hope that you can help me for my further research.

As a great-granddaughter of EM, I have a great interest in dealing more with his experiences, intentions, and actions in Greenland. I have grown up with the tales of *Farlig Tomandsfaerd* and the work he participated in during the Eastern Greenland case in The Hauge. But unfortunately, I do not seem to have encountered the Greenlanders' stories about him, and their views on the various polar explorers and scientists. Is there any material available about this issue? Or can you recommend some actors I can turn to, who knew EM and other polar explorers who had contact with the local population in Greenland or in the rest of the Arctic region?

Looking forward to hearing from you, and will be available at any time if you require further information.

Kind regards, Gudrun Havsteen-Mikkelsen

From: Danish Arctic Institute Sent: November 11, 2019, 10:57 To: Me

Subject: Regarding EM and his deeds in Greenland

Hi Gudrun

It's an interesting question you ask – and important too. We would encourage you to continue to work on Greenlanders' opinions on EM and the polar explorers, and try to get the local/Greenlanders' voice into the stories. Unfortunately, we do not have that kind of material in Danish Arctic Institute – even though we really have a lot to do with EM specifically, and your family more broadly. There could be something in A 094 lb. 41 (allegedly a story by Henrik Høegh) and perhaps in A 056 Kateket Seier Abelsen (catechist who was ordained a priest in Iceland on the way to the establishment of Scoresbysund). We have a couple of diaries (in Greenlandic) of the Greenlandic participants in the Literaere Ekspedition (A 194 lb. no. 28 Gabas diary (in Danish translation)) and 5. Thule Expedition (A 243 lb. 1-4 Jakob Olsen, in Greenlandic). There are also some lb.no., where there are only letters or correspondence – you have to go in and look further to see if there could be something. But try searching the register https://arktiskinstitut.dk/arkiverne/dokumentarkiv/soeg-i-dokumentregistranten/?tx_ogarktiskdocarchive-frontend_pi1%5Bsearchtype%5D=full. We have rich collections in the archives, which you can see more about through our website and from there click on to the 'Document Archive and Photo Collection'.

If there should have been something in the Greenlandic newspapers it can be searched: https://timarit.is/search_init.jsp?lang=da&orderby=score&q=ejnar+mikkelsen

We also know that there is a collection about EM at the Royal Library.

One last option could be Greenland's National Museum and Archives https://da.nka.gl/digitale-samlinger/qangagooqgl/ // https://da.nka.gl/

We assume you have contact with the rest of the family – XM, as far as we know, also has some material lying around.

Otherwise what we could also recommend to you is to get in contact with the local museums in Tasiilaq and Ittoqqortoormiit (and Qaanaaq). Of course, the most obvious and important thing would be to conduct fieldwork in East Greenland and interview

people there. Hope this can be of some help
– otherwise write again.
Best regards, Danish Arctic Institute

From: Me Sent: November 25, 2019, 17:08 To: Danish Arctic Institute

Subject: Regarding EM and his deeds in Greenland

Dear Danish Arctic Institute,
Thank you for your nice feedback with the many good references and suggestions! Your archive has certainly been useful to me, to get an insight into the amount of material, the person, and the time. As well the Icelandic search base, timarit.is, has really been interesting to get a visual impression with newspaper articles etc. Thank you! I have just finished *EM – A Biography,* by Frederiksen. Unfortunately, it does not give any impression of what the East Greenlanders really thought about EM, and I have therefore contacted museums in East Greenland to get their view on the case. I have interviewed people I met in Greenland in 2017 who knew about EM, Though most of the people that knew EM in Greenland are no longer alive (apart from EM's descendants) I interviewed people that knew about EM and his deeds by trying to give them space to remember, express experiences and emotions. but that information is something the people themselves now question, whether what they described was true or not ... I met with a woman who believed that EM had hunted the Greenlandic women, with enthusiasm, against the women's consent. When I contacted the woman again this fall, she wasn't sure if it was Lauge Koch or EM. Is this a story you know anything about at Danish Arctic Institute? I deliberately did not want to involve the family too much, since their memories of or attitude towards EM may be less critical of his behaviour. However, his grandson, Father, has said that EM could crack walnuts in his armpit.
Thank you ever so much for your help!
Best regards, Gudrun

From: Danish Arctic Institute Sent: November 26, 2019, 09:24 To: Me

Subject: Regarding EM and his deeds in Greenland

Dear Gudrun,
Lovely it could be useful. Regarding the 'rumours' about the hunt for the local women we have heard several loose comments about this, both in relation to EM, Lauge Koch, and Knud Rasmussen – but not really anything concrete.
Good luck for your project!
Best regards, Danish Arctic Institute

When visiting Danish Arctic Institute in June 2020 it was articulated in conversation that ethical measures are taken, which the archivists in dialogue together decide, regarding what material should be hidden and what should be included in the digital archive before making the material digitally accessible. These decisions are something the archivists specify and decide among themselves inside the archives; it is usually not commonly known to the public that these decisions are made, and with what guidelines. Manual or automatic digitisation of archives with colonial content may be just as well subject to 'blindness' and the reproduction of discourses of colonial memory and nostalgia. Have archival purposes changed since the establishment of Danish Arctic Institute? Would the polar explorers have been satisfied with critical changes in archival practices of today, and how would that be applied to Danish Arctic Institute, Royal Danish Library, Greenland's National Museum and Archive, or National Museum of Denmark, etc.? And if the shifted role of archives results in the existence of flexible systems in the digital realm, where content is constantly re-contextualised, where new users can approach the previously unavailable content in different manners, how will ownership and copyright of the material be upheld?

It seems impossible to imagine archives without their relation to geography and history, as the artist duo Nasrin Tabatabai and Babak Afrassiabi also explains in a conversation with Annet Dekker. Tabatabai and Afrassiabi believe it is more interesting to think of the historical (or geographical) 'situations' rather than 'contexts':

> 'Context operates according to precedence and priority; it is a closed system, which places complexities of conditions under a single totality. Whereas situation is open and indeterminate. It is what is not contextualized.'
>
> Annet Dekker, "Permeable Archive" in Dekker, *Lost and Living (in) Archives*, 220.

These 'situations' in comparison to the contextualised 'contexts', which already exist in archives, could allow for experimentation, collaborations, and a plurality of voices. I would argue that both ways of thinking about historical and geographical perceptions are relevant in the archives, as the existence of each – their co-existence – does not have to reject the other, but instead can allow for the possibility for opacity, and can allow for different (design) processes and media to interact. As the conversations with the descendants of EM, Father, archivists, museums, artists, Greenlandic locals, etc. indicate, 'situations' and 'contexts' often coexist inside the archive and the 'collective memory', depending on the specific understanding and perception of the past.

The process of getting material from third-hand sources, such as the archives, relied to a large extent also on the co-existence of 'situations' and 'contexts', and the confusion of the in-between, while still maintaining honesty to the provider, the archival service and gatekeepers, and to continue the research of *Snowblindness*.

From: Me Sent: January 20, 2020, 14:37 To: Danish Arctic Institute

Subject: image material Arctic Institute

Dear Danish Arctic Institute,
I have contacted you previously regarding the archive material dealing with EM, as I am conducting a research on his doings in Greenland seen in a post-colonial context. I am making a small booklet (about the different narratives associated with EM) for an exam moment at Sandberg. For that booklet, I will need some of the visuals from your archive. It is about 23-25 pictures. As the booklet is only for private consumption, and as it will only be printed in two copies, would it then be possible to get a reduced student price for the photo material? I have been in Father's archive over Christmas. He also has some material, but unfortunately not everything was equally relevant or sufficient to the subject I am investigating. Should I request access to the images individually through your website, even if I have a user ID?
I look forward to hearing from you.
Kind regards Gudrun

From: Danish Arctic Institute Sent: January 21, 2020, 10:34 To: Me

Subject: image material Arctic Institute

Dear Gudrun,
Using pictures from our digital archive for education purposes is something we catego as private use – so it is for free.
We would recommend that you log in and t save the pictures you would like to use in a folder/collection on your profile at 'arktiske billeder.dk'. In 'actions', you can then select 'order all', which will be one total payment, which we will then approve, and you can at that moment download the pictures when yo are logged in. Otherwise, let us know if you have any questions or difficulties.
Kind regards, Danish Arctic Institute

Some of EM's photographs are also archived at Danish Arctic Institute, and a selection of those are also shown in this publication. The copyright holders to these photographs, Danish Arctic Institute, also preserves them. Most often, museums, libraries, and archives do not own the copyright to the works in their collections. The sales service at Danish Arctic Institute provides external users the right to use the photographs but not to buy ownership of them. As mentioned in 'Terms and conditions regarding purchase and use of the digital records and material from Danish Arctic Institute';

> 'All users are welcome to download photographs with Danish Arctic Institute's logo and use them in all relevant contexts free of charge. For access to photos in highest resolution without the logo, users must be logged in and request the photos from the database. For private use this is free of charge. For use in commercial and institutional contexts, payment is required before access to download is given.' Danish Arctic Institute, accessed April 12, 2020, https://www.arktiskebilleder.dk/pages/home.php#.

These precautions between an archive and the public are standard practice in order to maintain a monopoly and security on reproductions and publishing. The archive can charge usage fees to pay salaries and fund projects within the institution.

In the making of *Snowblindness*, issues pertaining to copyright between institutions, companies, publishers, family members, and colleagues were unavoidable. Given the fact that a large amount of the image material needed for making this publication came from EM himself, and was later donated by EM's descendants to Danish Arctic Institute, it was necessary to find an agreement, ask and buy permission, to then use the photographs in the publication, as the project developed into something more than just private use, from a booklet in the academy domain to a published book.

In *Snowblindness* some of the images are marked by Danish Arctic Institute's logo, while other photographs are provided and bought with a permission to use, without a watermark or pixelated resolution.

When one assigns copyright to an institution or another individual, one typically lets go of a large amount of control. It's the new owner who can decide to accept translations or adaptations, and they can license out copyright material to be reprinted or used in other contexts Eric Schrijver, *Copy This Book – An artist's guide to copyright* (Eindhoven: Onomatopee, 2018), 17-18, eBook edition. without remuneration. The new owners can thereby determine the conditions of access and use of the material. It is especially important to be aware of copyrights in large-scale productions, such as Netflix's feature film *Against the Ice.* A production company such as Netflix, together with the publisher Gyldendal, will require all five descendants of EM to sign over their copyright to Gyldendal, while Gyldendal profits as much as possible from EM's written work and life. As for EM's closest descendants, including Father, it is most important for them that EM's work continues to be known and respected. However there are no large profits from Gyldendal's royalty payments to EM's descendants. I expect Gyldendal will be profiting at lot more from the collaboration with Netflix on *Against the Ice* than with EM's books. But who is left behind, and on whose expenses?

Unfortunately, it is not possible to share the full version of the conversation between the descendants and heirs of EM in this publication, due to reasons of privacy and due to agency contracts between the descendants and the publisher. The information I can share is that the conversation contains information about Netflix's release of *Against the Ice* in the early spring of 2022 instead of December 2021, to give themselves more time to gain attention for the film as a Netflixproduction in collaboration with Gyldendal. The conversation also contained information regarding the re release of the book *Farlig Tomandsfaerd* in 2022.

How confident can we be of the nature of publishers' agreements with companies like Netflix when some agreements are not made transparent? This is something the chapter

INVOLVEMENT OF NETFLIX

also questions. The processes of contract agreements or transparency with the publisher's and archive's material are relevant to engage with and to question, since these contract agreements often correspond to an overarching and dominating structure that keeps the dominant 'collective memory' alive and thereby perhaps also structures of coloniality. It has been important to discuss and question these in the *Snowblindness* research too. When information is kept private, the design-making must account for this absence or 'gap'. It must implement this 'gap' in the design and editorial translations. That is one of the reasons why the empty spaces and the metallic layered spaces occur throughout the book, as 'blindspots', and allow other narratives to co-exist and space.

EDITING & SHARING

Unfortunately, it is not possible to share the full version of the conversations below between the descendants and heirs of EM and the publisher in this publication, due to reasons of privacy and due to agency contracts. The information I can share is the publisher Gyldendal's excitement to launch the upcoming Netflix film *Against the Ice,* and that they are trying to get the internationally famous Danish actor Nikolaj Coster-Waldau – cast as EM in the film – to write the foreword in the re-release of the book *Farlig Tomandsfaerd.* Furthermore, the conversation includes details of a new republishing contract for EM's work outlining the percentage handed out to the descendants for every sold copy, and the need for all the descendants to sign the contract as soon as possible.

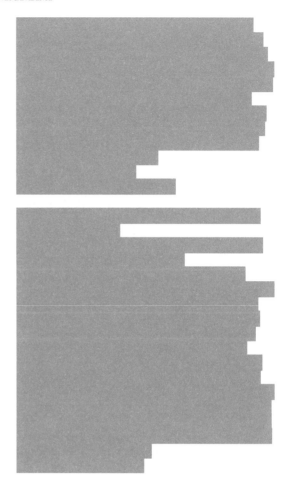

Unfortunately, it is not possible to share the full version of the conversations below between the descendants and heirs of EM due to reasons of privacy and due to agency contracts. In the conversation between the descendants it is stated that the director of the Netflix film *Against the Ice,* at that moment in time (January 2021), was filming in Iceland and will also make a few recordings in Greenland. The conversation ends with the following link:

Article by Netflix: Nikolaj Coster-Waldau hijacks giant Netflix role https://about.net

en/news/nikolaj-coster-waldau-and-joe-cole-star-in-netflix-feature-film-against-the

The Berne Convention specifies that copyright lasts for a minimum of fifty years (70 years in Denmark) after the author's death, with copyright ending on the first day of January of the year following this anniversary. Schrijver, *Copy This Book*, 16. eBook edition. This means that copyright does not last forever, and it could imply that EM's writings and images would be accessible for me to use freely in this publication after January 1, 2041, if it becomes part of the public domain. By then, it might be possible that other publishers can make editions of the same work, leading to a possible loss in profit for the original publisher or current rights-holders. Schrijver, *Copy This Book*, 148. eBook edition. This could explain the recent rush of interest in EM and the involvement of publishers and streaming companies such as Netflix in EM's work and adventures.

As a designer and editor, it is important to become familiar with the law on copyright as it can function as a tool when dealing with archives and institutions or when publishing work, and the responsibility that follows. This is especially important when it is a self-initiated project executed in a medium that allows for easy distribution and sale of copies, Schrijver, *Copy This Book*, 45. eBook edition. such as this project itself.

In the case of images inside *Snowblindness,* most of the images are provided by Father's private archive and my own footage. Another large amount is from Danish Arctic Institute, including other archives and institutions, such as Gyldendal. Other images are from private sources that wish to remain unknown. I have, as much as it was possible in terms of tracing origin, listed all the images sources in the

IMAGE INDEX.

From: Rights & Permissions at Gyldendal Sent: July 16, 2021, 13:54 To: Me

Subject: SV: re. pictures in EM's book 'Farlig Tomandsfærd' from 1962

Dear Gudrun,

Thank you for your inquiry. Do you know if the pictures you are referring to are privately owned or transferred to a museum or the like. If possible, feel free to send me an image of the book's colophon and if possible, the image overview.

Kind regards, Rights & Permissions at Gyldendal.

From: Me Sent: July 20, 2021, 12:33 To: Rights & Permissions at Gyldendal

Subject: SV: re. pictures in EM's book 'Farlig Tomandsfærd' from 1962

Dear reader at
Rights & Permissions at Gyldendal
Thank you for your response. Parts of the pictures are privately owned by the family's archive, others are owned by Danish Arctic stitute, and some are from other actors EM knew, since many of the pictures EM took ing his time in East Greenland in the period 1910-1912 were destroyed. Since I would like use scanned images from Gyldendal's book rlig Tomandsfærd by EM, I am interested in with whom the copyrights belong? Is it Gyldendal? EM's family? Danish Arctic Institute hich received a large part of EM's works and graphs from EM and EM's family)? Or is it unknown third party? Attached is an image the book's image information, as well as the page and the picture examples, since there unfortunately was no colophon in the edition from 1962.
Best, Gudrun

From: Me Sent: July 31, 2021, 11:39 To: Rights & Permissions at Gyldendal

Subject: SV: re. pictures in EM's book Farlig Tomandsfærd from 1962

Dear reader at
Rights & Permissions at Gyldendal
have now got an overview of which pictures belong to Danish Arctic Institute (the copyright holders) and which pictures are not in Danish Arctic Institute's archive and among Danish Arctic Institute's copyrights. The three (3) attached pictures can be found in EM's book *Farlig Tomandsfaerd* from 1962 published by Gyldendal. In this connection, I would like to k you at Gyldendal if I may use these images in my publication *Snowblindness* (project developed in design studies). *Snowblindness* will reportedly e printed in small edition through the Dutch lisher Onomatopee in Eindhoven, around the eginning of December 2021. The book is in nglish and will be about 250 pages. It is very portant to me to credit the copyright holders rectly through the execution of the book and the associated research. The pictures will of se be referred to Gyldendal in the colophon, ences, and in an image index. Hope to hear m you, and greatly appreciate your consideron and approved permission (see appendix of contract form, if you find it necessary).
est regards, Gudrun Havsteen-Mikkelsen

From: Rights & Contract Manager at Gyldendal Agency Sent: Aug 13, 2021,

Subject: SV: re. pictures in EM's book Farlig Tomandsfærd from 1962

Dear Gudrun,
Thank you for your email. Since it is a very old title, and even older photos, it has been difficult for us to examine the propriety of the photographs in depth. Therefore, I can only say that the publisher does not mind you using the images below, however, I cannot sign your contract form.
The copyrights to all of EM's own photos belong to the heirs, including your father.
I'm sorry we could not be more helpful.
Kind regards,
Rights & Contract Manager at Gyldendal Agency

Methodologies used in design and in journalism are variable elements when working with archives, also in the development of this work. Methodologies and historical writings in design are not 'designed' for long-term storage, but for reproduction, re-contextualisation, and for endless circulation between different people, networks, and locations. Dekker, *Lost and Living (in) Archives*, 17. These changes in history-writing or the locations of history preservation may affect people's relationships to the past and the future, and thereby also 'collective memories'. The same changes can portray the generational gaps in perception of history on colonial matters, as this research has already expressed. History, with a capital H, can also be debated in the design discipline, but what design can bring to the debate on History is the implication of memory both within and outside structures, systems, and medium. Certain visual decisions and edits can highlight what is suppressed, when the regulations and structures are adhered to, when the traditional role of the archivist, as the gatekeeper, is lost. This issue is also raised in the chapter MY STRUGGLE WITH SEEING CLEARLY, how can I or they determine what narratives should be erased, forgotten, and neglected?

Sampling archival documents as a designer practising Aesthetic Journalism opens up for new insights to be revealed, since it has generally been accepted that archives construct a specific account of History; many things end up in an archive, but even more information remains outside and forgotten. Dekker, *Lost and Living (in) Archives*, 18-19. Here especially oral history and storytelling have lacked attention and care, since throughout history the oral has often been declared invalid, unappreciated by the 'civilised' and 'scientific' Western world. Annet Dekker et al. "The hidden value of oral history in an 'open' society" in Dekker, *Lost and Living (in) Archives*, 129. Written stories are often categorised as 'true', while oral stories are categorised as 'false'. Minh-ha, *Woman, Native, Other*, 126.

Throughout their existence, the Inuit population in Greenland used oral communication to relay and preserve messages to and for the next generations. Oral storytelling is lesser archived in part due to lack of equipment, as well as its very nature, so it was previously looked upon as something not true or not worth caring for. Even though the Inuit were able to read and write before a large part of the European population, it was only the 'civilised' narrator who could renew his mind and exercise the power of his intellect through writing, Minh-ha, *Woman, Native, Other*, 126. as Trinh T. Minh-ha describes. Many voices and stories have been lost, and for that reason it is important to pay careful attention to oral storytellers and the means with which one documents and remembers those storytellers' voices.

Regarding the matters of decolonising design and challenging archival practices it is important to reflect on how the discipline can be inclusive and open to suggestions and changes. How can oral stories and voices be preserved institutionally? And how can I, as a designer and as a citizen, treat and interact with this material?

The media theorist Katrina Sluis suggests that the archive must place more emphasis on transfer, rather than storage, since memory is 'collectively (re)-constructed (and re-contextualised) in the present rather than collected and preserved from the past'. Katrina Sluis, "Accumulate, aggregate, destroy" in Dekker, *Lost and Living (in) Archives*, 35. This is something I believe Greenland will pay much more attention to in both the present and the future Through the digitalisation of Inuit artefacts from a Greenlandic interest and perspective at Nunatta Katersugaasivia (Greenland National Museum and Archive). – an archive for transfer, while focusing on repatriation and forgotten voices.

The Snowblindness Podcast Series also discussed this with the Greenlandic photographer Inuuteq Storch:

> "Usually when we [Greenlanders] read about ourselves, we are actually seeing us through the foreigner's eyes. My mom took a lot of photos when we were young and it's really common that someone independent takes photos of family gatherings or anything, I mean family albums basically. So I was like 'OK when I get back to my hometown I'm going collect photos from my account and make a book.' And then when I got home I naturally started with my parents' archive, and I was like, 'oh this is cool. I can actually divide this project into a bigger one, and I can make more books instead of one. I can actually map the years, this book is from this year to this year, kind of'."

Implementing multiple voices in research and design work is especially important when dealing with colonial pasts, divisive territories, and 'collective memory', since written and archived History cannot stand alone as the only source of evidence. It is just as important in this process to cherish the subject, project, and network by building a community of – and collaboration between – investigations and stories, and to find ways in which untold or oral stories can take space. A strategy of making visible must be established, while still respecting the presence of opacity for the people and cultures involved. *Snowblindness* is trying to obtain this, while working with and in-between the oral, written, and visual storytelling.

From: Rasmussen, Ammassalik Museum Sent: November 20, 2019, 13:55 To: Me

Subject: About research on EM

Hi Gudrun,
The last supply ship before next year in Jun
2020 should have sailed yesterday, which is
now postponed until this noon Greenlandic
time. It has therefore been a few chaotic days
at the museum, as the museum stands for
salutation with our small signal cannons. It i
an old tradition that signals that contact with
the outside world is gone in winter, as the ic
off the East coast of Greenland makes sailin
impossible until June. In addition, there is a
opening ceremony with the exhibition of Eig
Knuth's busts from the Ammassalik Distric
this afternoon, so we have been busy gettin
the last of the exhibition built up. But back t
EM and your interest point. His own writing
is really a good documentation of what his
general doings were all about. There are m
accounts of EM's behaviour from more than
half a century in East Greenland. If I were y
I'd split my research into two or three tracks
1. EM's own writing gives insight into what
underlies some of his decisions, which were
sometimes controversial, but basically mad
on a selfless basis. 2. Other people's descriptio
of him and the significance his decisions ha
for the East Greenland community. 3. Indirec
sources discussing the community in East
Greenland's development for better or worse
Here I refer especially to Pia Arke, see litera
ture reference.
Literature: Frederiksen, Kurt L. 2015. EM –
Biography. http://www.historie-online.dk/
boger/anmeldelser-5-5/biografier-erindring-
er-60-60/ejnar-mikkelsen-en-biografi
Various literature references: http://denstore-
danske.dk/Dansk_Biografisk_Leksikon/Sam
fund,_jura_and_politik/Eddagelsesrejsende/
Polarforsker/Ejnar_Mikkelsen
Inspiring gl./dk Artist: https://www.hakaima
azine.com/features/unforgettable-pia-arke/
She has also written the book *Stories from*
Scoresbysund, which is worth reading. Much
of the colonial heritage's inheritance is bein
addressed.
EM (Danish book titles): *Fra Fribytter til*

Embedsmand, De Østgrønlandske Eskimoers historie, Breve fra Nordøstgrønland, Nogle afrevne blade af mit livs historie. I hope you can use the above for something and that you can immediately proceed with your research. Otherwise, feel free to contact us again. Have a good day.
Kind regards, Rasmussen
Ammassalik Museum

m: Me Sent: November 25, 2019, 12:39 To: Rasmussen, Ammassalik Museum

Subject: A: Regarding research on EM

Dear Rasmussen,
Thank you very much for your answer and thank you for taking the time to answer my questions, and thank you for the references. I just finished reading *EM – A Biography* by lenriksen that you recommended. It certain- resents interesting stories and connections. m familiar with Pia Arke but I have not yet ved into her work. Your help is definitely to e benefit of my research. I am actually most erested in getting the Greenlanders' view of m, while he was staying in East Greenland. I have the impression that he was a very nourable person, and perhaps lacked some f-criticism ... I wondered if you know of any ner sources describing the locals' perception of him, other than a 'father figure'? I hope ings went well with Eigil Knuth's busts last ek. Hope sometime to have the opportunity to visit East Greenland and Tasiilap Katersugaasiva/Ammassalik Museum.
Kind regards, Gudrun

From: Rasmussen, Ammassalik Museum Sent: November 25, 2019, 8:12 To: Me

Subject: SV: About research on EM

Hi Gudrun,
I just now remember that there is a depiction of EM's visit to Ittoqqortoormiit in 1958–59. He was on a summer visit and there were some festivities. This is all described in Jens Nielsen's diary. It was published in 2013. Father showed me a copy of that book in July 2020, where he is mentioned as well. See p. 86-89 in *Dagbogsbreve fra Scoresbysund 1957-59* by Jens Nielsen (Skjern: Det Grønlandske Selvskab, 2012. See link:

https://www.saxo.com/dk/dagbogsbreve-fra-scoresbysund-1957-59_epub_9788787925471.

Nikolajsen's film about EM is maybe also worth watching: https://km.gl/da/nyheder/ejnar-mikkelsen-elsket-eller-hadet.
Kind regards, Rasmussen,
Ammassalik Museum

In February 2020 in the moving image *Aftermath: Narratives on EM* Father said: "Shall I start putting notes in here?"

157.JPG

158.JPG

EM was a polar scientist. Accord-ng to several Greenlanders, hunters and fathers died of influenza. As a consequence, EM introduced a pri-ate paternity for the children who had become orphans. EM was my great-grandfather (source from Frederiksen's book).

EM was a colonist. He became an honorary citizen in Scoresbysund, the colony he built. He financed a youth community house andgot his nephew and my uncle, an architect, to design it. The house is called *Mikis Hus*. EM was my great-grandfather (source from my Father and Frederiksen's book).

In April 2020, Father wrote: Grandson, your uncle. Three of his great-great-grandchildren in front of his bust [out of the frame] in Langelinje, Copenhagen.

159.JPG

160.JPG

161.JPG

DANMARKS STATSMINISTER,

under hvilken Minister Grønlands Styrelse er henlagt, gør herved vitterligt:

at Hr. Kaptajn Ejnar Mikkelsen, Inspektør for Østgrønland, hvis Fotografi findes nedenfor, er bemyndiget til paa den danske Regerings Vegne at udøve politimæssig Øvrighedsmyndighed i Østgrønland.

To whom it may concern be it known that

I, THE UNDERSIGNED PRIME MINISTER OF DENMARK,

under whose department the Greenland Administration is placed, do hereby make known:

that Captain Ejnar Mikkelsen, Inspector of East Greenland, whose photograph is found below, is authorized to excercise police authority in East Greenland on behalf of the Danish Government.

STATSMINISTERIET, den 3.August 1934.

Under Haand og Embedssegl.

162.JPG

163.JPG

In April 2020, Father wrote: Is this a myth?

Unknown citizen from Ittoqqortoormiit in Nikolajsen's film *Scoresbysund – kolonien er mit eget barn*: "It is the first time that I have heard that EM should have slapped one of his minions."

EM was a police officer in Ittoqqortoormiit. He once slapped a Greenlander in his face because he refused to shake hands with him. EM was my great-grandfather, but not by blood (source from local Greenlanders and people interviewed in Nikolajsen's film *Scoresbysund – kolonien er mit eget barn*).

164.JPG

165.JPG

the German colonial administration in 1904; the Japanese onslaught in China, notably the massacre of nearly four hundred thousand, and the rape of eighty thousand, Chinese in December 1937, the so-called Rape of Nanking; the rape of some one hundred and thirty thousand women and girls (ten thousand of whom committed suicide) by victorious Soviet soldiers unleashed by their commanding officers in Berlin in 1945 – seem more remote. These are memories that few have cared to claim.

The familiarity of certain photographs builds our sense of the present and immediate past. Photographs lay down routes of reference, and serve as totems of causes: sentiment is more likely to crystallize around a photograph than around a verbal slogan. And photographs help construct – and revise – our sense of a more distant past, with the posthumous shocks engineered by the circulation of hitherto unknown photographs. Photographs that everyone recognizes are now a constituent part of what a society chooses to think about, or declares that it has chosen to think about. It calls these ideas 'memories', and that is, over the long run, a fiction. Strictly speaking, there is no such thing as collective memory – part of the same family of spurious notions as collective guilt. But there is collective instruction.

All memory is individual, unreproducible – it dies with each person. What is called collective memory is not a remembering but a stipulating: that *this* is important, and this is the story about how it happened, with the pictures that

74

lock the story in our minds. Ideologies create substantiating archives of images, representative images, which encapsulate common ideas of significance and trigger predictable thoughts, feelings. Poster-ready photographs – the mushroom cloud of an A-bomb test, Martin Luther King, Jr. speaking at the Lincoln Memorial in Washington, DC, the astronaut walking on the moon – are the visual equivalent of sound bites. They commemorate, in no less blunt fashion than postage stamps, Important Historical Moments; indeed, the triumphalist ones (the picture of the A-bomb excepted) become postage stamps. Fortunately, there is no one signature picture of the Nazi death camps.

As art has been redefined during a century of modernism as whatever is destined to be enshrined in some kind of museum, so it is now the destiny of many photographic troves to be exhibited and preserved in museum-like institutions. Among such archives of horror, the photographs of genocide have undergone the greatest institutional development. The point of creating public repositories for these and other relics is to ensure that the crimes they depict will continue to figure in people's consciousness. This is called remembering, but in fact it is a good deal more than that.

The memory museum in its current proliferation is a product of a way of thinking about, and mourning, the destruction of European Jewry in the 1930s and 1940s, which came to institutional fruition in Yad Vashem in Jerusalem, the Holocaust Memorial Museum in Washington, DC, and

75

Susan Sontag in *Regarding the Pain of Others:* The familiarity of certain photographs builds our sense of the present and immediate past [...] And photographs help construct – and revise – our sense of more distant past. All memory is individual, irreproducible – it dies with each person. That is called 'collective memory'.

In March 2020, Gudrun wrote: Also, something which is discussed today in the article *Besaettelsestiden som kollektiv erindring*.

Susan Sontag in *Regarding the Pain of Others:* Ideologies create substantiating archives of images, representative images, which encapsulate common ideas of significance and trigger predictable thoughts, feelings.

166.JPG

167.JPG

In February 2020, Father wrote: Iver had this car who passed it over to Aksel who gave it to me in 1960. Picture is taken outside Johannes Larsen's home in Kerteminde where my father visited him. M was a captain. Him and Iver Iversen vere all alone, captured, exhausted and ear death for almost more than two winers in East Greenland. Iver did not have ny children, but he gave my dad a car for is birthday. EM was my great-grandfaher (source from Father).

EM was a polar explorer. He hoped that the lead-mine in Mestersvig could pave the way for other mineral explorations that could attract global investment and labour in Greenland. EM was my great-grandfather, and I have his eyebrows (source from Frederiksen's book).

In April 2020, Father wrote: Is this a myth? That you have his eyebrows.

168.JPG

ANOTHER SILVA RERUM?

Definition The Latin *silva rerum* (English translation: forest of things) was a specific type of book made by noble families from Poland and Lithuania between the 16th and 18th centuries. It was a multi-generational chronicle, written as a diary or memoir for the entire family, recording family traditions among many other matters. Silvae rerum were not intended for a wider audience or for printing, but were instead lent to friends of the family, who were allowed to add their comments to the book. The silva rerum contained information on wealth and status. There were often diary-like entries on events, memoirs, letters, political speeches, copies of legal and financial documents, anecdotes, advice, poems, and genealogical trees, just to mention a few examples. The books contained anything that the authors wished to record and preserve for future generations. Wikipedia, "Silva rerum," accessed January 3, 2021, https://en.wikipedia.org/wiki/Silva_rerum.

Act I

Me: I would like to develop these old negatives Father and I found in his archive. One negative is from around the 1910s and is black and white. The others are from the late 1960s and are mostly in colour.

Photography expert: Yes, that is possible. You will have to decide how you want to develop the negatives; analogue or digital? If you decide to develop them analogue, you will have to spend the whole day making one good photograph. It is a slow process to get the right exposure if you are not used to working in the dark room. If you decide to develop the negatives digitally, you will only have to adjust the curves and levels of light in Photoshop after scanning the negatives in our pro-film scanner. With digital development you can control the process much better. But in both cases I will only encourage you to develop the black and white negatives.

Me: I would like to make big prints. Is it possible to include all the details and texture in the digital process? Will the paper quality be as good if developing digitally?

Photography expert: You can develop big prints regardless of which technique you choose. On the matter of the paper, the analogue baryta paper contains silver gelatin, which gives the image another appearance. However, the current techniques on digital prints are now the same quality as the analogue. We have quite good paper here, which also contains silver gelatin. Let us first scan the negatives and see how many details there are.

The pro-film scanner is a black box with a small narrow opening that allows the 35mm negatives to enter. A slightly bent positioning during scanning ensures that the negatives are not crooked. Immediately you can see a high-resolution preview of the negatives on the computer screen. Behind liquid crystals we are able to travel back in time to 1912 and to the 1960s.

Photography expert: Aha, I can see you will need to remove some dirt from the image.

Me: I would prefer not to remove the dirt. I like all the details and all the traces the negative holds and carries with it. It is not my intention to remove traces or manipulate the images.

Photography expert: Yes, but the spectator might concentrate only on the traces of dirt if you decide not to clean it. This is easy to do through the digital development of your negatives. Can you see the dirt on his forehead? It is better to remove it.

The interface on the computer allows me to remove dirt and to make the image – whole or specific areas – brighter. If the image has a certain tone, I can also adjust the colour. I can scroll up and down within different parameters to manipulate the image from the original negative. All this happens in the software's interface until the image reaches the printer. The faces are brightened with the brush tool and then the printer mechanically prints out the 1912 image onto thick paper. It is now all about keeping the new print away from dust, damage, and direct sunlight.

Act 2

Act 2 and Act 3 are primarily based on conversations I had with tutors and fellow students at the Sandberg Instituut. The conversations' participants are in fluid, shifting positions.

The booklet, *Narratives on EM,* presents various stories and myths around EM followed by various images that contribute to the visualisation of the narratives. The images are not necessarily from the exact moment in time or place that the narratives represent, but they allow other perspectives to co-exist, and the reality of the written narrative is not necessarily reflected in the combined image. The memory of narratives and images can blur the line between fiction and facts, and can make substantial contributions to historical discussions, generating new meanings that change over time. V. Goethem, "Screening the City," 44-45.

Me: I want to make a book in order to collect my research and contextualise its material. I wish to publish the findings to bring forward various perspectives on the subject matter. I wish to make the book accessible for the public outside of the archival domain.

Critics: Why?

Me: It will give me an opportunity to think differently and to ask questions. I feel there is a necessity to stress the discussion around Nordic colonialism in relation to my own design practice, and a strength in including the problematic elements of making findings public. I can potentially challenge the notion of the designer as the one who finds solutions; the designer who has the answers to the questions.

Critics: So, you want to become an initiator of patch-working a convoluted past by acknowledging the gaps and incompleteness that we have to learn how to deal with?

Me: I do not think I can offer any solution to 'snowb lindness' as a phenomenon, but I do believe it is necessary for me to deal with this subject at this moment before I can move on.

Critics: How do you want to progress now with making this book? What is your strategy?

Me: I see a potential in the tension of pauses

in the moving images. Moving image *Aftermath: Narratives on EM* (4.06 min., colour and B/W. 2020) based on interviews with Father, own footage, and found footage. I see a potential to make a strategy that is based on these pauses or spaces in the book, and formulate a voice that can freely ask questions and present other narratives and new voices that previously have been silenced or erased.

Critics: Interesting. How do you do that, by giving more spaces in between, where it can work as a statement in itself or a lingering question, allowing the viewer to 'breathe'? By paying attention to the relations between film editing and editing a book? Both formats play with the edit-ability of the medium.

Me: More interventions in editing could help to communicate the stories. So, hearing something while seeing something else? Or keeping things ephemeral?

Critics: That is possible. So far, you practise acts of making visible, and making editing visible. The notes Father made in the booklet *Narratives on EM* shows how effective this is, and shows the way we discuss reality (at large) is always highly ideological. The research also shows the crumbling of the old world of male heroes with medals on their chests and the emergence of a new one in which these achievements are completely illegible, as they create an obscured view and a kind of 'blindness'. It is about the fading-out of the European nation state and the way in which this connects to its achievements of un-discussed coloniality.

Me: Yes, all this is very relevant, but for that reason I have also been in great doubt. To what extent do I have the right to make this book? Making a book is first and foremost interesting for my practice as a designer, when re-contextualising the materials of graphics work, photography, and written text. Second of all, it is important for me to present and make this book before I can continue my practice as a designer, if I want to interact with the Arctic region, simply because it interests me, not because of my colonial heritage or name.
The hidden concern of making this book is situated in what happens after the book is published; the consequences that occur when these personal stories, these fictional truths that were created in someone's imagination for no harmful reason, start to take on an

unexpected and uncontrollable life of their own. Stefan Vanthuyne, "Fiction as a Visual Strategy in the Photobook" in Wynants, *When Fact is Fiction*, 99.

Critics: For that reason, you have to reflect on how you want to tell the stories and for whom you are making this book. A way to answer these questions is to open up the editorial process to others, and to collaborate.

'Trust your graphic designer'; an advice given by Finnish artist Elina Brotherus. Louisiana, "Advice to the Young," accessed Jan 22, 2021, https://channel.louisiana.dk/video/elina-brotherusadvice-to-the-young.

Act 3

Walter Benjamin argues in *The Author as Producer* that the book as a medium can be the creative strategy in itself (the technique of the work), which refers to both aesthetic choices and the means of production. Vanthuyne, "Fiction as a Visual Strategy in the Photobook," 110.

Me: I need to make aesthetic choices in order to continue with the content and the making of a publication of some sort.

Graphic designer: There is a lot of potential; the archives, the findings of material and narratives and discussion in the research process, all of that allows for interesting aesthetic interventions. As I understand it, this project is about a messy history, dealing with personal, but also global, concerns, politics, and narratives – a project that deals with colonial actions and moral conflicts.

Me: Indeed, but also how I as a designer and a great-granddaughter can justify this project when diving into private and public archives and making work around a former Danish colony. I think a contextualisation of the material will help me progress with this research when making a book.

Graphic designer: Have you considered forms of publication other than a book?

Me: No, I have not.

Graphic designer: The content could potentially exist better in another format – stacks of paper, posters, newspapers, websites, etc. – where it is possible to shuffle the material around due to being un-bound. This introduces the possibility for the spectators to rearrange the narratives themselves, and to interact with the material in a way that is completely different to a book.

Me: For me, a book has narrative unity, and so does this unfurling story and body of research. That format speaks also to the colonial actions I am questioning, when dealing with 'collective memory' and publishing it. Making a book seems to me like the best medium to both communicate and question in my research. I will however just have to be careful when deciding on the various aesthetic choices, that does not speak into the discourses I am questioning or criticising.

Graphic designer: Yes, I agree. The book is a good and strong medium in which you can contextualise your work. The idea of another format than a book also calls for accidents and clumsiness, which the materials do not ask for. However, the material needs to be arranged on the pages to create a unity between the medium and the subject. As it is now, a lot of things are happening when we put it together in all its volume.

Me: Yes, I find it hard to remove and exclude material.

Graphic designer: The image material is massive; you will have to edit it, and choose what not to integrate. You will need to create space for interventions and interpretation. You need space for the narratives to evolve between image and text, which will draw the spectator in. You also need to experiment with how the different texts can be visualised, so that the spectator knows that the format of the content has changed; that they are reading other voices.

Me: Some information revealed in the text must not be seen. Is there a way we in collaboration can construct the visual language while thinking along the subject of the research, 'colonial memory', and subjectivities?

Graphic designer: Yes, let us work in a patchy way and embrace the gaps in time and content. I believe you will need to involve Father more on this matter, to have a dialogue about the material and the editorial process, which will make it easier for us to leave out material and create space for new narratives. You asking for help is just an act of love.

EDITING & SHARING

As the Filipino publishing and graphic design duo *Hardworking Goodlooking,* led by Clara Balaguer and Kristian Henson, formulates: '... For research to be taken seriously it must be published and reviewed. Making something public brings narratives into new contexts, in which they can be accessed, viewed and interpreted; it adds something that bookstores don't provide.' Annet Dekker, "Copying as a way to start something new" in Dekker, *Lost and Living (in) Archives*, 188. The central premise of this book relies on the notions of 'editing' and 'sharing', and making these processes visible with care. Editing and sharing have sculpted this research and its outcome in an inclusive yet critical manner. As the concept of the research circles around interactions, sparring, and contacts, this book has been brought to life with two essential collaborations: Anna and Father.

The collaboration with graphic designer, friend, and colleague Anna helped me to expand the responsibility for the process of an artistic research. It was in dialogue with Anna that my struggles with deciding what *Snowblindness* as the book lacked and what it could include were resolved. The book-making collaboration with Anna became much more than just a way to translate the mythmaking and the configurations of 'collective memory' in relation to a visual design practice. The book also became evidence, or a fruitful example, of what can happen when information, material, and narratives are shared between colleagues. Through our dialogue, I could see the value of working with texts as images, and of incorporating the practice of writing into a visual language with aesthetic choices. The collaboration on the book became an excuse for my own design practice to address collaboration as a subject, since this research and its concerns also generated meaning for other people and for Anna, and dealt with something contemporary and urgent in the design discipline too. It was crucial for me to understand that collaborating and engaging with others could only benefit the work, pushing it beyond my usual understanding of how artistic work comes to exist (namely through an individual mind, or the notion of the designer or artist as a 'singular' entity). In the collaboration, I came to another understanding of what my design practice could evolve into, how it could develop, and how it could engage its spectators.

The collaborations throughout the *Snowblindness* research, with individuals and institutions, opened up for different ways of positioning as designers, and different ways of positioning the book. Institute of Network Cultures: *Here and Now? Explorations in Urgent Publishing* (Amsterdam: Institute of Network Cultures, 2020), 70-71. Including the editorial voices and dialogues, which the research already benefited from, also called for new modes of structuring the material and presenting aesthetic choices, and thereby influenced the visual identity of the project itself with other media (podcast, objects, and moving image).

Anna and I felt a shared responsibility towards the research's material, for it to find its final form as a book. In the process of sharing material and exchanging ideas on how the research could be visualised, we found the excitement to work together, and the grounds on which to do so. Apart from sharing the responsibility for the visual outcome, the collaboration also resonated with both of our divergent practices. By exploring the various projects that we had previously been working on throughout our experiences as designers and makers, we found a way to help, learn, and benefit from each other. The collaboration became a sort of 'intersection between the commons and the underground' on various levels, Agustina Andreoletti, "Shadow Publishing", 2 as described in Agustina Andreoletti's *Shadow Publishing*, during professionalised education at the Sandberg

Instituut, the privatisation of knowledge and material, and later during our collaboration with Onomatopee – all in a generous exchange.

Through the making of our self-constructed archive (consisting of shared digital drives which included raw moving-image footage, audio recordings, photographs, documents, letters, etc.), we re-shuffled, divided, and re-contextualised the material into a new filed system. We started to make new connections; aesthetic strategies on how to read and how to encounter the material on page spreads. We started to create building blocks between the images and texts. These moments of sharing between Anna and I with our self-constructed archive, with our material, our knowledge, and our experiences within the design field, allowed for experimentation, design interventions, different kinds of knowledge-production, and even misinterpretations, where other 'realities' and narratives could unfold themselves on the pages of the InDesign document and other printed matter. The re-location (moving from one self-constructed archive folder to another) helped us with structuring the format of the book, and brought new ways of deciding content. This is implied in the creation of our podcast, *Snowblindness Podcast Series,* and the structure of the image-flow in the book. Anna being outside of the family (EM, Father, and I) also helped with regard to 'seeing clearly', and introduced a professional distance to the images and the subject.

From the beginning we were interested in creating new narratives by having one photograph followed by another sequence of images or empty spaces that would spark a tension and dialogue on the topics treated in the texts. With this composition it created a narrative leap that allowed multiple images to be seen and sensed as one connected entity, Vanthuyne, "Fiction as a Visual Strategy in the Photobook," 103-104. and created the feeling of one 'storyline' containing a plurality of voices, while still giving space for new encounters in the empty spaces.

Since I am not a trained graphic designer, I have learned about graphics mostly through working with Anna. In dialogue about how she interacts with materials, grids, typography, fonts, etc., our collaboration became a sort of graphic education for me, giving me the possibility to navigate, with her, in the graphic domain and logic both on screen and in print.

The collaboration started thanks to a tutor of ours at the Sandberg Instituut who suggested that I start a collaboration with a trained graphic designer in order to make decisions regarding what to keep and what to leave out of my research when producing printed media. In the early stages, Anna had been interested in the material and the subjects I was investigating, so I invited her to be a part of the *Snowblindness* project and she, to my great delight, accepted. Anna did not only contribute with a graphic 'service' to the project, but she became a collaborator. Anna joined the project with an agenda, too: to develop meaningful collaborations in the sculpting of printed matter. This created a need and a space for implementing new forms of negotiation and interaction with the subject, research, and its material. This is also something that Carmen Dusmet Carrasco recognises in her work *The Swimming Pool,* Carmen Dusmet Carrasco. 'The Swimming Pool,' https://vimeo.com/510747679. which she talked about in the *Snowblindness Podcast Series* in April 2021, referring to the collaboration with composer Lola de la Mata:

029.JPG

"I realised that I wasn't working with somebody that was basically providing a service for me, I was working with another artist. I wasn't working actually – I was collaborating. I think it took me a bit of time to understand that as much as these are my images and this is my mum and this is my movie, the moment that I brought Lola into the project, it was also her project. It was just a bit hard for me to let go in terms of deciding what was fading and what wasn't. But I guess once I realised you're not working with the service-provider, you just have to believe the fact that also the project is not hermetic to your own experience and I think a really beautiful thing was also that we – it felt that we – could kind of understand what certain images and what certain editing did to us, but then that was, like, translated in very different ways for both of us. I think allowing her own voice in her own way of interpreting the images that I was working with... I think it really transformed the film into something that I was not expecting. So, I think it took a while for me to let go of my initial idea of what I thought the film had to be. It was an intense collaboration, but it was great." *Snowblindness Podcast Series* 'Let's talk about how it is to collaborate with your mum' in conversation with Carmen Dusmet Carrasco.

The collaboration between Anna and I took its first steps by being an exchange of references and material, to then brainstorming what could be interesting for the visual concept of the book and for the continually evolving research. Through several moments of discussing content, material, meaning, and collaboration, we quickly found our way together, understanding how this research could be sculpted in an honest, sensitive, and reflective manner, while giving agency to the findings to unfold new realities and voices throughout the book, and still maintaining a certain level of opacity towards the contributors' shared narratives and reflections.

[April 20, 2020, 20.56] Anna Bierler:
gudruuuuuun! how long is this shitty upload!
i am excited and want to see things!

[April 20, 2020, 21.57] Gudrun Havsteen-Mikkelsen:

yes! i am so sorry - this seems to take ages! have moved on to we-transfer. you will probably receive an email the next half hour still working on the google drive – massive amount of time left before it is uploaded

[April 21, 2020, 11.26] Anna Bierler:

if it doesnt work you can also just send me
few things, you think are most important

[April 21, 2020, 11.33] Gudrun Havsteen-Mikkelsen:

i have tried to separate the two different sources. in public (dropbox) and private (google drive)

[May 5, 2020, 11.44] Gudrun Havsteen-Mikkelsen:

dear anna hope you had a good birthday sunday! i have the content order in written words, not yet visualised. you would like some kind of image visualisation as well to work with for the draft when we talk with anja next tuesday?

[May 5, 2020, 11.57] Anna Bierler:

nice!
no its fine if you send me a list -- and may
text and then i can take it from there and
you sth before friday so we can discuss it

[May 11, 2020, 16.12] Anna Bierler:

ciao gudrun! developed the layout further
did a few things: i got rid of the colours for
now because i think there is enough going
with text and also the very different styles
pictures
there are two main things: a vertical line
of for text and a horizontal line for images
images can lay on top of each other, to also
point to the direction of "the paper stack"
text can also disturb each other
on the text pages there are small images,
like footnotes, that can be found again on
image pages
ok!
i'm very excited about what you think
is it too boring for you now?
ah and what is also important: text is cut
sometimes showing that there cannot be a
clear objective look into history

[May 22, 2020, 11.14] Gudrun Havsteen-Mikkelsen:

dearest anna! hope you are good! i am done with the file. still some images needs to be filled in and texts need to be edited/translated but the basics are there. but let me know if this is not enough for you to work with.

[May 23, 2020, 09.26] Anna Bierler:

my idea of beauty

[May 23, 2020, 09.27] Gudrun Havsteen-Mikkelsen:
damn, what a grid!

[May 23, 2020, 09.27] Anna Bierler:
yes!
and i always change the colours
when i'm back in june i can show you how it's
done if you want
i think it's nice if this collab is also about
knowledge exchange

[May 5, 2020, 09.31] Gudrun Havsteen-Mikkelsen:
gree, storytelling and myths are also kind
n exchange! but yes tell me what you want
to learn from me also.

[July 18, 2020, 11.14] Gudrun Havsteen-Mikkelsen:
hat. but history is also a solid streamline
events. the images are a documentation of
is there, but also what is not-there. when
ade the white box in the image document
I wanted to make it correspond to the text
layout. but i am wondering if too much is
ering. showed it to a couple of people and
ey were a bit hard to convince. it has really
en a puzzle to put it together, because the
fferent image texts also talk to each other,
if there is not space on a page, let's say if
put in a white box on the page before and
it around, it can change a lot on the next
69 pages ... does it makes sense?
you know how "visible"/present the white
boxes are on the text pages...?
can also talk (tomorrow or monday) if it's
better to have a dialogue about this ...

[July 18, 2020, 11.18] Anna Bierler:
i agree and i totally think that it's a crazy
puzzle and a lot of work to put together
– but i rather also go this extra round and
rather work more on it to make it really nice :)
i showed it also to two people and they were
more for the white boxes
yes! skype about it tomorrow would work for
me si si!

An important factor in our collaboration was the urge to publish the book as printed matter. This was important for three reasons; firstly pertaining to how we saw our design practices evolve and how a published book could benefit our different practices, secondly due to the urgency of our collaboration and its final outcome as a book, and thirdly, due to the need to experiment and translate the research into a printed publish media, that could all at once guide the form, layout, and content. Vanthuyne, "Fiction as a Visual Strategy in the Photobook," 110. Another perception of ours, shared with Minh-ha's writings, was that 'unpublished writings do stink. A publication means the breaking of a first seal, the end of a "no-admitted" status, [...] and the start of a possible sharing with the unknown other – the reader, whose collaboration with the writer alone allows the work to come into full being.' Minh-ha, *Woman, Native, Other*, 8. We wanted to publish the artistic research and its material, as we believed *Snowblindness* had the right to exist and the right to question, while sharing our work, the process, and collaboration for more than two years. Still, when making something public, other concerns around privacy, opacity, ethics, and copyright invariably came into play, as is treated in the chapter

ARCHIVES & EVIDENCE,

especially when considering personal material, and/or the levels of intimacy cultivated during the video and sound recordings between 2019 and 2021 with Father.

Making this book engaged us as designers in dialogue about how we understand and interact with archives, and also how we can invite family members into our practices, and thereby also include our own backgrounds in our work, making it autoethnographic. In the process of revisiting the various image, sound, and text material, it became an urgent concern of ours to explore and reveal embedded struggles in any design process; the ethics behind personal encounters when making work public. The act of publishing can in itself be seen as a testimony to the archive, and we discussed the embedded paradoxes of re-contextualising material in a book format. However, at the same time the relationship between publishing and leaking has never been in a more critical state than it is now, Dekker, "Permeable Archive," 219. as we have seen information escaping institutions, regimes etc. For that reason, we saw an opportunity to strengthen the process by making *Snowblindness* public, by sharing the content in the form of a book containing a plurality of voices and reflections, allowing the spectator to interact and comment on the content or write new stories. We saw that this option – a materialised research in a physical form – provided a way for us to stay with the questions and to continue to debate the narratives and media while leaving space for multiple interpretations. It was an opportunity to be leaving spaces for opacity for the spectator (and the contributor), without giving a platform to expose comments and edits as in the digital domain (where everything is accessible and circulating). One could say that we encountered our own paradox when not making all information free or transparent in an accessible format. This also became quite present when unexpected demands arose, for example leaving conversations between the descendants, Gyldendal, and Netflix out of this book just before the first typesetting. We decided then to cover those conversations with metallic ink. Based on our concerns and fears of causing conflicts, for whatever reason in relation to EM or his work, we chose to reveal and sculpt the research in a printed form and insisted again on opacity for the involved contributors and the spectators in the materialisation. We insisted on the appearance of dialogues, edits, and comments inside the book, and to work *with* the paradox, as a design challenge and obstruction.

In our dialogues, Anna and I reflected on various ways of producing and publishing *Snowblindness*. We discussed the impacts of timelines and the policies of publishing, and how this could bring challenges with regards to the appearance of the book.

What is a book? Is a book papers bound together with openings and endings, openings and endings, etc.? Should the content be stacks of paper? Should it have a binding, a spine, or none of it? We discussed what it means that the production of a book will always have some sort of fixed timeline. The design choices and decision-making *around* the book became highly relevant to the content *in* the book. We discussed various typefaces, font sizes, and placements of footnotes, images, and sources – and empty margins and 'white' spaces. We wanted to draw attention to feminist practices, proper crediting, the importance of paying for work. We began to include critics connected to the subject, and divide roles for further translations and voices of the subject and 'landmarks'. We planned how we could include other media to support our content in the book; broadcasts and newsletters. Meanwhile, I applied for funding, and we established contacts with publishers for the production and the distribution of the book at quite an early stage. We discussed how this book could challenge our ideas to develop into something that others would relate to as well, as in its first appearance it could seem like 'navel-gazing'. However, our mission was to be 'navel-expanding', and to create something that would be relevant for others too, while reaching into a design discipline. All of the above concerns were constantly present as a huge part of our reflections on our vision of the book and its various modes of collaborative production.

Based on the findings in the research and the embedded conflicts within the material, we began to make a strategy and logic on grids, sizes, and interaction between images and texts on the pages, by sketching horizontal and vertical '(story)lines'. As the written content was being formed and the self-constructed archives as a whole were being shared, we decided to let the texts and images coexist, as two interconnected narrated stories. These interconnected stories would link, cross-reference, and be in dialogue with each other in the image texts as the content would be connected through referenced numbers in the

IMAGE INDEX

where sources, origin, and credits would be revealed.

We discussed ways of receiving content. We discussed that there is often not only one way to interact with a book, and that we wished to guide the reader differently, through a rhizomatic reading, 'Rhizomatic' reading allows for multiple, non hierarchical entry and exit points in data representation and interpretation. which could be made possible by linking and cross-referencing images, texts, and other media. This was essential to our ability to shift from the notion of a linear way of understanding and reading, to reading the content as a contradictory flux of signs and meanings, Cramerotti,

Aesthetic Journalism, 70. and gave us an opportunity as both makers and spectators to think, design, and read differently.

We talked about the 'white spaces' or 'empty spaces' in the book, 'White spaces' meaning, in this context, empty spaces on the pages referencing snow, and the eye disease where you are blinded and only see white. and how they functioned as a synopsis, corresponding to the notion of 'snowblindness' when 'not seeing clearly or not seeing at all', and how this 'blindness' has occurred throughout colonial history-writing and 'collective memories'. The 'white spaces' visualised an understanding before it was put into words for us. We experienced that the 'white spaces' had a similar function to margins when reading through the book's 'storyline' as implemented in the final version of the book. It was these spaces of emptiness that allowed us to see other interpretations of history and to hear new voices in the silence – a silence that, especially in Greenland, has been sustained by shame and trauma. The notion of allowing new voices to be heard worked as a comment on and a critique of 'collective memory'. Mapping the 'white spaces' Referring to Kimberlé Crenshaw's book title *Mapping the Margins: Intersectionality, Identity Politics, and Violence Against Women of Color* from 1991. helped us to define and question the design decisions and edits of the book. The 'white spaces' functioned like a landscape – a map – of memories. And the book somehow became an agent that could tell us something, not only about the research as it took shape, but about the questioning of our own positions and practices.

As the 'white spaces' interrupt the narratives in the texts and the fixed grid on the page, the footnotes do something similar, and should not be overlooked. The footnotes play a crucial part in the dialogue and content, as they function as an editorial voice in conversation, reflection, and as inspiration. The footnotes in *Snowblindness* can be compared with the comments one writes in the margins in the pages of a book; comments that one wishes to return to, or reflections one simply feels the urge to add in the attempt to remember and, crucially, to make the content relevant to oneself. Just as the creators of a book cannot control how the content will be received, it is also difficult to control the spectators' interaction with the book's format, margins, and 'white spaces'. Anna and I discussed how we could invite the spectator to take part in the reflections, conversations, and semi-fictional texts in order to challenge the epistemic violence of 'collective memory' that indicates the silencing of the colonial other, as Gayatri Chakravorty Spivak also talks about in her article *Can the Subaltern Speak?: Reflections on the History of an Idea.* We discussed how the various footnotes, 'white spaces', and interconnected patchy sections could contribute to a broader understanding and experimentation for us with regard to what it means to decolonise design practices. We discussed how aesthetics could guide interaction with the book, and how we, in collaboration, could remove a 'blindfold' without practising the same mechanisms that we sought to challenge and change; previously universal design mechanisms that were dictated by the Western world, and mechanisms of modernist and postwar heritage that rest on colonial and imperialist foundations, Mareis and Paim, *Design Struggles*, 15. as discussed in *Design Struggles.*

Finally, the collaboration with Anna on the visual language – of intertwined and diverse materials and connections – became a sort of a meta-medium that shaped a world of images, logics, and structures. Matthew Fuller, "Nobody knows what a book is any more" in *Archive has left the building. Report from Gutenberg Galaxy (Blaker)*, eds. Karin Nygård and Ellef Prestsæter (Oslo: Blaker gml. meieri, 2017), 8. It guided the project as a whole; the moments of sharing, editing, and dividing roles within the collaboration throughout the research, execution, and possibly in the afterlife of the book.

Trust is the basis for sharing content. The collaboration with Father was essential to this project, however there was always a certain element of risk when sharing the research findings with him. From the beginning, my assumption was that Father would never accept a critical investigation into the colonial actions of his beloved grandfather and his deeds in Greenland, and the implications of these stories when communicated by others. I thought that 'trust' could be questioned, and access to the material about EM, Greenland, and Nordic colonialism denied. My assumptions were very wrong. Our collaboration was based on respect and solidarity for and with the ethical positions and subjects we discussed. As the 'domestic ethnographer' acknowledges, collaborations with close family members bring other considerations of care and involvement into the work. This is something Anna and I discussed in conversation with Carmen Dusmet Carrasco in the *Snowblindness Podcast Series* regarding Carmen's collaboration with her mother, and how some moments were similar to the collaboration I had with Father:

173.JPG

Hello, and we're back now. We were ...dering, Gudrun and I, if you could tell us ...ore in terms of collaboration. I mean you ...ollaborated of course with Lola, but then ...f you think about it basically the biggest ...oration of the movie [*The Swimming Pool*] was the ...oration with your mom. I also remember ...ese scenes where your mom like directly ...s to you, and you are not in the frame but ...nd the frame or outside of the frame but ...irectly you are in the frame, and she sort ...irects you. Also there's the scene where ...are standing at some edge, I think it's on ...ountain and looking to the sky, and then ...ur mom says; 'Yeah, I think it's time to go ...', and yeah, I was wondering if you could tell us a bit more about this process.

Carmen: Well, I think luckily the whole process of shooting was not planned. There was no storyboard, nothing was scripted, so that made it kind of OK to deal with, like a lot of those situations you know, where kind of like. I mean obviously, like my mom in her head she had a different conception of what mak a film is, so a lot of times she would for exa ple also be like; ‘film this box with my ear rings,’ you know and I was like; ‘why?’ and would say; ‘because you know then people see the jewellery that I like to wear.’ It’s lik ‘OK mom I’ll do it you know but ...’ Or ther a scene that I actually put in the film but it at the pre-wedding and then she’s like; ‘oh f these shoes and then let’s pretend that they’ for the wedding, but I’m actually not going wear them you know.’ And she actually do end up wearing them at the end. I don’t kno collaborating with her was, I think, ultima the main collaboration between us obvious besides the fact that she was the main subje of the film, you know. I feel like she was rea always kind of ready to go where we had to go to shoot things, no matter how many tim we had to shoot them so she was constantl willing to give her everything 100--200% al the time. I mean, I could constantly also fee how proud she was that I needed her, you know, even if it was just like for this, so I t for me that was like the biggest collaborati I feel that we could unite forces to invest tim together on doing something and kind of striving today, trying to do the best we coul with the means that we had. Apart from tha she obviously had a lot of requests in terms like music that she wanted to be in the film My mom is really into Trance, I’m just goin drop that bomb. She wanted a lot of Trance songs in the film that unfortunately didn’t make it through.

Anna: Yeah but on that note, I’m also wondering, I imagine, you maybe also had a conflict about what to put in the film and what to leave out. I don’t know if I remember correctly, but I think there was like one scene, that she asked you not to put in and you respected that, but maybe you want to speak to that a bit?

Carmen: Yeah I mean I guess this is one examp of where this like embodied annunciated ro of you know being both, kind of like let’s say, filmmaker, outsider framer, but then al really much kind of involved in the actual li reality that is happening in front of you. So there were some conflicts where I really ha to learn how to snap out of the ‘I’m kind of filming-situation’ or ‘the maker perspective’ and really remember that you know, in the end of the day, that she's my mom and I'm her daughter. So there was one scene that got lost in the broken hard drive [a reference to a conversation earlier in the podcast] where we were by the pool and we were sunbathing and then my mom like took her top or bikini part off, because that's how we sunbathe, and then I turned the camera on but as I would have turned the camera on at any other moment, and then my mom all of a sudden she was like, she asked me; 'oh are you filming me?' And then she kind of put her hands on her breasts to cover up, and she got really shy and she was like can you turn it off and I was like; 'but why?' you know, and then we had this kind of discussion where I was like; 'but mom, who cares? Just forget about the camera' you know. I just saw a beautiful image, it wasn't about like the nudity or anything, you know, I just saw an image, that I wanted to capture and then I just left the camera rolling and then my mom kind of pretended that, you know, instead of just arguing with me to turn the camera off, she just pretended that she fell asleep, you know, just pretended to ignore me or something, and then the camera kept rolling and after a while I think she really did forget, you know, that like the camera was there, and we started talking about her family in Chile, and it evolved into a very like intimate kind of personal conversation about, you know, the situation with her family and, yeah, basically like a lot of drama and very bad things were happening at that time with her family, so she kind of just broke down, and I felt also, you know that a part of my brain was kind of like acknowledging the fact that how could this fit into the story, you know, how could this be part of the narrative and then another part of me was almost like feeling guilty for having those thoughts immediately. So that was a bit of a thing to juggle with, and then at some point my mom stood up and she remembered that the camera was on and then she stood out of the frame and she was crying a lot and she just says, you can hear her in the back, like asking me; 'can you please not put this in the film, and just turn the camera off.' And so then I turned the camera off, and obviously I was never going to use that, but yeah it was one of those examples where you kind of like have to remember also that, you know, you have this double responsibility not only to the world but also to the people that you're working with, especially with her being my mom.

Before it was even my ambition to make a book, the various texts and images I had collected went through several editing moments together with Father. The booklet, *Narratives on EM,* was the dummy for the first phase of the research, through which I shared the different narratives on EM with Father. Here, Father started to comment on, edit, and correct the various stories in the booklet using small yellow sticky-notes. The stories presented in the booklet were either told to me by Father, came from other sources that I had found in written publications about EM, or were stories that I had heard through oral channels among locals in Greenland. This editing moment of the booklet with Father took place for a second time two months later in April 2020. This time, new edits and corrections were made on orange sticky-notes. As the research evolved, along with my acknowledgement of what this project and its methods could ask of a design practice, all the content (the written texts, images, methods of getting access, documenting, editing, and sharing, etc.) was shared with – and ultimately created in collaboration with – Father. For three days in July 2020, in December 2020, and again in July 2021, Father and I sat together to read, discuss, correct, and edit the texts and images all present in this book. It was an experiment and a crucial moment in the argument for making the book, as the Anonymous family members most certainly questioned. The shared moments with Father became a milestone for me while designing and pushed me to further understand the subject. The collaboration presented ethical questions in relation to 'navel-gazing'/'navel-erasing', and notions of family privacy, as also demonstrated above by Carmen. The collaboration also required Father and I to reflect upon what it means to create content as both an active spectator and an active creator (and almost as the indirect subject). In the collaboration with Father, I too encountered moments where my recorder and film camera were rolling, where Father talked, got emotional, and joked, consciously or unconsciously, knowing or not knowing that I could need that material in my moving-image edits, translations, and dialogues for the book. However, honesty and trust were the key elements of the collaboration, and in the making of *Snowblindness*. Having honest and trustful conversations with Father that did not try to normalise or reduce different understandings, but tried to 'focus on the texture of the weave and not on the nature of its components' as Édouard Glissant writes in *Poetics of Relations*, Édouard Glissant, *Poetics of Relation*, trans. Betsy Wing (Michigan: University of Michigan Press, 1997), 190. was a crucial part of the collaborative process, and the key when engaging with Father's memories and communicating my reflections on his perceptions. These moments of sharing content took place nine times from January 2020 to January 2022, from diving into Father's archive to Father being the external editor of the manuscript for *Snowblindness.*

The notion of opacity became an important factor when working with Father's private belongings connected to EM, as opacity is a strategy for making stories visible and invisible, and translating these stories with care. Or, as Agustina Andreoletti writes, 'opacity transforms visibility from a source of vulnerability to the active production [the publication *Snowblindness*] of a visible but unreadable image.' Andreoletti, "Shadow Publishing," 7. Opacity, or the right to opacity, was always at stake when discussing with Father the material and narratives in question together with the need to publish the research.

Throughout the making of this book (from February 2020 and onwards), Father was informed about what my intentions were in relation to our collaboration, whether going through his archive with him, interviewing him, filming him, or editing with him. Throughout the research I strived to be caring in our conversations, particularly in relation to uncomfortable narratives, and before and after recording I always asked for his consent for me to use the material.

I wanted to practise the concept of opacity when recording as a strategy to rethink the relations between what remains visible and what is invisible. Father knew that he could control what he would keep 'invisible' and how he could avoid certain stories being recorded or further discussed, and what should not be included in this book of texts and images. As the interview footage was in English, which Father can speak fluently, he knew which parts of the footage I could use for my moving image translations, and which parts I could not use (when he spoke Danish). In these moments of changing language it was as if the discussed matter moved out of the viewfinder's frame. In our conversations Father and I, together with the other contributors involved in the research, had the right to opacity. I acknowledge that some conversations (with institutions or companies) have been more exhibited than others, due to their content, while other conversations were treated more with care, due to their sensitive or private nature. In the moments where sensitive content was captured in the camera or recorder, being the daughter of Father and being able to continue the beautiful collaboration meant that, for me, the right to keep certain things invisible was valued higher than the need to expose all material. I would argue that this does not necessarily support the agenda of challenging the 'collective memory' fully, but more the urgency to practise opacity towards contributors, and honour their investment and willingness to collaborate. For that matter I could have involved Father and Father's stories much more, thanks to his high-level storytelling capacity.

As the conversation below indicates, when Father became an active collaborator in the *Snowblindness* work, it allowed the research to continuously ask questions of the content, while still insisting on opacity throughout, which was important for understanding each other. The conversations are extracts of hours and hours of conversation with Father from the period of February 2020 to January 2022 about memories of childhood, EM, colonialism, Greenland, and on the matter of commenting on narratives – narratives that either support or challenge the perception of the 'collective memory':

Father: There were places where nobody had
so he wanted to discover the land. In those
days there were places on Earth that were
white, and that was land that had not been
colonised or not been visited, you see.

Father: This a good picture.

Me: I got acquainted with a narrative through this book, and it says that EM and some other people shot these thirty-eight Inuits ...

Father: He didn't shoot anybody, but he moved them to Scoresbysund (Ittoqqortoormiit).

Me: Yeah.

Father: That could be the misunderstanding,

Me: And the designer's practice ... It's my understanding that it's always creating work in between what's fake and what's real, and dealing with the especially colonial ...

Father: Times ...

Me: ... Issues.

Father: My father writes to EM
"You see poorly, but you are not blind".

Father: It can be fake then?

Me: Yeah.

Father: I'm not so keen on fake news.

Father: Maybe we should go through this [the dummy booklet *Narratives on EM*] together?

Me: Yes.

Father: Shall I start putting notes in here?

Asking Father to help with *Snowblindness* was an act of love. Father's engagement with the project happened out of interest and love, and I am very thankful for that, even though there were moments in which certain information was difficult to confront, which, in light of the events discussed, was due to our generational gap and political differences in our understandings of Danish colonialism in Greenland over the last 300 years, and how that was situated in the Greenlandic society today. Though my perception is that these conversations also really moved Father and his interpretation of Nordic colonialism.

In the process of working with both Father and Anna, the moments of sharing were essential not only for the making of the book, but also for the research and for my practice as a whole. Sharing content, valuing opacity, but still trying to be transparent as a designer and an editor when working with different narratives became a way to understand the context and the situations that the work operated in. In the process of editing, a common understanding evolved, which created a respectful relationship between the different parties, and allowed for a space where new or other stories, values, and opinions were discussed. Even though neither opacity nor transparency were a high priority at the beginning of the research due to my own assumptions and fears of harming people I loved and respected, the opacity (and additional transparency) nevertheless found its way through writing, making visuals, and sculpting a graphical structure. Through an unexpected understanding in an unexpected open dialogue with Father, (a dialogue I thought was not possible because of the generational gap, but became possible due to a foundation of trust and solidarity), and in collaboration with Anna (even in moments of confusion and lack of vision), trust and opacity became the main ingredients in the argument for continuing *Snowblindness,* and for continuing to question the perceptions and role of 'collective memory'. Leaving comments and edits in collaboration became the underlying reason for making the research, publishing the book, and developing the strategies necessary for doing so in order to talk about storytelling, colonialism, Netflix, and EM.

Since it is my story and reflections combined with several other voices, the book values co-authoring; the act of several actors – a plurality of contributors – deciding what to leave out and what to include. Through these co-authoring edits, my own perspective on design was challenged. In collaboration, we developed strategies to increase the visibility of what is invisible Andreoletti, "Shadow Publishing," 11. to the 'collective memory'. *Snowblindness* tried through its collaborations to bring diverse sources and narratives into an artistic research and design practice. As *Snowblindness* wishes to include other narratives and voices, it tries to make cross references between disciplines and material. It is a practice that wishes to decolonise through conversation.

EM was a polar scientist. He knew that there was gold and other valuable minerals in the Greenlandic mountain-material and under the icecap. EM was my great-grandfather, and I have his eyebrows (source from Father).

In February 2020, Father wrote: The last picture taken of EM.

169.JPG

170.JPG

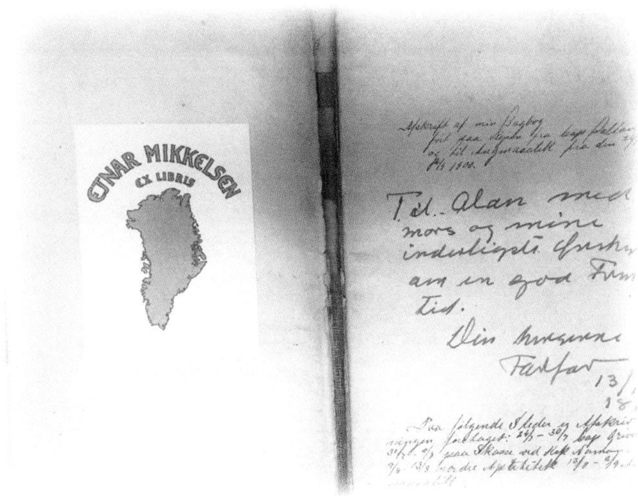

171.JPG

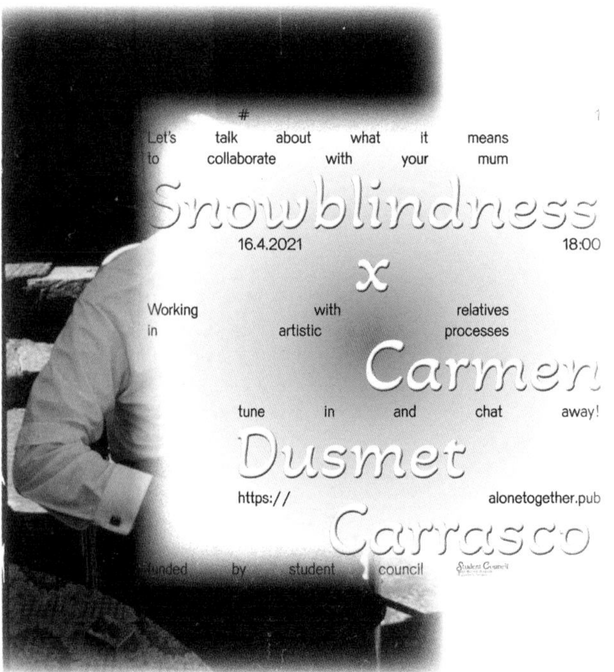
#
1
Let's talk about what it means
to collaborate with your mum
Snowblindness
16.4.2021
18:00
x
Working with relatives
in artistic processes
Carmen
tune in and chat away!
Dusmet
https://
alonetogether.pub
Carrasco
funded by student council

172.JPG 173.JPG 174.JPG

In 1997 Pia Arke visited her birthplace, Scoresbysund/Ittoqqortoormiit, for the first time in 35 years since she had moved away at the age of four. The trip marked the beginning of her extensive research for her 2003 book work *Stories from Scoresbysund*, and with her she brought copies of some of the more than 1,000 photographs taken by Danish colonists and migrant workers in Scoresbysund during the period 1924-32 that she had located in Denmark. Arke had no personal recollection of her birthplace and found that the settlement's history was also absent in the collective memory of many of its inhabitants. So with the help of different town members, she set about identifying the people and events in the photographs, and exhibited the result at Ittoqqortoormiit Kalersungaasiviat [Ittoqqortoormiit Local Museum] in 2001, when she made yet another trip to the town (see photo above). Arke's intention was for the photographs to form the basis for a very first archive in Ittoqqortoormiit. She also had plans to ship her large pinhole camera to the town, but died before she was able to carry out her plans. Collection of Søren Arke Petersen. Photo: Unknown

114

Stories from Scoresbysund: The Assertive Force of Method

by Kuratorisk Ak

Taking its departure in Pia Arke's principal work, the Danish-language book *Stories from Scoresbysund: Photographs, Colonisation and Mapping* (published by Borgen Publishers in 2003 and republished in a trilingual edition (English, Greenlandic, Danish) by Kuratorisk Akti in conjunction with the 2010 *TUPILAKOSAURUS* exhibition), this section considered the asse tive force of Arke's method. What was it that her artistic research succeeded in saying some-thing decisive about?

The section was, save your reverence, filled with main works: *Dummy* (1997-2003) (see pp. 128-129), the comprehensive image and text work which, as its title indicates, is a direct precursor for *Stories from Scoresbysund* and a work of art in its own right: the photographic work *Telegraphy* (1996) (see pp. 122-123); and a reconstruction of the lost 'coffee-recycling-work' *Soil for Scoresbysund* (1998) (see pp. 125 and 271).

About the last mentioned work, Arke writes in a letter to her co-author of *Stories from Scoresbysund*, Stefan Jonsson: "One may say that the work is anecdotal because it is linked to my stay in Scoresbysund, where my sister-in-law noticed me throwing out the used coffee grounds."[1]

The coffee had to be thrown out, but through the window – to compost on the town's otherwise barren stony ground. "I thought that was interesting in various ways. Scoresbysund was founded there where it is situated today because of a misunderstanding. And with the whole idea of Denmark's rights to Greenland's underground, etc., the work has quite a lot of depth historically. But it can also be viewed without knowing these things."[2]

With 151 old coffee filters wound about with string and laid out in a square, Arke practices the art of the impossible: she reaches a potentiality, a space of possibility without a predetermined goal. A space where linear history cannot be written, but where temporary histories are negotiated and created; histories that depart from the logic of conventional time to embrace subjective experience.

She articulates the silence that surrounds the bond between Greenland and Denmark. This is clearly seen in a work like *Telegraphy*, which addresses how t meeting of opposites and the communication acro distances and abysses change forever those, who m and that which is communicated. And she articula the silencing of the fact that the bond between pas and future – the progress of history and what unde pins the present – ties itself into knots when it has find room for individualized, subjective time.

Arke remains cool and does not try to cut the kno with a heroic stroke of the sword, even though th sword that was called *postcolonial studies* was on offer from abroad. Instead, she slogged away in o work after the other to loosen that knot and, if pos sible, arrange it a little more humanely.

Stories from Scoresbysund is in many ways Arke crowning work. The work was occasioned in 199 her finding of four photo albums in the home of th son of Danish ship master and polar explorer Ejn Mikkelsen, whom she laconically called "the inve tor of Scoresbysund town,"[3] as it was he who was charge of the colonization of Scoresbysund/Ittoq toormiit with inhabitants from Ammassalik (toda Tasiilaq). The photos put her on the track not onl lost time but also of a de facto historical lacuna.

In and around the Danish capital, Arke unearthe thousands of archival and amateur photos taken the town by colonists and migrant workers from D mark and populated by unidentified Greenland- subjects. But since they were not provided with e proper names or place names, "the photographs in principle valueless," as she wrote.[4]

So Arke set about identifying them. Initially, she interested in the period around 1924-32, i.e. from

In January 2020, Gudrun wrote: Ask XM if she knows about Pia Arke.

Kuratorisk Aktion on Pia Arke's work: Arrange it a little more humanely [...] The work was occasioned in 1996 by her finding of four photo albums in the home of the son of the Danish ship master and polar explorer EM, whom she laconically called "the inventor of Scoresbysund town".

In May 2020, Gudrun wrote: Pia Arke did never acknowledge to the public that she got help from EM's son, and only because of EM's photo album she was able to make her work *Dummy* and *Stories from Scoresbysund: Photographs, Colonisation and Mapping*.

In November 2020, Gudrun wrote: Maybe it is not for me to judge what and how Pia Arke tells or perceives history. But rather to give other actors the space to comment and ask questions, and the opportunity to debate the 'collective memory'.

Kuratorisk Aktion on Pia Arke's work: She articulates the silence that surrounds the bond between Greenland and Denmark. This is clearly [...] how the meeting of opportunities and communication across distances and abysses change forever those, who meet, and which is communicated [...] the bond between the past and future – the progress of history and what underpins the present [...]

Pia Arke in Tupilakosaurus: "Scoresbysund was founded there where it is situated today because of a misunderstanding."

EM was a polar explorer. He got his gravestone from his colony Scoresbysund, Greenland. EM died in 1971 and is buried in Ordrup, Denmark. EM was my great-grandfather (source from Father).

176.JPG

177.JPG

Father said: "Well, I am not so keen on fake news."
Gudrun said: "Yes."
Father said: "It can be fake then?"
Gudrun said: "issues."
Father said: "times."

n February 2020 in the moving image *Aftermath: Narratives on EM* Gudrun said: "It is ny understanding in the designer's practice :hat it is always creating work in-between vhat is fake and what is real ... and dealing vith, especially colonial."

;coresbysunds ældste ıfslører buste af Miki

Scoresbysundime utorkaunerssap ulèrpâ Ejnar Mikkelsen-ip kinâta kiperordlugo âssinga Mikkelsenivdle nalia pexkinginine pivdlugo najûsineusimângilax — agdl.: Ole Juhl, âss.: Grete Juhl, Scoresbysund

Miki-p åssinga ulêrnekart

Ny overlæge

Otte har bestået fiskerifagligt grundkursus

12 kvinder på rengøringskursus

178.JPG

EM was a captain. He had a swinging temperament and could have tyrannical behaviour. EM was my great-grandfather (source from Frederiksen's book).

179.JPG

180.JPG

181.JPG

EPILOGUE

Snowblindness – Let's talk about storytelling, colonialism, Netflix, and my great-grandfather is a multitude of images, narratives, and conversations. It is a translation of materials and reflections that contains many various stories connected to a personal colonial past in the North (Nordic colonialism) but which also speaks to the methods used in editorial design practices of today, and especially practices of collaboration.

The making of the book *Snowblindness* provided tools for me as a designer with which to navigate the notions of research, writing, and visualising, and helped me to implement these into my design practice. The work included reflections on how to research; how to document; how to make selections, edits, comments; how to formulate, collaborate, listen, visualise, present, and debate content with care. As the book tries to indicate, the texts do not appear in a 'logical' order, but instead are presented as a contradictory flux of signs that are trying to engage the reader by leaving 'empty' white spaces for comments, edits, and opacity. The flows of images/storylines work in the same way, as they suggest another way to read stories and to understand narratives by suggesting other 'realities'. This re-contextualisation, the interpretation of the past and the present, is essential for design practices that seek to contribute more pluralistic perspectives and include un(der-)heard stories. The designer is well-placed to carry out this task, due to their artistic and interdisciplinary skills, by working in collaboration and paying attention to the visual and audial communication and meanings for the receiver on the 'realities' of the past and the future.

The ability to draw connections between 'realities', and the act of displacement of archived material as it is discussed in this book, can be seen as tools to challenge 'collective memories' and to include new voices and narratives. This is the essence of this design translation. It is the vision of *Snowblindness* to reflect on design methodologies and on how visual interventions are situated in design research. It is my understanding that the contemporary designer's task is to visualise possible futures, to move between experimental scenarios. It is my understanding that the contemporary designer's task is to draw lines and connections with different narratives and debate those. This research is debating the mechanisms within a design process and practice, though still to a large extent this design work is incomplete, as it could have involved more sources (the inaccessible sources too) and a larger variety of contributors. Openly, *Snowblindness* leaves space for comments, edits, and opacity. It debates how design can be seen as an act of decolonising our futures, through aesthetic storytelling and listening.

Thanks to the collaboration with Anna, this book creates space for a multiplicity of voices and visions, both *in* and *outside* of itself, by using and debating the methodologies of Aesthetic Journalism and autoethnography. In this collaboration, *Snowblindness* became an argument for staying reflective and constantly questioning our own positions and practices of research and design-making. *Snowblindness* was made with curiosity and care for the collaborations, the topics, and the methods that evolved. On this note, it is important to mention that my family and I are on good terms, and that I have tried to uphold and respect the right to opacity for the people who did not want to be involved in this project. *Snowblindness* was made with love.

In February 2020 in the moving image *Aftermath: Narratives on EM* Gudrun said: "I got acquaintance with that narrative through this book, and it says that EM, ooh ... and some other people, shot these thirty-eight inuits."

In February 2020, Father said: "He did not shoot anybody. But he moved them to Scroesbysund (Ittoqqortoormiit) that could be the misunderstanding, yes."

The visual material is from various archives and private collection;
Arktisk Institut, Greenland National Museum and Archive, Olaf Ejnar Havsteen-Mikkelsen private collection and home, Pia Arke's book *Scoresbysund historier*, Nanna Ánike Nikolajsen's film *Scoresbysund – kolonien er mit eget barn*, Kurt Frederiksen's book *Kaptajn Ejnar Mikkelsen*, and Ejnar Mikkelsen's own publications and images.

Gudrun,
I spell my
name with
an Einar like
your younger
brother.

February 2020, Father wrote: Gudrun, I spell
ny name with Einar like your
ounger brother.

184.JPG

185.JPG

In January 2020, Gudrun wrote: But true stories? She does not even cred the source she [Pia Arke] has the material from.

Kuratorisk Aktion on Pia Arke's work: The decision meant that Den mark, which had not only planted its flag but also it colonised subjects at the spot, could make the fina moves in a game that gave the nation sovereignty ove 'all' Greenland. A collage of personal stories soundin from the past and the present, from inside and outsid Greenland.

In January 2020, Gudrun wrote: Because they were starving else where.

Kuratorisk Aktion on Pia Arke's work: ... Her investigation int what happened to the Greenlanders, who ha been promised a life of plenty (good hunting) if the would leave Ammassalik/Tasiilaq and settl in the Danish colony.

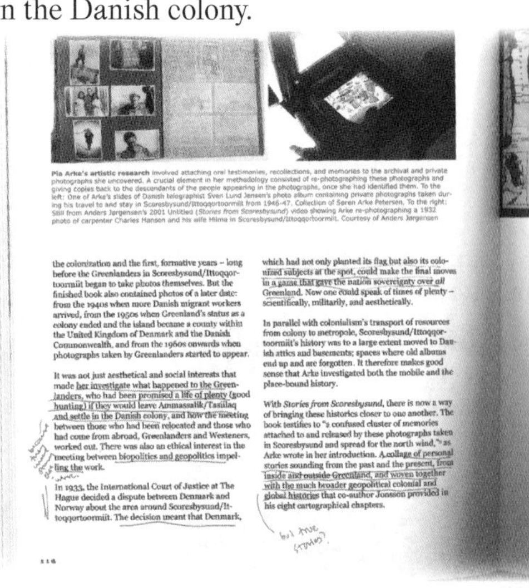

Pia Arke's artistic research involved attaching oral testimonies, recollections, and memories to the archival and private photographs she uncovered. A crucial element in her methodology consisted of re-photographing these photographs and giving copies back to the descendants of the people appearing in the photographs, once she had identified them. To the left: One of Arke's slides of Danish telegraphist Sven Lund Jensen's photo album containing private photographs taken during his travel to and stay in Scoresbysund/Ittoqqortoormiit from 1946-47. Collection of Søren Arke Petersen. To the right: Still from Anders Jørgensen's 2001 Untitled (*Stories from Scoresbysund*) video showing Arke re-photographing a 1932 photo of carpenter Charles Hansen and his wife Hilma in Scoresbysund/Ittoqqortoormiit. Courtesy of Anders Jørgensen

the colonization and the first, formative years – long before the Greenlanders in Scoresbysund/Ittoqqortoormiit began to take photos themselves. But the finished book also contained photos of a later date: from the 1940s when more Danish migrant workers arrived, from the 1950s when Greenland's status as a colony ended and the island became a county within the United Kingdom of Denmark and the Danish Commonwealth, and from the 1960s onwards when photographs taken by Greenlanders started to appear.

It was not just aesthetical and social interests that made her investigate what happened to the Greenlanders, who had been promised a life of plenty (good hunting) if they would leave Ammassalik/Tasiilaq and settle in the Danish colony, and how the meeting between those who had been relocated and those who had come from abroad, Greenlanders and Westeners, worked out. There was also an ethical interest in the meeting between biopolitics and geopolitics impelling the work.

In 1933, the International Court of Justice at The Hague decided a dispute between Denmark and Norway about the area around Scoresbysund/Ittoqqortoormiit. The decision meant that Denmark, which had not only planted its flag but also its colonized subjects at the spot, could make the final moves in a game that gave the nation sovereignty over *all* Greenland. Now one could speak of times of plenty – scientifically, militarily, and aesthetically.

In parallel with colonialism's transport of resources from colony to metropole, Scoresbysund/Ittoqqortoormiit's history was to a large extent moved to Danish attics and basements; spaces where old albums end up and are forgotten. It therefore makes good sense that Arke investigated both the mobile and the place-bound history.

With *Stories from Scoresbysund*, there is now a way of bringing these histories closer to one another. The book testifies to "a confused cluster of memories attached to and released by these photographs taken in Scoresbysund and spread for the north wind," as Arke wrote in her introduction. A collage of personal stories sounding from the past and the present, from inside and outside Greenland, and woven together with the much broader geopolitical colonial and global histories that co-author Jonsson provided in his eight cartographical chapters.

but true stories?

116

EM was a conqueror. He got milder and softer over the years. EM was my great-grandfather (source from Father).

In February 2020, Father wrote: Me as 9 years old with my Napier tie, taken in 1950.

186.JPG

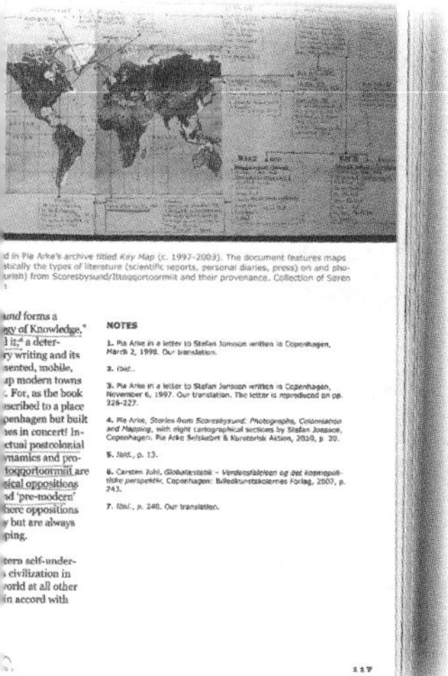

d in Pia Arke's archive titled *Key Map* (c. 1997–2003). The document features maps
atically the types of literature (scientific reports, personal diaries, press) on and pho-
urish) from Scoresbysund/Ittoqqortoormiit and their provenance. Collection of Søren

und forms a
gy of Knowledge,"
l it;[4] a deter-
ry writing and its
sented, mobile,
up modern towns
. For, as the book
scribed to a place
penhagen but built
hes in concert! In-
ctual postcolonial
ynamics and pro-
toqqortoormiit are
sical oppositions
d 'pre-modern'
here oppositions
y but are always
ping.

tern self-under-
civilization in
vorld at all other
in accord with

NOTES

1. Pia Arke in a letter to Stefan Jonsson written in Copenhagen, March 2, 1998. Our translation.

2. *Ibid.*.

3. Pia Arke in a letter to Stefan Jonsson written in Copenhagen, November 6, 1997. Our translation. The letter is reproduced on pp. 226–227.

4. Pia Arke, *Stories from Scoresbysund: Photographs, Colonisation and Mapping*, with eight cartographical sections by Stefan Jonsson, Copenhagen: Pia Arke Selskabet & Kuratorisk Aktion, 2010, p. 20.

5. *Ibid.*, p. 13.

6. Carsten Juhl, *Globalæstetik – Verdensfølelsen og det kosmopolitiske perspektiv*, Copenhagen: Billedkunstskolernes Forlag, 2007, p. 243.

7. *Ibid.*, p. 240. Our translation.

117

In February 2022, film instructor Peter Flinth said: "EM was a very private person, and in that regard, we are very thankful that we can draw on his love relation to Naja."

187.JPG

188.JPG

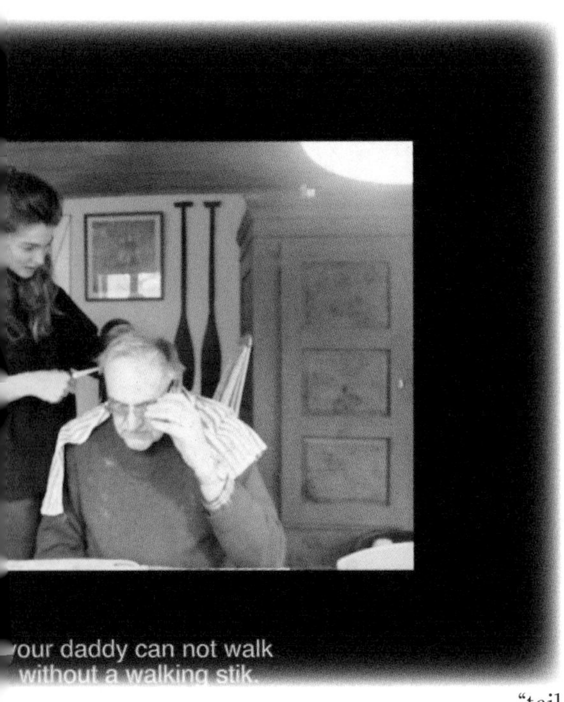

your daddy can not walk
without a walking stik.

In February 2020 in the moving image *Aftermath: Narratives on EM* Father said: "tail tail tit your mother cannot knit, your daddy cannot walk withyt a walking stick." (quoting a childhood poem from Scotland).

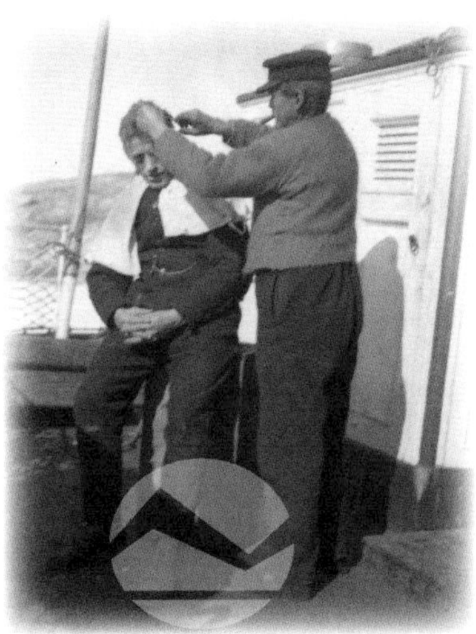

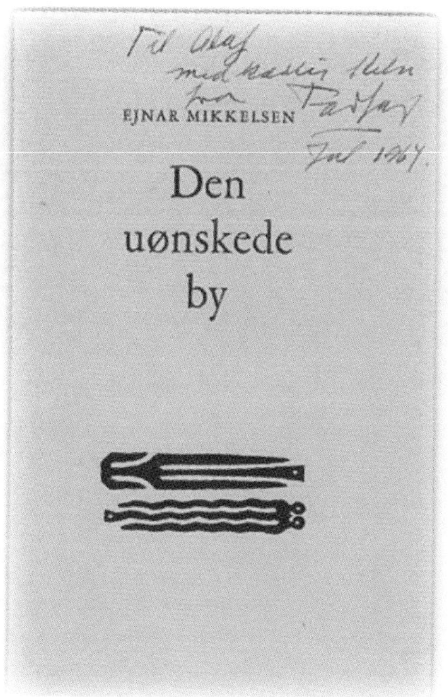

In December 1964, EM wrote: To Olaf with love from grandfather, Christmas 1964.

190.JPG

191.JPG

192.JPG

APPENDIX

FILM
within *Snowblindness* Project

Havsteen-Mikkelsen, Gudrun. *Aftermath: Narratives on EM.* Found footage and own footage, colour and B/W, 4:00 min., 2020.

Havsteen-Mikkelsen, Gudrun. *Dialogue w. EM through Father.* Found footage and own footage, colour and B/W, 01:35 min., 2020.

Havsteen-Mikkelsen, Gudrun. *Process images for the book Snowblindness.* Found footage and own footage, colour and B/W, 01:00 min., 2020.

PODCASTS
within *Snowblindness* Project

Bierler, Anna and Gudrun Havsteen-Mikkelsen. *Snowblindness Podcast Series w. Carmen Dusmet Carrasco #1,* April 16, 2021. https://extraintra.nl/initiative/student-council/event/snowblindness-podcast-series-1.

Bierler, Anna and Gudrun Havsteen-Mikkelsen. *Snowblindness Podcast Series w. Inuuteq Storch #2,* April 30, 2021. https://extraintra.nl/initiative/student-council/event/snowblindness-podcast-series-2.

IMAGES AND OBJECTS
within *Snowblindness* Project

Bierler, Anna. *"Poster" for the Snowblindness Podcast Series w. Carmen Dusmet Carrasco #1, 2021.*

Bierler, Anna (with photography by Inuuteq Storch). *"Poster" for the Snowblindness Podcast Series w. Inuuteq Storch #2, 2021.*

Havsteen-Mikkelsen, Gudrun. *Engraved map of EM's travels in East Greenland in granite* included in the chapter TOP VIEW & INFORMATION CARRIER, 2020.

Havsteen-Mikkelsen, Gudrun. *Frame of wood and glass* included in the chapter NOTIONS ON CANNIBALISM. 2020.

Havsteen-Mikkelsen, Gudrun. *Shrimp-ring of brass and Greenlandic ruby* included in the chapter SHRIMP PARADOX. 2020.

Havsteen-Mikkelsen, Gudrun. *Glasses of plexiglass* included in the chapter I THINK I GOT IT, SNOWBLINDNESS. 2020.

Havsteen-Mikkelsen, Gudrun. *Booklet and development of negatives* included in the chapter ANOTHER SILVA RERUM? 2020.

BOOKS & CHAPTERS IN BOOKS

Alter, Nora M. and Timothy Corrigan. *Essays on the Essay Film.* New York: Columbia University Press, 2017.

Andreoletti, Agustina. "Shadow Publishing: Opacity, Reproduction, Circulation and Legitimation of Knowledges." Postgraduate Thesis, Academy of Media Arts Cologne, 2019.

Arke, Pia. *Scoresbysundhistorier – fotografier, kolonisering og kortlaegning.* Copenhagen: Borgen, 2003.

Arke, Pia. S*tories from Scoresbysund – Photographs, Colonisation and Mapping.* Copenhagen: Pia Arke Selvskabet & Kuratorisk Aktion, 2010.

Bourriaud, Nicolas. *The Radicant.* New York: Lukas & Sternberg, 2009.

Breum, Martin. *Hvis Grønland river sig løs.* Copenhagen: Gyldendal, 2018.

Bryld, Claus, and Anette Warring: *Besaettelsestiden som kollektiv erindring – Historie- og traditionsforvaltning af krig og besaettelse 1945-1997.* Roskilde: Roskilde Universitetsforlag bind 5, 1998.

Carrasco, Carmen Dusmet, "A Matter of Optics." In *We Must Begin Somewhere,* Design Department Issue 5, Master Thesis, Sandberg Instituut, 2020.

Cramerotti, Alfredo. *Aesthetic Journalism: How to Inform Without Informing.* Bristol: Intellect, 2009.

Dekker, Annet, ed. *Lost and Living (in) Archives: Collectively Shaping New Memories.* Amsterdam: Valiz, 2017.

Frederiksen, Kurt. *Ejnar Mikkelsen – En biografi.* Copenhagen: Gyldendal, 2015.

Glissant, Édouard. *Poetics of Relation.* Translated by Betsy Wing. Michigan: University of Michigan Press, 1997.

Gulløv, Hans Christian, ed. *Grønland – Den Arktiske Koloni.* Copenhagen: Gads Forlag, 2017.

Hastrup, Kristen et al. *Ind i verden - en grundbog i antropologisk metode.* Copenhagen: Reitzels Forlag, 2003.

Kalaallit Nunaata Katersugaaivia. *Gustav Holm Samlingen.* Nuuk: Kalaalit Nanatta Katersugaasivia/Grønlands Landsmuseum, 1985.

Koch, Palle. *Kaptajnen.* Viborg: Gyldendal, 1980.

Kuratorisk Aktion. *TUPLIAKSAUROS: An Incomplete(able) Survey of Pia Arke's Artistic Work and Research.* Copenhagen: Kuratorisk Aktion, 2012.

Lewis, G. Malcolm et al. *The History of Cartography,* Vol. 2, Book 3. Chicago: University of Chicago Press, 1998.

Lorusso, Silvio et al., eds. *Here and Now? Explorations in Urgent Publishing.* Amsterdam: Institute of Network Cultures, 2020.

Mareis, Claudia, and Nina Paim, eds. *Design Struggles: Intersecting Histories, Pedagogies, and Perspectives.* Amsterdam: Valiz, 2021.

McDonald, Kevin, and Daniel Smith-Rowsey, eds. *The Netflix Effect: Technology and Entertainment in the 21st Century.* London: Bloomsbury Academic, 2016.

McGhee, Robert. *The Last Imaginary Place: A Human History of the Arctic World.*
Chicago: The University of Chicago Press, 2007.

Mikkelsen, Ejnar. *Farlig Tomandsfaerd.* Copenhagen: Gyldendal, 1962.

Mikkelsen, Ejnar. *Fra Fribytter til Embedsmand.* Copenhagen: Gyldendal, 1957.

Mikkelsen, Ejnar. *Lost in the Arctic.* London: William Heinemann, 1913.

Mikkelsen, Ejnar. *Svundne Tider i Østgrønland – Fra stenalder til atomtid.* Copenhagen: Gyldendal, 1960.

Mikkelsen, Ejnar. *Ukendt Mand til Ukendt Land.* Copenhagen: Gyldendal, 1966.

Minh-ha, Trinh T.. *Woman, Native, Other: Writing Postcoloniality and Feminism.* Bloomington: Indiana University Press, 1989.

Morris, Rosalind C, ed. *Can the Subaltern Speak? Reflections on the History of an Idea.* New York: Columbia University Press, 2010.

Naylor, Simon, and James R. Ryan, eds. *New Spaces of Exploration: Geographies of Discovery in the Twentieth Century.* London: I. B. Tauris, 2010.

Nielsen, Jens. *Dagbogsbreve fra Scoresbysund 1957-59.* Skjern:

Det Grønlandske Selvskab, 2012.

Nygård, Karin, and Ellef Prestsæter, eds. *Archive Has Left the Building. Report from the Gutenberg Galaxy (Blaker)* no. 3. Oslo: Blaker gml. meieri, 2017.

Pouplier, Erik. *Uden for Tredje revle.* Rungsted Kyst: Anders Nyborg AS, 1984.

Renov, Michael. "Domestic Ethnography and the Construction of the 'Other Self'." In *Collecting Visible Evidence,* edited by Michael Renov and Jane Gaines, Chapter 7. Minnesota: University of Minnesota Press, 1999.

Sandell, Hanne. *Kortlaegning af Kulturhistoriske interesser i Jameson Land og Scoresbysund 1982-84.* Nuuk: Kalaallit Nunaata Katersugaasivia/Grønlands Landsmuseum, 1985.

Sontag, Susan. *Regarding the Pain of Others.* London: Penguin Books Ltd, 2019.

Spivak, Gayatri C. *A Critique of Postcolonial Reason.* Cambridge: Harvard University Press, 1999.

Steinberg, Phillip E. et al. *Contesting the Arctic: Politics and Imaginaries in the Circumpolar North.* London: I.B. Tauris, 2015.

Schrijver, Eric. *Copy This Book: An Artist's Guide to Copyright.* Eindhoven: Onomatopee, 2018. eBook edition.

Thompson, Rob. *Manufacturing Processes for Design Professionals.* London: Thames & Hudson, 2012.

Wekker, Gloria. *White Innocence: Paradoxes of Colonialism and Race.* Durham: Duke University Press, 2016.

Wynants, Nele, ed. *When Fact is Fiction: Documentary Art in the Post-Truth Era.* Amsterdam: Valiz, 2020.

ARTICLES & JOUNALS

Agostinho, Daniela. "Archival encounters – rethinking access and care in digital colonial archives." In *Archival Science,* vol. 19. no. 2. (2019): 141-165.

Agostinho, Daniela et al. "Archives that Matter – Infrastructures for Sharing Unshared Histories. An Introduction." In *Nordisk Tidsskrift for Informationsvidenskab og Kulturformidling* vol. 8. nr. 2. (2019): 1-18.

Ahmed, Sara. "A Phenomenology of Whiteness." In *Feminist*

Theory vol. 8 (2) (2007): 149-168. SAGE Publications.

Alves, Barbara Neves. "Relocations – The Idiot as a Figure of Miscommunication" In *Parse Journal* Issue 3 (2016): 85-98.

Christen, Kimberly. "Does Information Really Want to be Free? – Indigenous Knowledge Systems and the Question of Openness." In *International Journal of Communication* 6 (2012): 2870-2893.

Hastrup, Kirsten. "Colonial Moments in Greenland: Mutable Tensions in Contact Zone." In *Itinerario* vol. 43, no. 2 (2019): 243-261.

Kristensen, Monica. "Noget om helte." In *Arktis Louisiana Revy* 54, no. 1 (September 2013): 54-67.

Odumosu, Temi. "The Crying Child – On Colonial Archives, Digitization, and Ethics of Care in the Cultural Commons." In *Current Anthropology* vol. 61, supplement 22 (October 2020): 289-302.

Odumosu, Temi. "What Lies Unspoken – A Remedy for Colonial Silence(s) in Denmark." *In Third Text, Informa UK Limited* (2019): 1-15.

Thisted, Kirsten. "De-framing the indigenous body." In *Nordlit* vol. 29 (2012): 279-298.

Wall, Sarah. "An Autoethnography on Learning about Autoethnography." In *International Journal of Qualitative Methods* 5 (2) (June 2006): 1-12.

WEB RESOURCES
(in order of appearance)

Kjærgaard, Thorkild. "Grønland og Hermod Lannungs private udenrigspolitik." Weekendavisen. February 24, 2017. https://www.weekendavisen.dk/2017-8/boeger/groenland-og-hermod-lannungs-private-udenrigspolitik.

Sontag, Susan. "The Decay of Cinema." The New York Times. February 25, 1996. https://www.nytimes.com/1996/03/17/magazine/l-the-decay-of-cinema-007358.html.

Arrouas, Michelle. "Danske stat lille naturfolk." Information. October 7, 2016. https://www.information.dk/kultur/2016/10/danske-stat-lille-naturfolk.

Ventegodt, Ole. "Danmark ekspeditionen." Den Store Danske Encyklopædi. August 23, 2013. https://denstoredanske.lex.dk/Danmark-ekspeditionen.

Blas, Zach. "Opacities: An Introduction + Biometrics and Opacity: A Conversation." 2016. https://zachblas.info/writings/opacities-introduction-biometrics-opacity-conversation/.

Bierler, Anna, and Gudrun Havsteen-Mikkelsen. "Snowblindness Podcast Series w. Carmen Dusmet Carrasco." Extra Intra, Radio Rietveld. July 9, 2021. https://extraintra.nl/initiative/student-council/event/snowblindness-podcast-series-1.

Danmarks Radio, ritzau. "Nye lufthavne i Grønland bliver realitet midt i politisk drama." August 13, 2019. https://www.dr.dk/nyheder/indland/nye-lufthavne-i-gronland-bliver-realitet-midt-i-politisk-drama.

Dunne, Anthony, and Fiona Raby. "Design for Debate." http://dunneandraby.co.uk/content/bydandr/36/0.

Carrasco, Carmen Dusmet. "The Swimming Pool." 2020. http://www.carmendusmet.net/video.

Havsteen-Mikkelsen, Gudrun. "Aftermath: Narratives on EM." April 14, 2020. https://www.youtube.com/watch?v=jQOcB4Zffts.

Wikipedia. "White Guilt." https://en.wikipedia.org/wiki/White_guilt.

Bierler, Anna, and Gudrun Havsteen- Mikkelsen. "Snowblindness Podcast Series w. Inuuteq Storch." Extra Intra, Radio Rietveld. July 9, 2021. https://extraintra.nl/initiative/student-council/event/snowblindness-podcast-series-2.

Havsteen-Mikkelsen, Gudrun. "Dialogue w. EM through Father." January 25, 2020. https://vimeo.com/388551320.

Wikipedia. "Cartography." https://en.wikipedia.org/wiki/Cartography.

Weiss, Daniel. "Wooden Inuit Maps." Archaeological Institute of America. May/June 2019. https://www.archaeology.org/issues/337-1905/features/7550-maps-greenland-wooden-inuit-maps.

Observatory of Economic Complexity. "Greenland." 2020. https://oec.world/en/profile/country/grl/.

Breum, Martin. "Grønland kortlagt." Weekendavisen. March 14, 2019. https://www.weekendavisen.dk/2019-11/samfund/groenland-kortlagt.

Knudsen, Anne. "Øm om hjertet." Weekendavisen. February 16, 2018. https://www.weekendavisen.dk/2018-7/boeger/oem-om-hjertet.

Louisiana. "Pia Arke." 2021. https://louisiana.dk/en/exhibition/pia-arke/.

Kunsthal Charlottenborg.
"Slow Violence." 2017. https://kunsthalcharlottenborg.dk/en/exhibitions/charlottenborg-art-research-slow-violence/.

Bjørnsson, Iben. "Arktiske
Historier." Danish Arctic Institute's Podcasts. https://arktiskinstitut.dk/index.php?id=102.

Wijnberg, Rob. “How the truth became whatever makes you click.” The Correspondent. April 16, 2020. https://thecorrespondent.com/410/how-the-truth-became-whatever-makes-you-click/9567807150-326405ae.

Wikipedia. “Cannibalism.” https://en.wikipedia.org/wiki/Cannibalism.

Wikipedia. “Silva Rerum.” https://en.wikipedia.org/wiki/Silva_rerum.

The International Trade Administration. “Denmark Doing Business in Grenland.” April 2, 2019. https://www.export.gov/apex/article2?id=Denmark-Doing-Business-in-Greenland.

Healthline. “Snow-blindness Causes.” https://www.healthline.com/health/snow-blindness#causes.

The Vancouver Maritime Museum. “Inuit Snow Goggles.” https://web.archive.org/web/20070314111555/http:/www.vancouvermaritimemuseum.com/modules/vmmuseum/treasures/?artifactid=77.

Olsen, Jan M.. “Greenland ready to take US aid but won’t accept conditions.” The Detroit News. April 23, 2020. https://eu.detroitnews.com/story/news/politics/2020/04/23/greenland-ready-take-us-aid-accept-conditions/111588328/.

Hessel, Niklas. “Det højspændte nord.” Weekendavisen. April 30, 2020. https://www.weekendavisen.dk/2020-18/samfund/det-hoejspaendte-nord.

Chivers, C. J.. “Russians Plant Flag on the Arctic Seabed.” The New York Times. August 3, 2007. https://www.nytimes.com/2007/08/03/world/europe/03arctic.html.

Arctic Council. “About the Arctic Council.” https://arctic-council.org/en/about/.

Breitenbauch, Henrik. “Et kig ned i afgrunden.” Weekendavisen. August 22, 2019. https://www.weekendavisen.dk/2019-34/samfund/et-kig-ned-i-afgrunden.

Danish Arctic Institute. “Articles of association / Vedtægter.” https://arktiskinstitut.dk/fileadmin/files/arktiskinstitut/pdf/Arktisk_Institut_Vedtaegter_2011_11_09.pdf.

Danish Arctic Institute. “Copyright.” https://www.arktiskebilleder.dk/pages/home.php#.

Brotherus, Elina. “Advice to the young.” Louisiana Channel. 202., https://channel.louisiana.dk/video/elina-brotherusadvice-to-the-young.

Carrasco, Carmen Dusmet. “Trailer, The Swimming Pool.” https://vimeo.com/510747679.

ARCHIVAL DIGITAL DATABASES

Danish Arctic Institute Archive: https://arktiskinstitut.dk/arkiverne/.
Document archive: https://arktiskinstitut.dk/arkiverne/dokumentarkiv/soeg-i-dokumentregistranten/.
Photo collection: https://arktiskinstitut.dk/arkiverne/fotosamling/.
Sound collection: https://arktiskinstitut.dk/arkiverne/lydsamling/.

Timarit.is (Digital collection from GL, FO, and IS): https://timarit.is/?q=Ejnar+Mikkelsen&size=10&isAdvanced=false.

Greenland National Museum & Archives: https://da.nka.gl/.
Digital collection: https://www.qangagooq.gl/main/thumbnailview/qsr=Ejnar%20Mikkelsen.

The Royal Danish Library: https://soeg.kb.dk/discovery/search?query=any,contains,Mikkelsen%20Ejnar&tab=Everything&search_scope=MyInst_and_CI&vid=45KBDK_KGL:KGL&facet=lds24,include,Manuscoll&lang=da&offset=0.

The New York Times Archives: https://www.nytimes.com/1912/07/29/archives/capt-ejnar-mikkelsens-own-story-of-two-years-of-arctic-torture.html.

Danish Film Institute & Danish Libraries "Filmstriben": https://biblioteket.filmstriben.dk/film/9000000082/to-maend-i-odemarken.

MOVING IMAGES

Danmarks Radio. *Grønlandsekspeditionen 1909: I farfars fodspor.* Documentary production by Danmarks Radio, 2014. 28 min. https://arenan.yle.fi/1-2414752.

Nikolajsen, Nanna Ánike. *Scoresbysund kolonien er mit eget barn.* 2010.

Roos, Jørgen. *To m nd i Ødemarken.* Documentary production by Minerva Film, 1972. 14 min. https://filmcentralen.dk/grundskolen/film/maend-i-odemarken.

DR-Derude. *Den sidste sl derejse* 6:8. Documentary production by Danmarks Radio, 1993. 30 min. https://www.dr.dk/bonanza/serie/548/den-sidste-slaederejse/68371/den-sidste-slaederejse-68.

PODCASTS

Harvig, Bjørn. "Den yderste grænse, S1E10." Vores Tid – National Museum Denmark & LOUD. https://open.spotify.com/episode/5cugPs6z-0lI9G1V4WctXWP.

Bjørnsson, Iben, and Mads Malik Fuglsang Holm. "Arktiske Hisorier." Danish Arctic Institute Podcast Series. https://arktiskinstitut.dk/index.php?id=102.

appendix
IMAGE INDEX

001.JPG
Front and back cover of booklet *Narratives on EM with edits from Father,* 2020, Gudrun Havsteen-Mikkelsen.

Narratives on EM

002.JPG
Narratives on EM with edits from Father, 2020, Gudrun Havsteen-Mikkelsen.

003.JPG
EM and Iver Iversen, Alabama-expedition, 1910, photo: unknown photographer, © Danish Arctic Institute.

004.JPG
EM at his summerhouse in Bornholm, ca. 1968, photo: Olaf Havsteen-Mikkelsen, Father's family album.

005.JPG
EM onboard Antarctica, 1900, photo: N. P. Sørensen, © Danish Arctic Institute.

006.JPG
Mylius-Erichsen's cairn at Danmark's Fjord, 1910, photo: EM, © Danish Arctic Institute.

007.JPG
EM and his family in Charlottenlund, ca. 1950, photo: unknown photographer, Father's family album.

He mostly talked about the stories, the success stories, he had.

008.JPG
Still image from the moving image *Dialogue w. EM through Father* (footage from Denmark's Radio Archive in 1961), 2020, Gudrun Havsteen-Mikkelsen.

009.JPG
Snow landscape in West Greenland, 2017, photo: Gudrun Havsteen-Mikkelsen.

010.JPG
Bust of EM in Ittoqqortoormiit/Scoresbysund, unknown year, photo: unknown photographer, Britannica.

011.JPG
EM, unknown year, photo: unknown photographer, Father's archive.

012.JPG
EM and his Leica camera, unknown year, photo: unknown photographer, Father's archive.

013.JPG
Quarry outside of Nuuk, 2017, photo: Gudrun Havsteen-Mikkelsen.

014.JPG
Image of EM from the publication *Kaptajnen,* 1980, Palle Koch, © Gyldendal (with permission from Gyldendal to use the illustration).

015.JPG
EM raising the flag in Ittoqqortoormiit/Scoresbysund, 1924, photo: unknown photographer, © Danish Arctic Institute.

016.JPG
Dummy for Stories from Scoresbysund by Pia Arke, 1997-2003, exhibited at Louisiana, 2021, photo: Gudrun Havsteen-Mikkelsen.

017.JPG
The Alabama cottage, during the Alabama-expedition 1909-1912, 1910, photo: EM, © Danish Arctic Institute.

018.JPG
Father with artefacts and documents from EM, 2020, photo: Gudrun Havsteen-Mikkelsen.

019.JPG
Still image from the moving image *Dialogue w. EM through Father,* (footage from Denmark's Radio Archive in 1961), 2020, Gudrun Havsteen-Mikkelsen.

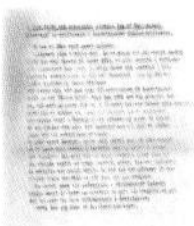

020.JPG
Speech held by Emil Madsen at the inauguration of Miki's House in Ittoqqortoormiit/Scoresbysund, 1958, Father's archive.

021.JPG
Scan of Father's family album, images from Greenland and Denmark, 1958, photo: Olaf Havsteen-Mikkelsen, Father's family album.

022.JPG
EM and the rest of the Alabama-expeditions members in Thorshavn, 1909, photo: EM, © Danish Arctic Institute.

023.JPG
Still image from conversation with Father while looking through his archive, 2020, photo: Gudrun Havsteen-Mikkelsen.

024.JPG
Still image from the moving image *Dialogue w. EM through Father,* 2020, photo: Gudrun Havsteen-Mikkelsen.

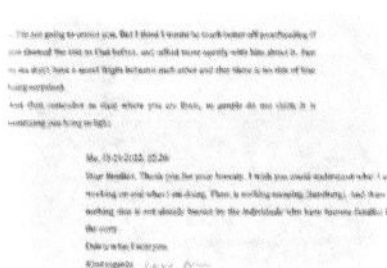

025.JPG
Manuscript of *Snowblindness* with Father's comments, 2020, Gudrun Havsteen-Mikkelsen.

026.JPG
Still image from the moving image *Aftermath: Narratives on EM,* 2020, photo: Gudrun Havsteen-Mikkelsen.

027.JPG
Ella in possibly in Ammassalik Tasiilaq, ca. 1926, photo: EM, Father's archive.

028.JPG

029.JPG
Snowblindness Podcast Series #1 during broadcasting w. Carmen Dusmet Carrasco interviewed by Anna Bierler, 2021, photo: Gudrun Havsteen-Mikkelsen.

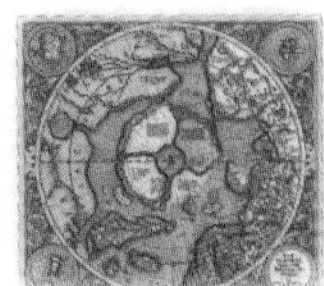

030.JPG
The second draft of the Septentrionalium Terrarum, the imaginary North Pole, 1606, Gerardus Mercator, Public Domain.

031.JPG
Father looking through his archive, 2020, photo: Gudrun Havsteen-Mikkelsen.

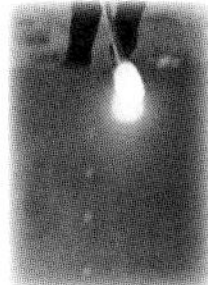

032.JPG
Process image, the making of snowgoogles in glass, 2019, photo: Gudrun Havsteen-Mikkelsen.

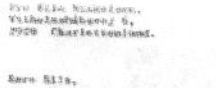

033.JPG
Letter to Ella from Ebbe Munck regarding a bust of EM at Langelinje after EM's death in 1971, Father's archive.

034.JPG
Still image from the moving image *Aftermath: Narratives on EM,* 2020, photo: Gudrun Havsteen-Mikkelsen.

035.JPG
Image from EM's publication *Svundne Tider i Østgrønland – Fra Stenalder til Atomtid,* 1960, © Gyldendal (with permission from Gyldendal to use the illustration).

036.JPG
Harbour area outside of Nuuk, 2017, photo: Gudrun Havsteen-Mikkelsen.

037.JPG
EM at the Amdrup-expedition in East Greenland (1898-1900), 1900, photo: Georg Carl Amdrup, © Danish Arctic Institute.

038.JPG
Polar bear skin at Ittoqqortoormiit/Scoresbysund, 1925, photo: EM, © Danish Arctic Institute.

039.JPG
Musk head Father bought in Ittoqqortoormiit/Scoresbysund, on the image musk head in Troense, 1958, photo: Olaf Havsteen-Mikkelsen, Father's family album.

040.JPG
EM at Bornholm, ca. 1965, photo: Olaf Havsteen-Mikkelsen, Father's archive.

041.JPG
Members of the Treårs-expedition (1931-1934), 1932, photo: Børge Andersen, © Danish Arctic Institute.

042.JPG
Ella and EM at Sven and Pamela's wedding in London, 1936, photo: unknown photographer, Father's archive.

043.JPG
Process image with artefacts in the development of the *Snowblindness* research, 2020, photo: Gudrun Havsteen-Mikkelsen.

044.JPG
I think i got it, Snowblindness: glasses, model Hanna Valle, 2020, photo: Gudrun Havsteen-Mikkelsen.

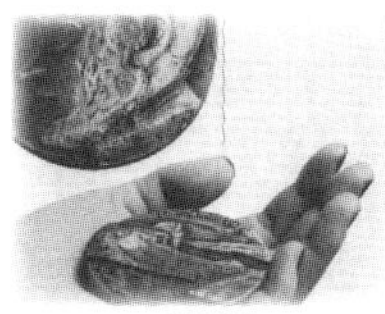

045.JPG
Medal of EM by Sven, image from the publication by Erik Pouplier, Uden for Tredje revle, 1984, publisher Anders Nyborg.

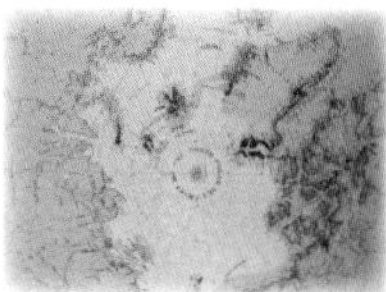

046.JPG
Chart of the North Polar Sea, 1855, Capt. Washington R.N. F.R.S, Helsingfors University Library.

047.JPG
Image from the publication Kaptajnen, 1980, Palle Koch, © Gyldendal (with permission from Gyldendal to use the illustration).

048.JPG
The Shrimp Paradox: ring, model Tali Liberman, 2020, photo: Gudrun Havsteen-Mikkelsen.

049.JPG
Image from the publication *Ejnar Mikkelsen,* Kurt L. Frederiksen, 2015, Gyldendal (with permission from the author and copyright holder to use the illustration).

050.JPG
Still image from the moving image *Aftermath: Narratives on EM,* 2020, photo: Gudrun Havsteen-Mikkelsen.

051.JPG
EM probably coming home from an expedition or travel, ca.1930s, photo: unknown photographer, Father's archive.

052.jpg
EM with Leica camera, unknown year, unknown photographer, Father's archive.

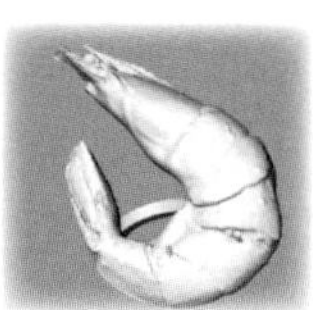

053.JPG
The making of the shrimp ring, 2020, photo: Gudrun Havsteen-Mikkelsen.

054.JPG
The making of Ittoqqortoormiit/ Scoresbysund Church, ca. 1928, photo: Charles Hansen Jarrill, © Danish Arctic Institute.

055.JPG
Dead whale alongside the ship, 1906, photo: EM, © Danish Arctic Institute.

056.JPG
Archive material on EM when visiting Danish Arctic Institute's archive in Copenhagen, 2020, photo: Gudrun Havsteen-Mikkelsen.

057.JPG

058.JPG
Father's boat, ca. 1955, photo: Olaf Havsteen-Mikkelsen, Father's family album.

059.JPG
Scan from *Kortlaegning af Kulturhistoriske interesser I Jameson Land og Scoresbysund (1982-84),* 1985, Hanne and Birger Sandell.

060.JPG
Speech given at EM's funeral, 1971, Ordrup Church, Father's archive.

061.JPG
Cod catch in West Greenland, 1925, photo: EM, © Danish Arctic Institute.

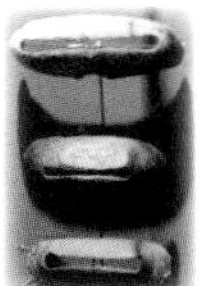

062.JPG
Snowgoogles exhibited at Greenland National Museum and Archive, 2017, photo: Gudrun Havsteen-Mikkelsen.

063.JPG
Miners examining rubies in Nuuk, 2017, photo: Gudrun Havsteen-Mikkelsen.

064.JPG
EM's file bag, which Father uses for choir notes, 2020, photo: Gudrun Havsteen-Mikkelsen.

FERIESMIL PÅ

065.JPG
Article from "Se og Hør" no.30 with Father, EM and Ella, 1966, Father's archive.

066.JPG
EM in 1937, scan from the publication *Ejnar Mikkelsen,* Kurt L. Frederiksen, 2015, Gyldendal (with permission from the copyright holder to use the illustration).

067.JPG
Process image with documents from Father's archive in the development of the *Snowblindness* research, 2020, photo: Gudrun Havsteen-Mikkelsen.

068.JPG
The sledge dog 'Girly', Alabama-expedition, 1910, photo: EM, © Danish Arctic Institute.

069.JPG
Process image with stacks of paper in the development of the Snowblindness book, 2020, photo: Gudrun Havsteen-Mikkelsen.

070.JPG
Kortl gning af Kulturhistoriske interesser I Jameson Land og Scoresbysund (1982-84) showing Inuit settlements and extinction, 1985, Hanne and Birger Sandell.

071.JPG
Dummy for *Stories from Scoresbysund* by Pia Arke, 1997-2003, exhibited at Louisiana, 2021, photo: Gudrun Havsteen-Mikkelsen.

072.JPG
Locals in Ittoqqortoormiit/ Scoresbysund, 1958, photo: Olaf Havsteen-Mikkelsen, Father's family album.

073.JPG
Local girls in front of Ittoqqortoormiit/Scoresbysund Church, 1958, photo: Olaf Havsteen-Mikkelsen, Father's family album.

074.JPG
Process image of the making of the shrimp ring, 2020, photo: Gudrun Havsteen-Mikkelsen.

075.JPG
EM and H. P. Nielsen onboard the ship Greenland, 1924, photo: unknown photographer, © Danish Arctic Institute.

076.JPG
Image from EM's publication *Farlig Tomandsfaerd,* 1962, Gyldendal, with comments by Gudrun Havsteen-Mikkelsen (with permission from Gyldendal to use the illustration).

077.JPG
EM writing at his desk in Charlottenlund, ca. 1958, Olaf Havsteen-Mikkelsen, Father's family album.

078.JPG
EM writing in Reykjavik, 1958, photo: Olaf Havsteen-Mikkelsen, Father's family album.

079.JPG
Dummy for *Stories from Scoresbysund* by Pia Arke, 1997-2003, exhibited at Louisiana, 2021, photo: Gudrun Havsteen-Mikkelsen.

080.JPG
Still image from the moving image *Aftermath: Narratives on EM,* 2020, photo: Gudrun Havsteen-Mikkelsen.

081.JPG
Manuscript of *Snowblindness* with Father's comments, 2020, Gudrun Havsteen-Mikkelsen.

082.JPG
Bluebook on EM, 1961, with a comment from Father, 2021, Public Domain.

083.JPG
Father, Mollie Butler, Ella and EM, 1963, photo: unknown photographer, Father's archive.

084.JPG
Front cover of the publication by EM, *Conquering the Arctic,* 1909, W. Heinemann, Father's archive.

Well, the Government, Danish Government,
where not so keen on him, doing what he was doing.

085.JPG
Still image from the moving image *Dialogue w. EM through Father* (footage from Denmark's Radio Achieve in 1961), 2020, Gudrun Havsteen-Mikkelsen.

086.JPG
Officers and crew of the Baldwin-Ziegler Polar Expedition, 1901, photo: unknown photographer, Wikipedia.

087.JPG
Peter Freuchen and EM, 1913, photo: John Møller, © Danish Arctic Institute.

088.JPG
Receipt from the small-scale mining company, Ice Cold Gems, Greenland, 2017, Gudrun Havsteen-Mikkelsen.

089.JPG
Father watching archive material of EM, 2020, photo: Gudrun Havsteen-Mikkelsen.

090.JPG
EM and Ernst de Koven Leffingwell pointing at Alaska, image from EM's publication *Ukendt Mand I Ukendt Land,* 1954, Gyldendal (with permission from Gyldendal to use the illustration).

091.JPG
EM at the Anglo-American Polar-Expedition in Alaska, 1907, photo: unknown photographer, Wikipedia.

092.JPG
Alabama's mast is falling during the Alabama-expedition, ca. 1909, photo: EM, © Danish Arctic Institute.

093.JPG
Film poster of *Against the Ice,* 2022, photo: The Netflix Team (with permission from the Netflix Team to use the illustration).

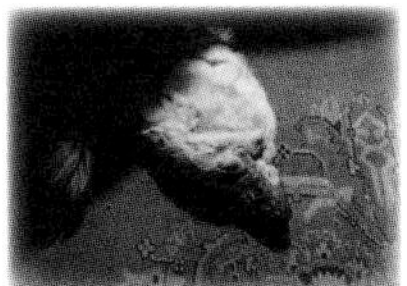

094.JPG
Polar bear from EM to Father, 2020, photo: Gudrun Havsteen-Mikkelsen.

095.JPG
Unknown girl in traditional costume of Greenland, on a back cover in a frame of another image, unknown year, photo: unknown photographer, Father's archive.

096.JPG
EM, 1907, photo: Ernest de Koven Leffungwell, © Danish Arctic Institute.

097.JPG
P571 EM Inspectorship, 2013, photo: unknown photographer, Søværnet.

098.jpg
Snowblindness Podcast Series #2 poster, photo by Inuuteqch Stoch (with permission from the artist to use the illustration), 2021, Anna Bierler.

099.JPG
Telephone and two bottles in Mestersvig, 1983, photo: J. E. Saaby-Hansen, © Danish Arctic Institute.

100.JPG
EM's expedition map 1909-1912 in the publication by EM *Farlig Tomandsfaerd,* 1962, Gyldendal, (with permission from Gyldendal to use the illustration) redrawn by Gudrun Havsteen-Mikkelsen.

101.JPG
Snowblindness artefacts, process image in the *Snowblindness* research, 2020, photo: Gudrun Havsteen-Mikkelsen.

102.JPG
Image of EM from the publication *Ejnar Mikkelsen,* Kurt L. Frederiksen, 2015, Gyldendal (with permission from the copyright holder to use the illustration).

103.JPG
EM with fellow traveller, 1907, photo: EM or unknown, © Danish Arctic Institute.

104.JPG
EM writing in Argentina, ca. 1923, photo: unknown photographer, Father's archive.

105.JPG
Inuit settlement during the expedition from Kap Dalton to Ammassalik , 1905, photo: EM, © Danish Arctic Institute.

106.JPG
Greenlandic woman and child, ca. 1961-1968, photo: Jette Bang, © Jette Bang/Danish Arctic Institute.

107.JPG
EM at Ittoqqortoormiit/Scoresbysund, 1926, photo: unknown photographer, © Danish Arctic Institute.

108.JPG
Ruined rudders at the ship 'Grønland' in Copenhagen from Ittoqqortoormiit/Scoresbysund, 1924, photo: unknown photographer, © Danish Arctic Institute.

109.JPG
Scan of EM's book spines, 2020, Gudrun Havsteen-Mikkelsen.

110.JPG
EM at Ittoqqortoormiit/Scoresbysund, Jameson Land, 1924, photo: unknown photographer, © Danish Arctic Institute.

111.JPG
Day of expedition departure in Alaska, 1906, photo: EM, © Danish Arctic Institute.

112.JPG
EM, unknown year, photo: unknown photographer, Father's archive.

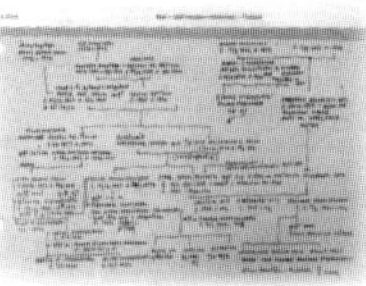
113.JPG
Family tree made by Alan, ca. 2000, Father's archive.

114.JPG
Capt. EM's own story of two years of Arctic torture; Disease, Hunger, and Cold Fought for Lives of Danish Explorer and His Comrade (July 29. 1912), 1912, The New York Times Archives.

115.JPG
EM, Aksel, Alan in Mestersvig, 1955, photo: unknown photographer, Father's family album.

116.JPG
The booklet *Narratives on EM* and EM's publication *Lost in the Arctic* (1913), 2020, photo: Gudrun Havsteen-Mikkelsen.

117.JPG
Interior of a house in Kap Hope (East Greenland, near Ittoqqortoormiit/Scoresbysund) with three locals, 1926, photo: unknown photographer (most likely EM), © Danish Arctic Institute.

118.JPG
Digging out a native grave at Kodiak Island, 1906, photo: EM, © Danish Arctic Institute.

119.JPG
EM, 1955, photo: unknown photographer, Father's archive.

120.JPG
Iver Iversen during the Alabama-expedition at Shannon Island, ca. 1910, photo: EM, © Danish Arctic Institute.

121.JPG
EM and Iver Iversen, image from the publication *Kaptajnen*, 1980, Palle Koch, Gyldendal (with permission from Gyldendal to use the illustration).

122.JPG
Tectonic map of East Greenland, 1970, Greenland's Geological Survey (today GEUS).

123.JPG
Still image from the moving image *Aftermath: Narratives on EM* (footage from Denmark's Radio Archive, ca. 1960), 2020, Gudrun Havsteen-Mikkelsen.

124.JPG
EM during the Alabama-expedition at Shannon Island, 1910, photo: Iver Iversen, © Danish Arctic Institute.

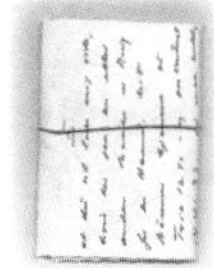

125.JPG
Letters from Ebbe Munch to Ella after EM's death, 1971, Father's archive.

126.JPG
Polar bears in East Greenland, ca. 1930s, photo: EM, Father's family album.

127.JPG
EM in East Greenland, 1958, photo: Olaf Havsteen-Mikkelsen, Father's family album.

128.JPG
Image from EM's publication *Farlig Tomandsfaerd*, 1962, photo: Børge Høft, Gyldendal (with permission from Gyldendal to use the illustration).

129.JPG
EM in Kangertittivaq, Ittoqqortoormiit/Scoresbysund, ca. 1934, photo: unknown photographer, © Danish Arctic Institute.

130.JPG
EM among others, 1924, Ittoqqortoormiit/Scoresbysund, photo: unknown photographer, © Danish Arctic Institute.

131.JPG
Quarry outside of Nuuk, 2017, photo: Gudrun Havsteen-Mikkelsen.

132.JPG
Anna Bierler and Gudrun Havsteen-Mikkelsen, 2020, photo: Rozemarijn Jens.

133.JPG
Dummy for *Stories from Scoresbysund* by Pia Arke, 1997-2003, exhibited at Louisiana, 2021, photo: Gudrun Havsteen-Mikkelsen.

134.JPG
EM at Shannon Island, 1909, photo: EM, © Danish Arctic Institute.

135.JPG
EM among others, image from EM's publication *Fra Fribytter til Embedsmand*, 1957, Gyldendal (with permission from Gyldendal to use the illustration).

136.JPG
The naming of the ship 'Duchess of Bedford' in Alaska, 1906, photo: EM, © Danish Arctic Institute.

137.JPG
Notions on Cannibalism: frame and photograph, 2020, photo: Gudrun Havsteen-Mikkelsen.

138.JPG
Dummy for *Stories from Scoresbysund* by Pia Arke, 1997-2003, exhibited at Louisiana, 2021, and image also used in *Narratives on EM*, 2020, photo: Gudrun Havsteen-Mikkelsen.

139.JPG
Scan from *Tupilakosaurus:* 2012, published by Kuratorisk Aktion, with Gudrun Havsteen-Mikkelsen's comments as a part of the *Snowblindness* research.

140.JPG
Tupilaq props, 2020, photo: Gudrun Havsteen-Mikkelsen.

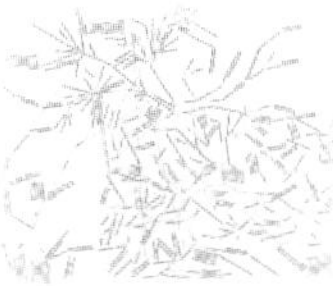

141.JPG
Mindmap of the *Snowblindness* research, 2020, Gudrun Havsteen-Mikkelsen.

142.JPG
Drum dance in Ittoqqortoormiit/Scoresbysund performed by Magnus and Ole, 1958, photo: Olaf Havsteen-Mikkelsen, Father's family album.

143.JPG
Thule Air Base, ca. 1961-1964, photo: Torben Gjerløff, © Danish Arctic Institute.

144.JPG
Josva, EM, and Ole in Ittoqqortoormiit/Scoresbysund, 1958, photo: Olaf Havsteen-Mikkelsen, Father's family album.

145.JPG
Image from *Dagbogsbreve fra Scoresbysund* 1957-59 by Jens Nielsen, 2012, publisher Det Grønlandske Selvskab.

146.JPG
Runway for airplanes at Kulusuk Kap Dan, 1940, photo: EM, © Danish Arctic Institute.

147.JPG
Runway near Tasiilaq, Ammasalik East Greenland, 1958, photo: Olaf Havsteen-Mikkelsen, Father's family album.

148.JPG
Ruby in a safe in Nuuk, 2017, photo: Gudrun Havsteen-Mikkelsen.

149.JPG
Clearing the deck on the ship 'The Duchess of Bedford' near Flaxman Island, 1907, photo: EM, © Danish Arctic Institute.

150.JPG
Mining machine in West Greenland, 2017, photo: Gudrun Havsteen-Mikkelsen.

151.JPG
Dummy for *Stories from Scoresbysund* by by Pia Arke, 1997-2003, exhibited at Louisiana, 2021, photo: Gudrun Havsteen-Mikkelsen.

152.JPG
EM with Narwhale tooth, ca. 1926, photo: unknown photographer, © Danish Arctic Institute.

153.JPG
Inuit wooden maps, ca. 1885 © Greenland National Museum and Archives.

154.JPG
Participant at the Arctic Circle Conference in 2018, Gudrun Havsteen-Mikkelsen.

155.JPG
EM, ca. 1960s, photo: unknown photographer, Father's archive.

156.JPG
Ameralik Fjord in West Greenland, 2017, photo: Gudrun Havsteen-Mikkelsen.

157.JPG
Still from the moving image *Process images for the book Snowblindness*, 2020, photo: Gudrun Havsteen-Mikkelsen.

158.JPG
A group of people near the bygd Kap Tobin, Ittoqqortoormiit/Scoresbysund, 1925, photo: unknown photographer, © Danish Arctic Institute.

159.JPG
Bust of EM at Langelinje with his great-great-grandchildren in the foreground, 2019, photo: Cecilia Havsteen.

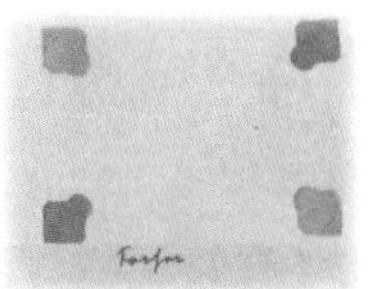
160.JPG
Image of a missing photograph titled 'grandfather' (EM), Father's family album.

161.JPG
EM with his parents, ca. 1912, photo: unknown photographer, Father's archive.

162.JPG
Image from the publication *Ejnar Mikkelsen*, Kurt L. Frederiksen, 2015, Gyldendal (with permission from the author to use the illustration).

163.JPG
Containers outside of Nuuk, 2017, photo: Gudrun Havsteen-Mikkelsen.

164.JPG

165.JPG
The Danish flag and the Greenlandic flag next to each other in Nuuk, 2017, photo: Gudrun Havsteen-Mikkelsen.

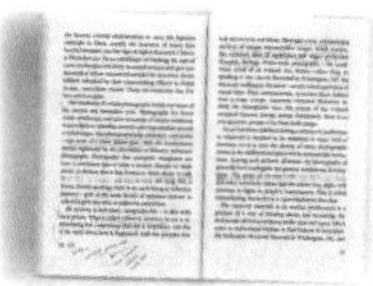

166.JPG
Image of the publication *Regarding the Pain of Others* by Susan Sontag, 2003, published by Penguin Books, with Gudrun Havsteen-Mikkelsen's comments as a part of the *Snowblindness* research.

167.JPG
Father with Iver Iversen's car, a Studebaker 1930, 1961, photo: Sven Havsteen-Mikkelsen, Father's family album.

168.JPG
Nikolaj Fleischer at work in the coal mine in Qullissat East Greenland, 1958, photo: Jette Bang, © Jette Bang/Danish Arctic Institute.

169.JPG
EM, late 1960s, photo: probably Olaf Havsteen-Mikkelsen, Father's family album.

170.JPG
EM's artefacts and Father's belongings, 2020, photo: Gudrun Havsteen-Mikkelsen.

171.JPG
EM's diaries at Danish Arctic Institute's Archive in Copenhagen, 2020, photo: Gudrun Havsteen-Mikkelsen.

172.JPG
EM with an unknown child, ca. late 1960s, photo: Olaf Havsteen-Mikkelsen, Father's family album.

173.JPG
Snowblindness Podcast Series #1 poster, 2021, Anna Bierler.

174.JPG
Top View & Information Carrier: engraved map of the Alabama-expedition, 2020, photo: Gudrun Havsteen-Mikkelsen.

175.JPG
Scan from *Tupilakosaurus*, 2012, published by Kuratorisk Aktion, with Gudrun Havsteen-Mikkelsen's comments as a part of the Snowblindness research.

176.JPG
EM's gravestone in Ordrup churchyard, 1980, photo: Olaf Havsteen-Mikkelsen, Father's archive.

177.JPG
Still from the moving image *Aftermath: Narratives on EM,* 2020, photo: Gudrun Havsteen-Mikkelsen.

178.JPG
"Atuagagdliutit" newspaper issue 166, 1976, photo: Grete Juhl.

179.JPG
EM, Ittoqqortoormiit/Scoresbysund, 1964, photo: Christian Vibe, © Danish Arctic Institute.

180.JPG
EM on board Islands Falk in Iceland, 1909, photo: H. Einarsson, © Danish Arctic Institute.

181.JPG
Stone quarry outside of Nuuk, 2017, photo: Gudrun Havsteen-Mikkelsen.

182.JPG
Still from the moving image *Aftermath: Narratives on EM,* 2020, photo: Gudrun Havsteen-Mikkelsen.

183.JPG
Scan of the booklet *Narratives on EM* with edits from Father, 2020, Gudrun Havsteen-Mikkelsen.

184.JPG
EM together with local Greenlanders from Tasiilaq/Ammassalik, 1924, photo: unknown photographer, © Danish Arctic Institute.

185.JPG
Father, EM, and Alan, 1950, photo: unknown photographer, Father's family album.

186.JPG
Scan from *Tupilakosaurus,* 2012, published by Kuratorisk Aktion, with Gudrun Havsteen-Mikkelsen's comments as a part of the *Snowblindness* research.

187.JPG
Premiere for EM's descendants of Netflix's film *Against the Ice* with an introduction by the film instructor, Peter Flinth, 2022, photo: Mette Eriksen Havsteen-Mikkelsen.

188.JPG
Still image from the moving image *Aftermath: Narratives on EM,* 2020, photo: Gudrun Havsteen-Mikkelsen.

189.JPG
H. P. Nielsen cuts EM's hair on board the ship 'Grønland', 1924, photo: unknown photographer, © Danish Arctic Institute.

190.JPG
Bluebook on EM, 1961, with a comment from Father, 2021, Public Domain.

191.JPG
Unknown 'Oncle' and EM, ca. 1913, photo: unknown photographer, Father's archive.

192.JPG
Ice of Greenland, 2017, photo: Gudrun Havsteen-Mikkelsen. appears on the cover, too.

193.JPG
Alan, Ella, Olaf and EM, ca. 1945, photo: unknown photographer, Father's family album.

Snowblindness would never have found its breeding ground without the discussions, help, and interest from various actors including my family who have contributed in many valuable ways. Tusind tak!

Firstly, the production of *Snowblindness* as a book would never have been possible without support from the Dutch funds Stichting Jaap Hartens Fund, Stichting Stokroos, and Cultuur Eindhoven, and the Danish fund Kaptajn Alf Trolles Legat. To all I am greatly thankful.

Secondly, I am humbled by and very grateful to Bent Nielsen, Jørgen Trondhjem, and Stig S. Rasmussen from Danish Arctic Institute, Lars Rasmussen from Ammassalik Museum, and Sille Radoor Larsen from Ærø Museum. My thanks go to Nikolajsen, Bendo Albertsdottir, Kurt L. Frederiksen, and Dr. Temi Odumosu for sharing their knowledge and memories. Also thanks to actors at Gyldendal, who brought me further in terms of sources, information, and anecdotes on the Denmark-Greenland relation, EM, and the upcoming Netflix film.

Anna and I are very grateful for the collaboration with Onomatopee and Freek Lomme and Dymfy van Meel for publishing *Snowblindness*, for thinking through the structure and content of the book, and for welcoming and finalising the project with enthusiasm. Many thanks to Sebastiaan Hanekroot for editing the images. We would also like to express thanks to Harriet Foyster for proofreading the texts, and asking relevant, sharp, and critical questions as an external actor in the production of the book.

Many thanks to the Rietveld/Sandberg Student Council for support in the making of the *Snowblindness Podcast Series*, and thank you to PUB for making the broadcasting possible at the Sandberg Instituut. We are also grateful for the contributions of Carmen Dusmet Carrasco and Inuuteq Storch in their taking part in the *Snowblindness Podcast Series,* and for the conversations we had before and during broadcasting. Also a warm-hearted thanks to Daniel Slats for helping with the postproduction of the podcast.

Our thanks go to Charlotte Rohde for providing *Snowblindness* with her beautiful typefaces, *Kéroïne Care Set* from 2020, which contains *Kéroïne Doux Etrême* and *Kéroïne Intense Légère*.

Sincere gratitude to the tutors at the Design Department of the Sandberg Instituut; Anja Groten (Head of Design Department), Tina Bastajian, Daniel van der Velden, Annelys de Vet, Nirit Peled, Silvio Lorusso, and guest tutor Anja Kaiser, together with my fellow colleagues for encouraging me to continue the research and work. I owe all of the above the most heartfelt thanks for their dialogue, critique, and support.

I would like to single out Anna Bierler for being a great, caring, and curious collaborator and friend in the making of this book as visual co-author, many warm-hearted thanks and wishes for many more collaborations to come.

And last but not least, utmost and eternal gratitude to Father, for his time, love, and willingness to debate, comment, and share.